Fabius M. Ray's
Story of Westbrook

Compiled by
Karen Sherman Ketover

HERITAGE BOOKS
2025

HERITAGE BOOKS
AN IMPRINT OF HERITAGE BOOKS, INC.

Books, CDs, and more—Worldwide

For our listing of thousands of titles see our website
at
www.HeritageBooks.com

A Facsimile Reprint
Published 2025 by
HERITAGE BOOKS, INC.
Publishing Division
5810 Ruatan Street
Berwyn Heights, MD 20740

Copyright © 1998 Karen Sherman Ketover

Heritage Books by the author:

Fabius M. Ray's Story of Westbrook [Maine]

Westbrook, Maine Cemeteries; Plus the Surrounding Towns of Cumberland, Falmouth, Gorham, Portland and Windham

— Publisher's Notice —
In reprints such as this, it is often not possible to remove blemishes from the original. We feel the contents of this book warrant its reissue despite these blemishes and hope you will agree and read it with pleasure.

International Standard Book Number
Paperbound: 978-0-7884-1019-2

A carbon copy of Fabius Ray's Story of Westbrook has been in the vault at the Walker Memorial Library for as long as anyone can remember. We have one photocopy of it in the library's Local History Room for general use. I have been asked many times over the years to retype this faded, hard to read manuscript and index it. I have prefaced his story with articles of Mr. Ray. As you read on, you will see what a remarkable man he was and he should be remembered for all he did for his community.

Further reading on City of Westbrook and surrounding areas can be found in the Local History Room of the Walker Memorial Library, 800 Main Street, Westbrook, Maine, 04092.

On a personal note, I have recently moved to Las Vegas. Julie Peterson is now the Curator for Walker Memorial Library. Julie is a native of Westbrook and has a great interest in genealogy.

Karen Sherman Ketover

The Saunterer

People He Meets and People He Remembers

Portland Sunday Telegram
September 22, 1912

The half-tone printed here is a good likeness of Judge Fabius M. Ray as he appeared several years ago. He is thinner in the face today, and the gray has crept into his full beard. But he is as good a specimen of a well-preserved man of 75 years as would be found in a day's walk about the City. Fond of historical reading, heis one of the few regular visitors at the library of the Maine Historical Society. Born in South Windham, March 30, 1837, young Ray was graduated from Bowdoin College in the class of 1861. Among the 51 graduated of this class were Frank L. Dingley, editor of the Lewiston Journal; Lucillus A. Emery,ex-chief justice of the Supreme Court;Gordon M. Hicks, Judge of the Municipal Court, Rockland; Dr. Charles O. Hunt, for many years superintendent of the Maine General Hospital; Moses Owen, the Bath poet, author of The Return Battle Flags; Edward Stanwood, long time editor of the Boston Advertiser, and Professor Alpheus S. Packard. The year following his graduation young Ray passed in Heidelbergand Geneva studying French and German. Returning home he took up the study of law, and in due time was admitted to the Bar of Cumberland County and opened an office in Saccarappa. In 1871-72 he represented the town of Westbrook in the State Legislature, elected on the Republican ticket. He was appointed judge of the Municipal Court of Westbrook in 1883 held the office one year, resigning to go to the Legislature as one of the senators from this County in 1885-86. From 1871 to 1876 he was the law partner of Colonel John C. Cobb, the firm name being Cobb & Ray, with an office on Exchange Street. From 1878 to 1880 he had Edwin L. Dyer for a partner, the firm name being Ray & Dyer. Since the dissolution of the last named firm Judge Ray has had no partner, but has practiced his profession alone, his office in recent years being at 181 Middle Street, though his residence has always been in Westbrook.

Judge Ray has nearly all his life been an occasional contributor to newspapers or magazines. Some of his historical articles have been of lasting value, owing to the patient which preceded the writing of them, while his poetry has been justly praised for its thoughtfulness, originality and mastery of difficult meters. In 1874 he collected a score or more of these fugitive children of his brain and published them in a small blue-bound book, with a fir tree on the cover, and called the publication The Christmas Tree. The poem of ten stanzas entitled On Loch Katrine is, to the mind of the Saunterer, the best in this little book. Here are two fine stanzas:

> But not a ripple stirs the tide
> Of Loch Katrine, the queenly lake,
> As o'er its silvery face we glide,
> Save those the highland oarsmen make.
> The autumn evening lingering low,
> Now hastens, ere the sun is set,
> To fling its last expiring minaret.

The memorial sonnets to Nelson P. Cram, Samuel Fessenden, John Rich and William W. Morrell, read by the author at the triennial meeting of the lass of 1861, Bowdoin College, August 1864, are appreciative and tenderly sympathic.

A more ambitious volume is that published by Judge Ray in 1904, modestly entitle Translations, Imitations, and a Few Originals. This is inscribed to the Elians, a college society of which he was a member. This neatly printed book contains about 60 poems, in various meters and on a wide range of subjects. Here is a quatrain with a moral that he who cares may read:

> Though scandal's tongue is never mute,
> One thought should always comfort bring:
> 'Tis not the sour and crabbed fruit
> That wasps delight the most to sting.

A good many of the poems in this book were originally published in the Home Journal of New York City. Judge Ray is a fine classical scholar and this accounts for the translations from Horace that add to the charm of the volume. His translations from the German poets are equally fine, while the original entitled To the Trailing Arbutus, is a fair specimen of the delicacy and beauty of the author's numbers.

At the commencement of 1911, the class of 1861 celebrated its fiftieth anniversary, and Judge Ray read a poem written by him for the occasion. As it has never been published and is more that ordinarily good verification, the poem is given here:

> "We're half way through. So sang our odist when
> The years gone by, like those to come, were twain,
>   and chose the happy phrase as fit refrain

To tell of years that ne'er should come again.
Since then we've more than halved the century;
But what of that? There's still no dearth of time,
Nor will be while the patient aeons climb
Toward the top round of eternity.
Nay, what of that or this? A hundred years
It will be all the same to you and me,
Whether we pledge the passing century
In aqua pure or the cup that cheers;
For years will go, and lives will multiply,
With earth below and overhead the sky.

We've reached the goal where all ambitions cease;
And now mid shadows lengthening like our days,
A paen to this year of Jubilee we raise,
And sit us down in idleness and ease,
Life's duties done, henceforth perennial peace
Is ours; and though not all our brows with bays
Are crowned, we fear not on the west to gaze,
Nor apples pluck of the Hesperides.
Since sad allusions hath our scribe forbade,
All sadness to the shades we'll relegate,
And laugh amain, like him of old, whose mad
Guffaw, for all life's ills was anodyne,
Whilst this long-looked-for day we consecrate,
With oft oblations of a classmate's wine.

Hon. Fabius M. Ray of Westbrook Died Today

Portland Evening Express
November 23, 1915

The death of Hon. Fabius M. Ray occurred at 12:35 today and the news came as a great shock to the citizens of Westbrook and will be heard with much sorrow throughout the entire State. The deceased was born in So. Windham, March 30, 1837. He graduated from Bowdoin College in the year 1881 and leaving college he spent a year aboard at Heidelberg and Geneva, studying French and German. He then entered upon the study of law, was admitted to the Bar and began his practice in Westbrook, then known as Saccarappa, which has since been his home. In 1867 entertaining the project of abandoning the law, he entered the senior class of the Divinity School in Cambridge, Mass., and graduated, but never received ordination, and in a year resumed a legal practice in Portland which he continued until Nov. 12 of the present year, when he was taken ill with a bilious attack, which so affected his heart that he was unable to rally. He represented Westbrook in the Legislature of 1871-1872. He taught school in Saccarappa in 1865, and in the Winter of 1869 and 1870, and has had several private pupils in modern languages and the classics.

He was the author of a volume of verse, published in 1874 and of numerous original poems and metrical translations in various periodicals. He was the editor of a journal kept by a medical ancestor, who accompanied the expedition against Ticonderoga in 1758, which makes the basis of a page in Parkman's Wolfe and Montcalm.

In 1904 he published a second book entitled Translations, and Imitations and a Few Originals. All of his poems show the keen observer and lover of Nature that he was.

He was Judge of the Municipal Court of Westbrook in 1883-1885, and was a member of the Maine Senate in 1883. Mr. Ray was twice married, his first wife being Mary Muzzey Marrett of Westbrook, who died January 27, 1877, and by whom two children were born. Sarah Adeline, wife of Doctor Albert H. Burroughs of Westbrook and William C. of Portland. His second wife was Josephine Isabel Tibbets, whom he married Nov. 22, 1883, who survives him and for whom much sympathy is felt by a legion of friends in this City and surrounding towns. No man in Westbrook, or perhaps the State, was more thoroughly educated or more generally cultured than he. He loved and read only the best literature. He was one of the best read lawyers in the State. He was always interested in the history of Westbrook and has written many articles of more than local interest. He had frequently been asked to publish in book form a history of the City, but as he was constantly adding to his material, he never considered it complete.

Coming to Westbrook as he did many years ago, he had been able to collect much from the older settlers, which it would be impossible at the present day to procure. Yesterday we the 22nd anniversary of his wedding day and he remembered and spoke of it to his wife, saying to her with a smile: "Happy, happy years."

He will be much missed on the street; on the cars; both in this city and Portland, while at his home his loss cannot be over-estimated, as he was, regardless of his many cares, a home man and there when business did not otherwise detain, he was most often found. He loved a joke; was quick to see a point; was loyal to his friends to an unusual degree and there is an aching void in many hearts, that he has passed on into the Great Beyond.

The funeral services will be announced later, but will probably be held Friday at 2 o'clock from his late home.

Portland Evening Express
November 26, 1915

A large number of old time friends, neighbors, acquaintances and members of Cumberland County Bar gathered at the home of Hon. Fabius M. Ray at 2 o'clock this afternoon to pay their last tribute of respect to their departed friend and honored citizen. The services were conducted by Rev. Dorr A. Hudson, pastor of the Westbrook Congregational Church, and Rev. Harry E. Townsend of the First Universalist Church. The floral tributes were most beautiful and the abundance of blossoms told their own story and were a sermon in themselves. The burial was at Evergreen Cemetery and the pall bearers were Arthur Chapman, Hon. Charles A. Strout of Portland, Hon. Charles M. Waterhouse and Postmaster Clinton S. Eastman of this city.

Westbrook, April 4th, 1927

My dear Mr. Haskell: - At your request I have written out at some length the facts regarding the Library. Of course I do not expect you to use but a small part, if any, of what I have written. But, I have always bitterly resented the treatment Mr. Ray received. He was the last man who would wish or expect praise for any service he was able to render; but I know he felt that he had never received justice in the matter from the hands of those whom he had every right to consider his friends. Mr. Fox expressed himself as feeling the same way.

                        Your most truly,
                        Isabel T. Ray

      This library of which we are all so justly proud would never have been given to the City of Westbrook had it not been for the influence of one man, the late Fabius M. Ray of the city.

      Mr. Joseph Walker, a resident of Portland, began his business career in the lumber industry, in which he amassed a considerable fortune, in Westbrook.

      Mr. Walker was a client of Mr. Ray's and one day brought to him a skeleton of a will which he wished put in proper form. There were a number of public bequests among them being the provision for setting aside a considerable trust fund to be used for the worthy poor of this community.

      Mr. Ray, realizing how much more good a really up to date library would do for the needs of the growing city, suggested to Mr. Walker that he give the proposed money for a library to be known as the Walker Memorial Library. At first the idea did not appeal to Mr. Walker and he refused to listen to Mr. Ray's arguments, saying that on a certain date he would like to have the will ready for his signature with the provisions as he had stated.

Seeing that he felt strongly on this matter, Mr. Ray did not urge him but simply said, "You think it over."

The day he was to come and sign the document, Mr. Ray received a letter from him saying that he had thought the matter was a good deal and talked it over with his wife who strongly approved of Mr. Ray's suggestion and that he would come the next day to talk the matter over still further. This was done and the will signed.

After Mr. Walkers death the executor, Frederick Fox, took the matter up. Here again, Mr. Ray gave his services gladly. It took considerable time and negotiation to finally obtain the present site. The matter hung fire for quite a little time owing to the unwillingness of Mr. Ferris W. Edwards to give a common right of way on the east side. This obstacle being surmounted, then came the building of the structure and finally the selecting of the books, several thousand in number. Many evenings did Mr. Ray pour over catalogues and lists - until he was able to present to Mr. Fox at his request a good working library with which to start.

The remnant of the old circulating library of Westbrook founded in 1802 had been for many years stored in Mr. Ray's barn. Some three of four years before the building of the Memorial Library a group of citizens interested themselves in running this old library and in various ways money was raised to purchase new books. Mr. Ray freely gave of his time as librarian on Saturday afternoons, later, others helped out and finally it was turned over to the Memorial Library.

Then came the dedication of the new library and although no man in town had been more responsible for it than he, the Committee10 saw fit to ignore him completely in its program, much to the surprise of a goodly number of the city residents.

Prominent Maine Judge Was Successful Wooer Of The Muses

March 4, 1928, Portland, Maine

Besides being a sound and conservative lawyer, Fabius Maximus Ray was a wooer of the Muses and during his life published two volumes of poems which received favorable notices from the critics, and gained quite a wide circulation

He was born at South Windham, March 30, 1837, and was graduated from Bowdoin College in 1861. Among his classmates were: Frank L. Dingley, Edward Stanwood, Moses Owen, Charles B. Rounds, Lucilius A. Emery, Merritt C. Fernald, Charles G. Haines, Thomas W. Hyde and Charles O. Hunt.

Went Abroad

Mr. Ray passed the year following graduation in Germany and Switzerland studying German and French. Before returning to the United States, he passed a month in Scotland visiting scenes immortalized by Sir Walter Scott. This visit was the inspiration of one of Mr. Ray's finest poems, On Loch Katrine.

Mr. Ray studied law in the office of Phinehas Barnes of Portland and on being admitted to the bar began practice in Westbrook, where he maintained an office until 1885. In 1871 he formed a partnership with John c. Cobb of Portland, under the firm name of Cobb & Ray which continued for five years. Later Mr. Ray took as a partner

Edwin l. Dyer, under the firm name of Ray & Dyer, and this connection lasted until 1885 when Mr. Dyer was made register of the municipal court.

In 1867 Mr. Ray entered the senior class of the Divinity School at Cambridge, Mass., and was graduated but never received ordination as he concluded that he was better fitted for a lawyer than for a minister.

Mr. Ray was a firm believer in the principles of the Republican party and for many years took an active part in politics. He was elected to the Maine house of representatives in 1870-1871 and to the Senate in 1884. From 1883 to 1886 he served as judge of the municipal court of Westbrook.

He was a charter member of the Maine Genealogical Society and its third president, serving in that capacity for two years. He was also a member of the Maine Historical Society and in his latter years a frequent and welcome visitor to its library. He contributed to the Evening Express a series of valuable articles on the history of Westbrook. He was the poet of his college class and during the larger part of his life contributed many poems of merit to different periodicals which he finally collected and published in book form.

Judge Ray had a charming home in Westbrook, including flower and vegetable gardens in both of which he was deeply interested and aided in their cultivation. A visit to his hospitable home was a source of pleasure to many of his friends. He died quite suddenly, November 22, 1915.

Fabius M. Ray's Story of Westbrook

	page
Story of Westbrook	1
Old Ironworks and First Westbrook Church	109
First Baptist Church in Westbrook	113
Westbrook Congregational Church	117
Warren Congregational Church	130
Methodist Episcopal Church	133
Universalism	139
Episcopalians	146
Advent Christian Church	150
St. Hyacinthe Catholic Church	153
Saw & Grist Mills, Mast Industry	157
Westbrook Manufacuring Company	165
Haskell Silk Mill	169
S. D. Warren Company	172
Dana Warp Mills	179
Pewter Manufacture	181
Lesser Industries	184
Underground Railroad	193
Cumberland & Oxford Canal	195
Col. Westbrook's Dam	200
Old North School and other schools	202
Archelaus Lewis	210
Martha Washington Charitable Society	212
Index	218

Chapter 1

The first 18 chapters of this story have been compiled wholly from manuscripts and printed articles written by the late Fabius M. Ray who spent long years of genealogical research into the past. It is wholly his, as was said, with the exceptions of a few additions. In explanation of this labor of love, Mr. Ray says, to quote, "It was not the purpose of the writer in the preparation of these chapters to lay before the reader anything like a history in the true sense of the word, but rather to furnish him, in methodical form, the results of researches covering many years which it was thought might be of interest, for present perusal, and afford material for the future historian. Now while the subject is far from being exhausted, this is not true of the material still available. Up to this time we have dealt for the most part with the history of families, avoiding as much as possible the dry detail of mere genealogy. The work of gathering the histories of early families is sadly incomplete and is given up at the present time, mostly for lack of data."

All good stories begin with "once upon a time," therefore, once upon a time this region now covered with substantial homes, varied industries, churches, schools, libraries, in short, all that goes to make up a thriving and well-to-do community, was virgin forest.

The Presumpscot river was then even more beautiful than it is today for its verdant banks, which cast unrivaled shadows in its clear and limpid waters, were unpolluted by the many industries which now dot its banks. Great trees of many years' growth here stood in majestic splendor until Time, that great destroyer, did its work, ably seconded by the destructive hand of the white settler.

It has been conjectured by some that Saccarappa, now known as Westbrook, was built in the depression of an ancient lake. However, historic investigation does not seem to bear out that theory. It is much more likely that early settlers built their crude cabins over one of these disturbances of the earth's surfaces, partly eruptive and partly subsidence, know in the Presumpscot valley as "landslides." This must have occurred in prehistoric times, and covered extensive territory much greater than the slide of later date.

This later one known as the Boody slide, from its having taken place largely on Boody property, was within the memory of some now living in Westbrook. This slide, although rather a misnomer, took place in the autumn of 1868, and is still called the Boody or Cumberland Mills slide. This without a doubt began in the bottom of the Presumpscot river about three quarters of a mile below the dam at Cumberland Mills where the single tax colony of Halidon is now located.

At this point there had been, from historic times, a rather sharp curve in the river toward the northern bank, at the foot of a steep embankment of earth. The ascent from the bed of the river was between 30 and 40 feet, and above was a large tract of level land covered largely with pine and fir trees intermixed with hardwood growth.

The season, in this fall of 1868, had been unusually wet, and as a consequence the earth was saturated with water and the volume and velocity of the Presumpscot was much increased. As this upland was heavily overcharged with water and the soil of the river bed had been softened by being constantly flooded, this great extent of level land rested on no better foundation than a semi-liquid mass of soft clay and quicksand. From some cause the liquid mass of earth finding vent upward through the bed of the river, after a renewal of the heavy rains of the season, soon filled the curve in both directions, and as the soft earth was forced upward there was a corresponding subsidence of the upland so that in a few hours about 30 acres of level land had settled down into a rough and broken area of sandy loam and clay, which had been forced upward through many fissures nearly on a level with the waters of the river, that now made a new channel to the bed of the stream below.

This subsidence took place largely in the night and Mr. James Roberts, whose home was on East Bridge Street, told the writer how astounded he was on going out of doors on the morning of the slide, on looking toward Cumberland Mills to see no familiar trees; the forest was no more. He thought for a moment that something was wrong with his eyes and called his wife who confirmed his vision. Perhaps she said, "for the land's sake;" anyway the land was gone.

To return to the prehistoric slide. That the slide took place before 1657 is certain from the fact that this year the attention of the English was turned to this region, and land extending from the Capisic river to the present Cumberland Mills was purchased from an Indian Sagamore. Of course it was long after the floating iceberg had ceased to make its mark upon the rocks, and the land had settled down to its present aspect of plain and hill, valley, lake and river. And it is probable, too, many, many years after the Presumpscot had been its winding course from Sebago Lake to the Atlantic ocean, by substantially the same route as that of today. And the Stroudwater river also began its way through the dense forest in the direction of the estuary that afterward played such an important part in the trade of the colonies as a safe harbor for the ships of Waldo and Westbrook.

At this point not then named, but afterward called in the Abnakis dialect, Sacarabeag, the Presumpscot river made a sharp turn "toward the rising sun" and flowed onward toward the rapids near the old Indianplanting ground at old Ammoncongin and thence through swamp and woody tangle to the ocean.

Reasoning from the know facts and the appearance of the country near the Boody slide, investigators conclude that the southern bank of the Presumpscot, before the great slide of unknown date, was about where the Boston & Maine, Nashua Division, stood until very recently at Westbrook. Southerly and westerly from this point was a large tract over which, as was said, the wild beasts of the forests roamed at large. Suddenly 200 or more acres subsided, carrying with this subsidence all that grew here and all life that roamed at will, damming the swollen waters of the river and changing the face of the ground from upland to meadow.

The contour of this subsidence is easily traced, its deepest part being still called the "Old cellar field," for many years the property of the late George and Lewis P. Warren. Within recent years streets have been opened and houses built there.

It should be said that all the conditions that prevailed in old Westbrook at the time of which we write, also were present in a large adjoining territory which later was incorporated under the name of Falmouth. That ancient township included, besides numerous islands in Casco Bay, the present city of Portland, including the Deering district, Westbrook, South Portland, and the towns of Cape Elizabeth and Falmouth.

The first settlement within the limits of Falmouth of recorded date that has come down to us was made at Richmonds' Island, which may still be seen off the Cape Elizabeth shore near the mouth of the Spurwink river. Here as early as 1628 lived Walter Bagnall, otherwise know as "Great Walt," who carried on a thrifty trade in fur with the Indians in exchange for English goods and other commodities.

For some reason he had incurred the hatred of the red men and was killed by them in 1631; a companion of his was also killed and their houses plundered and burned.

This crime was supposed to have been the deed of a chieftain named Squitterrygusset and his men. This did not seem to have come to the attention of the English for a year or more. Then, however, in January of 1632, the crew of a vessel which was cruising along the coast in pursuit of pirates, put in at Richmonds' Island where they found a sachem from Massachusetts known as Black William of Nahant, whom they proceeded to hang to the nearest tree, notwithstanding his vigorous protests of innocence, and who was know to be friendly to the Whites. Meanwhile Squitterrygusset, for whose crime Black William of Nahant suffered an ignominious death, was spared to go down in history as the first to give a deed of land within our city to the white land speculator.

This sachem is said by the historian, Hon.William Willis, to have ruled over a tribe or clan of Abnekis known as the Aucociscos, from which is derived our familiar name of Casco. This is thought to have been the same tribe which fished and hunted along the Presumpscot river, and whose squaws planted in Springtime at the old Ammoncongin planting ground, and over which in later years reigned Polin who was shot by Manchester at New Marblehead, now Windham, in 1756. Descendants of this Stephen Manchester are still living in our city.

As places in and around Saccarappa still preserve in their local names the tradition of the beaver, and as this small animal furnishes the most valuable fur for the fur trader which was obtained by trade or barter with the Indians, it is highly probable that during these years that Walter Bagnall lived and carried on trade at Richmonds' Island, the Red Man hunted over this very territory where the beaver was plentiful, as evidenced by the name still used by us of today. Any inquiries as to why the large pond or sheet of water between Spring and Church Streets in Saccarappa is called Beaver Pond have received no satisfactory answer. I, therefore, assume, but it is only an assumption, that some time, years ago, in an age long gone by, the beaver built his dam on the little rill that empties into the Pond near the dwelling house, formerly the home of William Phinney on Spring Street. Also the Beaver Dam Brook, so-called, on Longfellow Street, within the limits of Gorham, was in the possession of these little animals when the white settler came. In fact, within the memory of some still living in Westbrook, Longfellow Street was called Beaver Road by the older people.

Other fur-bearing animals lived within the limits of the present city of Westbrook, in that far off time. A gentleman who lived until a few years ago is authority for the statement that up to the beginning of the past century the bears were so numerous in the vicinity of Saco Street that they made great havoc in the corn fields of the farmers, and the then familiar way of destroying them was by setting a rude trap known as the figure 4. This was the method of catching them practiced by the Johnson brothers who lived on Saco Street and whose farm was where the late Rufus Johnson, remembered by many, lived and died.

An old lady living in that vicinity told the writer that she well remembered as a child hearing her mother tell how on moonlight nights in the early Fall the bears would be heard in the corn fields. The fence around this field had a loose board which she would go out and flap back and forth to scare them away, which often proved effective.

The deer, the moose, and the caribou roamed over this territory and their flesh was a valued article of food then as now. They also furnished clothing and strings for the Indian's bow and arrow, and thongs for his snowshoes.

And now the White Man appears and this paradise of the Red Man gave way before the hand of progress. The stately forest trees that counted not at all in the Indian's mind, the European saw as a source of wealth. For a few beads of glass, or something of as little value, he gave up his ancient heritage and the White Man took possession.

Chapter 2

It is very probable that there was settlers within the limits of our present territory who came with the intention of remaining permanently, but were driven off by the Indians before 1650, the year of the destruction of Fort Loyal at Falmouth, now the city of Portland. Fort Loyal stood approximately where the Grand Trunk Station now stands.

At Ammoncongin, now Cumberland Mills (the older inhabitants were loath to relinquish the Indian name which they shortened to Congin oftentimes), the Indians from time immemorial had a considerable clearing which they used as a planting ground.

This land was included in the tract of a mile square or more which George Munjoy, under date of June 4, 1666, had purchased of the Indian Sagamore. Previous to this, as has already been said, in 1657 the famous chieftain, Squitterrygusset, had deeded lands within our present limits to a white man. The buyer in this transaction is described in the deed of conveyance as "Francis Small of Casco Bay, fisherman" and the territory described as "all that upland and marshes at Capisic lying up along the northern side of the river, unto the head thereof, so to reach and extend into the river side at Ammoncongin."

The consideration for this large tract of land, which Mr. Willis, the Portland historian, greatly underestimates as two miles, was "one trading coat a year for Capisic and one gallon of liquor a year for Ammoncongin," and on this same authority, too, we are justified in saying that this is the first Indian Deed extant of land in old Falmouth, and that Small, who was 30 years old at the time, settled on his purchase where he remained several years. In May 1658, Small sold one half of his Squitterrygusset purchase to John Phillips of Boston, who was the father-in-law of George Munjoy in whose behalf the purchase seems to have been made. Unfortunately it is quite impossible to determine from data available after this long lapse of years whether it was at Capisic or at Ammoncongin that Small lived. It is not probable that Robert Lawrence, who married Munjoy's widow and succeeded to his agricultural operations at Ammoncongin, ever dwelt at Capisic. Nor did Small ever live at old Congin, where he was succeeded by Munjoy, who in turn was succeeded by Lawrence and their servants. If so, Small was the first settler in that part of the present Westbrook. In this connection it is worthy of mention that his kindred and descendants are with us in considerable numbers today.

According to the well remembered correspondent of the Argus, "L.W.S.," Francis Small was born in England in 1620 and came to America in 1632 with his father who is thought to have borne the name of Edward Small. Francis Small was living at Dover, New Hampshire, in 1648, and died at Truro or Provincetown on Cape Cod in 1713. He had a house and trading camp where the village of Cornish, in York County, is now situated, and received a deed from the famous Captain Sunday of a large tract of land known as the Ossipee lands. Through one of his sons, Samuel, he was the ancestor of numerous families of Smalls in Limington and other town in York County.

George Munjoy, who received the deed of the "mile square", was the same individual who gave the name to the present Munjoy Hill of Portland. He seems to have been a man of considerable enterprise, who was with a prophetic vision that the land to which the Indians attached little value, being willing to give up their precarious titles for a few trinkets or a coat of many colors, to say nothing of the strong waters which undoubt-edly prepared the way for a sharp bargain on the part of the white man, would in the years to come be of great a value, if not to himself, to those coming after him.

But the ancient planting ground that was already cleared seemed especially attractive to the English speculator. According to an old deposition Munjoy and his wife Mary "had a home and some improvements on the southwest side of the river at Ammoncongin" where the said Munjoy and his servants used to go in planting and reaping times, and where they usually tarried about a week at a time.

It seems that a dispute had arisen concerning the ownership of the Capisic and Ammoncongin lands, and testimony was now being taken "in perpetual memory of the thing" by some of the claimants; hence "this deposition further saith that the home last mentioned was opposite to said Munjoy's planting ground on the northerly side of the river at Ammoncongin which said Munjoy to the deponent's certain knowledge, improved many years, sowing peas and wheat without interruption."

After Munjoy's death, which happened here in 1685, his widow married Robert Lawrence who in 1690 was the officer in command and lost his life at the taking of Fort Loyal. Lawrence also improved his wife's property, which she had received from her first husband, Mr. Munjoy, for several years, and lived on the southwest side of the river in the manner Munjoy did. Said Lawrence rebuilt the house after it was burned by the Indians. It is a matter of history, therefore, that both Munjoyand Lawrence lived, temporarily at least, at old Ammoncongin.

It was in 1658, the year following that in which Francis Small acquired title to his Ammoncongin land, that the name of Falmouth was first applied to the ancient township by joint compact between the inhabitants and commissioners appointed by the General Court of Massachusetts. "These places formerly called Spurwink and Casco Bay shall run back eight miles from the east side of Spurwink to the Clapboard in Casco Bay, shall run back eight miles into the country, and hereafter shall be called by the name of Falmouth." It was thus an article numbered 8 of this agreement read; and from this time the scattered settlements of Spurwink, the Neck, Presumpscot river (Lower Falls), Capisic and Back Cove commenced the business of self government under the unique form of the republic, the town with its board of selectmen and other necessary officers.

From this time, until the abandonment of this territory by the Whites in 1690, was a period of 32 years which, but for the trouble with the Indians, was marked by much prosperity. Saw and grist mills grew in the forest and it is probable that the export of grain and fur brought large profits to the enterprising business men of these days.

It is evident that the farming operations of both Munjoy and Lawrence were not confined to the old Indianplanting ground from the fact that in 1734, after the organization of the old town when lands between Saccarappa and Ammoncongin were laid out by the proprietors' committee to Samuel Waldo, mention is made of "Old Ammoncongin Farm" as being, by implication at least, on the southern side of the river.

Robert Lawrence, as has been said, lost his life in the defense of old Fort Loyal in 1690. By the calamities of this and succeeding years up to 1703 inclusive, the white settlers were driven away from Falmouth for the second time. The wife of Lawrence, who had probably returned to Boston at the commencement of Indian troubles about 1680, finding herself a widow, married as her third husband Stephen Cross, and continued to live in Boston where she died in 1705. The lands at Saccarappa and Ammoncongin now passed into the hands of a Boston merchant named Cooper, and by subsequent conveyance came into the possession of that great landed proprietor, Brigadier Samuel Waldo. This tract was long known as the "Cooper Claim" and is mentioned by that name in deeds of real estate in the first years of the 19th century.

The years from 1690 to 1730, a period of 40 years, is barren of interest as far as this region is concerned. Probably the red man held way here and his squaws again cultivated the old Ammoncongin planting ground. But it is probably that the woodlands round about did not escape the attention of the King's Mast agents, and that many of the gigantic pine trees bore the sign of the broad arrow.

For the little that can be learned of George Munjoy, who seems to have built first in Westbrook, then Falmouth, we are indebted to Willis. That he was a man of intelligence and business acumen goes without saying. It was quite the fashion for the historian of that day to assume that any man who achieved success in his day and generation had come to this new world from some part of the old world, preferably from England.

Of Colonel Westbrook and Brigadier General Waldo, it is related by both Willis and Williamson that they were both natives of America, and came of old families that had lived for several generations on New England soil. But there is better reason for believing that Munjoy was born in England, his birth taking place half a century at least before that of Westbrook, while he had been dead several years when Waldo was born in Boston in 1796. According to well established authority George Munjoy was the son of John Munjoy of Abbottaham in Devonshire, England, where he was born in 1626. What year he came to America is not known but he was admitted free man in Masschusetts in 1647. He married Mary, daughter of Deacon John Phillips of Boston who, as was said, after his death married Robert Lawrence, and after Lawrence's death, Stephen Cross.

Munjoy and his wife had several children, viz; John, born in Boston and killed by the Indians at Falmouth Neck in 1657; Mary, who married John Palmer; John, born in Boston and died at Braintree in 1698; and others.

It was stated by Mr. Willis that the name was extinct. Such is not the fact, however. A rather curious happening brought this fact to light. A member of the family of the chronicler of these by-gone events is a bird student, hence seeing an unusually fine bird chart, the maker's name was noted as being John Mountjoy whose residence was in the vicinity of Chicago. He was written to and one of these charts obtained. A correspondence followed which brought to light the fact that the John Mountjoy of Chicago was a lineal descendant of George Munjoy of old Falmouth. The descendant spells the name Mountjoy instead of Munjoy. The name is said to have been of Norman French origin and formerly written Mountjoie. The elder George Munjoy had a sister who married John Saunders of Braintree.

Much speculation has been indulged in regarding the meaning and derivation of the so-called Indian names in and about this locality. The name Saccarappa has undergone one important change since it was first written in the deed from the Indian Sagamore to George Munjoy. There can be but little doubt that the word contains the same root as Saco which has also undergone important changes and curtailments. It may be, as some have thought, that the waterfall "toward the rising sun" in both cases gives the name to the locality. Others maintain that the common "sac" or "ak" in both names should signify "burnt district." According to Rev. Dr. Ballad of Brunswick, Ammoncongin was also written Ammoncoggin, but it is hardly probable for only once, after most diligent search, has that spelling been found to exist. During the Indian wars, when Falmouth was deserted by the white settlers, one deed was given which was recorded in the York records, and only one in which a former inhabitant conveys land on the Ammoncongin river near Presumpscot Falls. Everywhere else the name is used the stream mentioned is manifestly the Androscoggin, a very natural mistake. According to Dr. Potter, another distinguished antiquarian, the word Ammoncongin is compounded of three Indian words: namaas--fish; kee--high; anke--place.

A vivid imagination surely is required to understand just how this connection is effected but it gives us in English either of three forms following from which to choose an equivalent for one of our best know historical names, to wit: a fish place, a fish drying place, and a high fish. It is said that the Indians were accustomed to fertilize their cornfields by placing under the seed at planting time one or more dead fish, a process which was called "fishing the corn." It is told that in Springtime alewives and possibly salmon were abundant in the Presumpscot in the day when the Indians planted there. There is a fast fading tradition which has been handed down for many generations that before the river had been obstructed by dams across the stream, shad and alewives were always abundant in season, and that salmon were so plentiful that when boys were appren-ticed to any of the trades that were pursed in these hamlets along the river, it was especially stipulated that they should not be compelled to eat salmon more than three days out of each week.

Chapter 3

Tradition, or records, are silent as to the exact time that the former settlers, or their descendants, ventured back to their old homes in Falmouth after their departure caused by the fear of the direful deeds of the Indians in 1703. The following from the book of the Church Records of the old First Parish in the hand writing of the Rev. Thomas Smith has been most fortun-ately preserved and will be read with added interest as the years go by.

"Anno 1716 on Ingersoll built a hut on Falmouth Neck, where he lived alone some time, and was thence called Governor Ingersoll. He was afterwards drowned at Presumpscot with one Millett by the damming of the ice, raising a head of water in the night while they slept. New Castle Fort being demolished by order of Government a few months after this, viz. 1717, Major Moody who had been the commanding officer, with Captain Larrabee who had been a sergeant, moved their families down to the Neck and built them houses. About this time, 1715, Mr. Skillin and Mr. Brackett settled on their fathers' old farms at Back Cove (near the present Oakdale in the Deering district.) Now came Captain Coller and built a house, as did one Proctor, Doughty, Rounds, Mills, Hall, two Scales (brothers), father Thomes, Wass (12 in all), and John Barbour and father Gustin (who died in 1718.)" The last two have descendants in Westbrook who served on the centennial committee in June 1914, for the Presentation of old Families, namely George E. Gustin and Herbert D. Barbour, who have both died since. Mr. Barbour left a son and two daughters. Mr. Gustin left no children.

It was now determined to petition the General Court of Massachusetts for the reincorporation of the old town, and the prayer of the petitioners was readily granted, after which the town entered upon an era of prosperity and growth that has always continued, although not always with the speed that many have wished.

But difficulties arose within the first decade that are fully detailed in the history of Portland by the late William Willis and need therefore only a passing mention. It was the controversy between the old and new proprietors, or owners of the common lands, which was adjusted by a union of the two parties in 1732, and the formation of a new proprietary that continued in active existence until about 1826 and has never as yet, it is believed, been formally dissolved. Its last clerk was Nathan Winslow of Westbrook who died in the year last named.

After the union the work of parceling out the lands to the inhabitants who had complied with the conditions went on rapidly, especially in the year 1732. Most of the titles of real estate in this vicinity have their beginning in the above mentioned grants which are to be found recorded in the Falmouth Proprietors' Records, now kept in the Cumberland County Registry of Deeds in the city of Portland.

Some of the grants, however, are to be found in the town clerk's records of the ancient town. One of these which should be of special interests to the citizens of Westbrook is as follows:

"According to ye vote of ye town, we ye subscribers to choose ye Falls, ye third Falls in Presumpscot River and known by ye of Sacarapese called by ye Indians.

"This report to ye Select Men of Falmouth as witness this 12th day of July 1728

>Benj. Ingersoll
>Robert Pearce
>Benj. Larrabee Jr.
>John Bayley

This was in accordance with a vote of the town at the previous annual meeting giving to these men their choice of certain of the great water powers.

There is a prevailing impression based upon traditional authority that the first saw mills were soon after erected upon the northerly side of the "Island" where the Dana Warp Mill now stands, and as soon as possible put in operation. An industry of so much importance in the midst of the wilderness would of necessity call in a considerable number of workmen, who naturally would bring along their families and erect dwellings in the near vicinity.

But to Joseph Conant born in Beverly on the 9th day of November, 1701, tradition gives the honor of having made the first permanent settlement in Saccarappa and probably the first within our corporate limits. Too often traditions are entirely baseless and misleading and should, therefore, always be received with great caution. But this one seems to be of historic verity; it has always been accepted by old families and when told is always the same.

Conant was the great grandson of Roger Conant, the first settler and governor of Naumkeag, now Salem. He married in Boxford on the 9th day of December, 1725, Sarah, daughter of Thomas and Hannah Jewett. Their first child, Hannah, was born in Ipswich December 27,1726. On November 7, 1728, a son, Lot, was born in Falmouth. The year of Conant's coming to Saccarappa tradition does not say but does say that he was the pioneer settler and brought his family and worldly goods up the river in a canoe. If nature was in a good mood that day a fair sight must have been spread out before their eyes for the Presumpscot is a beautiful river. In 1728 two lots of land were assigned to him, which he appears to have been obliged to give up, probably because they were claimed by old proprietors. In 1730 he was granted a ten acre lot at the head of Fore River. This, too, seems to have been upon a former grant, for in 1734 there was laid out to him a tract of 43 acres on the northerly side of the Presumpscot river, in lieu of his thirty, ten and three acre grants, which he had reconveyed to the proprietors. At the same time he was also granted 60 on the southerly side of the Presumpscot which has never been located, but the tract of 43 acres is without doubt in the William Walker farm near Pride's bridge, and was the same which Conant sold to John Webb in 1761. In 1734 he was most likely living in Saccarappa where he had already resided for some years.

Would that we might record which one of Conant's children, if either, was the first child of European descent to be born in Westbrook. But it is recorded that a son Thomas was born in Falmouth December 2, 1731 and died young; but whether Conant had already made his memorable trip up the Presumpscot at this time cannot be ascertained with any degree of certainty. But it is fairly safe to assume that he had come here and was housed under his squatter roof on the 3rd of October, 1733, the date of the birth of his twin daughters, Elizabeth and Sarah. The subsequent career of Sarah is unknown, but Elizabeth, before July 1759, had become the wife of Ezekial Jones who appears later to have emigrated to Royalsborough, now Durham, where bother he and his wife were living in 1800.

Of Conant's son, Lot, born in 1732, no more has been learned, but two younger sons, Barthelomew and Joseph left numerous posterity, although none of them bearing the family name are now left in Westbrook. Barthelomew Conant lived near Duck Pond, now known as Highland Lake. He married Anna Frink of an old Falmouth family, and had five children, one of whom, Eunice, was the second wife of Daniel Lunt, a prominent and active man in the affairs of the town in the latter part of the 18th century, of whom more will be said later.

Joseph Conant, Jr., had sons, Barthelomew and Thomas, and a daughter Anna, who married Nathan Partridge. He married Hannah Shackford June 10,1782, and died in Portland June 17,1816 while attending court as a witness. On the 10th of June 1740, Joseph Conant, "husbandman" as the deed has it, sells to Thomas Conant "my dwelling house that stands on the northerly side of the Presumpscot river near Saccarappa Falls in Falmouth." It seems that the conveyance had something to do with the compromising of a law suit. In the deed which was not acknowledged until May 16,1762, no mention is made of the land on which the house stood, which was probably a part of the old Cooper or Munjoy claim. From recitals of a deed from Haskell to one of his sons made in 1764, it would seem that he had previously received from the proprietors a grant of a hundred and three acres on the northerly side of the river at Saccarappa, which had been recovered against him in suit by one Mary Waters of Sturbridge, Massachusetts, widow, and which he had subsequently purchased from her.

It seems that Conant still continued to reside at Saccarappa after selling his home to Haskell, and to diversify his farming pursuits with the management of saw and grist mills, for in 1755 he sells one-eighth of a saw mill at Saccarappa to Enoch Freeman. The recitals in a deed from Conant to Francis Peabody of Middleton under date of March 25, 1758, are of interest as showing the manner in which mills and water powers were deeded in those days. The interest conveyed by this deed is "one-half of one-thirtieth of the mill privilege of Saccarappa Falls with the privilege of setting mills on both sides of the river, which was granted to Benjamin Larrabee and others, together with half the dwelling house and half the grist mill thereon standing, being part of the privilege I purchased of Thomas Smith." the other half of the thirtieth part was owned at this time by his brother, Samuel Conant, whose wife was a sister of the grantee, Peabody, and from whom the Conant family of this city descended, and for whom also the street extending from Main Street to the Gorham line was named.

On the 27th of November, 1761, Joseph Conant conveyed land near the Duck Pond to his sons, Joseph, Jr. and Barthlolmew. This was probably done in anticipation of a surgical operation from which he did not recover as is shown by the following extract from the journal of the Rev. Thomas Smith. "27th (November, 1764) I rode with Mr. Deane to Conant's and Proctor's I prayed with the former who had his leg amputated by Nathaniel Coffin, and Mr. Deane with the latter who had his arm broken in two places."

At a time when the only anesthetics known were spirituous liquors, it is not strange that a man of Mr. Conant's years should not withstand the shock of so severe an operation as the removal of a leg. From the journal of Mr. Deane this extract is taken which concludes the life drama of this enterprising pioneer: "2 (January 1765), attended the funeral of Mr. Conant."

Mr. Conant seems to have yielded up his life under the best surgical skill nearer than Boston. Dr. Nathaniel Coffin who performed the operation was no doubt the younger of that name now living in Falmouth Neck, where he was an eminent practitioner under date of August, 1764, about three months before the operation of Mr. Conant. Parson Smith made the following entry in his invaluable journal: "Captain Haggett in a mast ship arrived with young Dr. Coffin." In a marginal note the information is given that he had been abroad to complete his medical education and had been studying in London in Thomas and Guy's hospital. Such advantages were very unusual with the young physicians in America where it appears there was no medical college whatsoever, the usual method of pursuing medical study being as an articled apprentice to an old practitioner, who at the completion of the term gave a written certificate as a sufficient diploma. Many of the pastors of the Congregational persuasion also practiced physics, and many laymen pursued blood letting and tooth pulling as subsidiary vocations, thereby acquiring the title of "Doctor," which contrary to English custom and etiquette, is now applied to men of the medical profession generally in this country.

Chapter 4

The mile square received from the Indian sagamore by George Munjoy, of which frequent mention has been made, was sold by Munjoy's widow and his son, George, to Thomas Cooper of Boston on April 5, 1692, and was thereafter called the Cooper claim. Finally through successive ownership's it passed into the hands of General Samuel Waldo from whom and his heirs the present owners of the most past derive their titles.

An early land survey was made by William Pote, a land surveyor of that time, of this tract, and a plan made by him is recorded in the Falmouth Proprietors' book of land grants. This survey was made in the Spring of 1743 for General Waldo who was then at the height of his prosperity, having recently accomplished the business ruin of his former partner, Colonel Westbrook, upon whose estate and lands he levied an execution for 10,500 pounds. The easterly boundary is, to quote, "by Mr. Phippen's land." The latter is probably the largest purchase made from the Indians in this vicinity. It is recorded that on August 14, 1672, Jenkin Williams, George Felt, and Francis Neale purchased from Nanaadonit and Waraad Button a tract of land on the northeast side of the Presumpscot river beginning at the easterly end of the "mile square" and extending down the river to John Wakeley's new dwelling house, and six miles back from the river. Wakeley's house was about three fourths of a mile below the Lower Falls. Felt's son, Neale and Williams conveyed this land to David Phippen before 1700. The Indian grantors probably claimed their right to convey in place of Squitterrygusset who had departed for "the happy hunting ground." It seems from an old deposition that the other Indians disputed their right to convey.

These two claims known as the "Cooper" and "Phippen" claims take in nearly all our original territory on the northerly side of the river, for New Marblehead, now Windham, was laid out on the 17th day of May, 1735, as follows: "We began at a place called Saccarappa Falls on Presumpscot River and as the river runs to a great pond call Sebago Pond; thence north 45 degrees, east 4 miles and 120 rods; thence south 45 degrees, east to North Yarmouth back line; thence 3 miles, 45 degrees west to the corner of North Yarmouth and Falmouth boundary; thence south 24 degrees, 20 minutes, 8 miles and 50 rods to Saccarappa Falls.

The boundary line between Windham and that past of Falmouth which is now Westbrook remained in controversy until November 27, 1761 when it was established as at present, existing by an act of the General Court. The first settlement in Windham is said to have been July 30, 1737 by Capt. Thomas Chute, who carried his family and effects up the river by the present route of the many canoes and small motor boats of today, and made a clearing and erected his log cabin where he afterwards kept an ordinary on land by the river side lately owned by the father of the late ex-mayor Mahlon H. Webb. But previous to this time, from July 8, 1735 to June 9, 1737, the grantees had spent considerable sums of money in building bridges over the Presumpscot River immediately above Saccarappa Falls, and on Inkhorn and Colley Wright's (now Dole's) brooks, and clearing a highway for the incoming of the settlers. That large tract of land was long in dispute between the proprietors of the tow towns, but none of the first home lots in Windham were laid out upon the same. It seems, however, that some encroachments were made thereon by the Windham grantees for it appears in an old deed that the farm formerly owned by the late Daniel B. Shaw was laid out to Richard Dana of Boston, to compensate him for a forest grant which he had been obliged to give up after the adjustment of the division line between Windham and Falmouth was found to be in Falmouth.

The bridge for which the Windham grantees made appropriation at Saccarappa, if ever built, probably did not long continue to be used, for at a town meeting held at Falmouth March 19,1759, it was voted that "The selectmen be directed to lay out the money assessed on the mills at Saccarappy and Ammoncongan that year to repair the Great Bridge at Saccarappy."

The same year a return was made of a road "beginning at Saccarappa Road at a pine tree, marked, near the corner of David Small's land at Deer Hill, thence by southeasterly course which are given till it intersects with a road that is laid out to Presumpscot River by Joseph Conant's land. Small is said to have lived on the same spot where the residence of the late Clement P. Maxwell now stands; and Conant's land was probably the tract of 60 acres laid out to him by the Falmouth Proprietors.

Whatever was done about the money assessed on the mills for the repairing of the "great Bridge" at Saccarappa seems not to have been satisfactory to the good people then living in Windham, at least not for any great length of time, for at a town meeting held in Falmouth, February 9, 1756 the selectmen were made a committee without pay to confer "with the inhabitants of New Marblehead and others to see how much they will advance toward building a bridge over the Presumpscot River and fix the most proper place therefore," and make report to the town at the ensuing annual meeting. When the annual meeting came in March it seems that the matter had already got into the Courts for Colonel Ezekiel Cushing was chosen "to make answer at the April term to the complaint exhibited by the inhabitants of New Marblehead, and to petition the sessions to establish a ferry over the river for their accommodation."

The proposal for a ferry over a comparatively narrow stream seems to have met with little favor apparently. The reply seems to have been to build a substantial bridge forthwith. Still, as the principal business of the town and town meetings were held at the "neck," while Saccarappa was only a small village in an outlying district, the disposition to temporize and evade seems to have continued for a year or more before the matter was finally disposed of. On the 30th of September, 1757, a town meeting was held for the sole purpose, it would appear, of hearing "the report of the committee chosen in May to view the bridge lately built at Saccarappa." This bridge, evidently, was not more acceptable than the report, but there is no recorded date respecting either except what may be inferred from the fact that at the same meeting it was "voted to give Solomon Haskell Fifty Pounds Lawful Money for the bridge he has lately built at Saccarappy, provided the court at sessions will accept the same as a good and sufficient bridge; otherwise he is to make it sufficient to the court's acceptance."

To the foregoing vote Solomon Haskell returned the following answer which, if tradition is to be credited, was characteristic of the man: "I consent to sell the bridge, I refuse making nay repairs or additions, bur relinquish my right to the above sum and reserve the bridge to myself, Solomon Haskell.

After two or three adjournments for short, short periods, evidently for consultation as the sufficiency of the bridge, the meetings died a natural death. This bridge was in the same place where the iron bridge stands today. Probably Haskell's terms were accepted for the bridge became the property of the town.

In a deposition given in 1805 and recorded in the Cumberland County Registry of Deeds he says that he was 79 years old and came to live in Saccarappa in February, 1740, and had resided here ever since, with the exception of 2 1/2 years that he lived at Ammoncongin. According to the inscription on the headstone in Saccarappa cemetery his death occurred May 22, 1816 when he was 92 years old. This makes a difference of two years as between the age given on the gravestone and that given in the deposition. Like many of the early settlers he was actively engaged in the operation of mills, which were made to yield handsome returns. He was one of the sons of Thomas Haskell, already mentioned, who purchased Joseph Conant's dwelling house in 1740, the same which his son came to Saccarappa to occupy. Thomas Haskell was born in Gloucester, Massachusetts, in 1689 and came to Falmouth Neck in 1726. His coming is spoken of in connection with the coming of others by Parson Smith; "also one Haskell, a sober sort of man, with his family."

From Batson's History of Gloucester it is learned that he was of the same family as Roger Haskell, an early settler of Salem, and was the son of Benjamin and Mary (Riggs) Haskell, and thus related to Jeremiah Riggs, the first of the name in this vicinity and an early settler at Capisic. Coming to Saccarappa Thomas Haskell not only obtained the house of Conant by purchase but he had a grant of 103 acres of land nearby, the title of a part of which involved him in litigation with the heirs of Thomas Cloice, an old settler, whose earlier claim in the township he finally bought of the heirs. He also had an interest in a grist mill on the northerly side of the river, probably on the Lower Falls, which was in existence as late as 1813.

On the 31st day of March, 1732, a grant of land containing one hundred acres on the southerly side of the river was laid out to John Tyng as follows: "Beginning at Saccarappa Falls and running down the river 126 1/2 rods to a stake, and back from the river 126 1/2 rods." Authorities do not agree as to John

Tyng's connection with the celebrated family of that name, but reliable investigation shown him to have been the brother of Sarah Tyng, the first wife of Rev. Thomas Smith, and the son of William Tyng of Woburn. He remained in Falmouth only a few years, subsequently settling in Tyngsboro, where descendants bearing the name of Brinley were living a few years ago. He long served as judge of the Court of Common Pleas for Middlesex County and was known as "the eccentric Judge Tyng of Tyngboro." His grant of 100 acres he disposed of a few years after acquiring it to General Samuel Waldo, who seems to have made this land an exception to his usual custom, selling it sometime before 1756 to Benjamin and Solomon Haskell, brothers, and sons of Thomas Haskell. Thus having large landed estates on both sides of the river, together with mills, so much frequented as grist mills were to a later day, the Haskells wisely connected their possessions by a bridge of their own, and so were independent of the caprice of the town meetings that were held several miles away, and were obviously controlled by voters who would not willingly tax themselves for needed improvements in a remote country village.

Benjamin Haskell, after a few years' joint ownership conveyed his share of the Tyng tract to his brother, Solomon, but continued to hold his interest in the grist mill, and to reside on the northerly side of the river until his death October 14, 1785, at the age of 60 years. His grave and that of his second wife, Lydia, marked by a double headstone, were to be seen for many years in the neglected burying ground on Scotch Hill. Some years ago when the property came into the possession of the S. D. Warren Company, Mr. John E. Warren had the remains removed to Woodlawn cemetery and the ancient headstone laid in cement over the grave. The inscription is "Doctr.Benjamin Haskell but in all conveyances he is mention as as "yeoman."

In the ledger of William Lunt, who in the last century resided at Prides Corner on the farm until recent years owned and occupied by the late Henry B. Walker, occurs an account of mutual dealing between himself and Benjamin Haskell. William Lunt was a shoemaker as well as farmer and in the debtor column of the ledger after sundry charges for mowing and for repairing foot wear for members of Haskell's family is following entry: "this 31st day of May, 1786, I settled all accounts with

Mrs. Haskell as this receipt will appear." It is a quaint relic. The "receipt" which was doubled together and stitched to the leaf with show thread where it had no doubt remained for more than a hundred years reads as follows:

                Falmouth, May 31, 1786

Received of Mrs. William Lunt four shillings in full of all accounts from the Beginning to Today.

        Lydia Haskell
        Administrix

The credit column which is transcribed as showing the nature of the latter's medical practice, as well as the price received in English money, viz.

1775

			s	d
	May 11	By bleeding me		0
			0	8
	Aug. 5	By haling a tooth	0	
			0	8

1777

			s	d
	June 7	By one visit & bleeding my wife & some roots	0	
	July 1	By 1 visit and some roots and arbs		0
	July 2	By one visit and some fisike	0	
	July 10	By one snuf Bottel of sorrup	0	
	July 11	By one visit and bleeding my wife	0	

1785

			s	d
	June 15	By one visit and bleeding me	0	1

Chapter 5

William Lunt, of whom we have spoken, had business dealing with most of the physicians who lived in the old town at that time, according to his ledger. He mowed their hayfields and mended their shoes for which he received their professional services and nostrums for himself and family. On the same page and immediately following his account with Dr. Haskell are debits and credits to Dr. Coffin who, as was said, was the leading doctor east of Boston. Among the items with which he is credited are the following: "1 visit, Som Salts, Som Snakeroot," and later, "Bleeding Me," thus making it evident that Haskell though only entitled to "yeoman" during his lifetime, did not differ in his medical practice from the regular physicians of that day.

Intentions of marriage between Benjamin Haskell of Falmouth and Abigail Parsons of Gloucester were entered with the town clerk on May 10, 1752. She was no doubt a relative, perhaps a cousin of Haskell, whose mother was Mary Parsons of Gloucester. The marriage probably took place, although there is no record, but Benjamin is said to have been married twice. His second wife was Lydia Freeman of a Cape Cod family of that name. She survived his death nearly 13 years, dying May 20, 1798.

Below the name of the parents on the double headstone are those of children. The only other headstone in that old neglected cemetery having an inscription was erected to a daughter of Thomas Haskell who married Z. Hunnewell, a native of Scarborough, who was the first of the name to settle in Windham. The inscription is as follows:

Here Lyes Buried
The Body of Mrs.
Hannah Hunnewell
Wife of Zerubabel
Hunnewell
Died July 26th,
1753
Aged 32 years.

This body and headstone was also removed to Woodlawn Cemetery where the other before mentioned were removed.

Dr. Benjamin Haskell had sons, Thomas, William, Barri and Parsons, and daughters, Hannah and Mary who survived him. Parsons at the time of his mother's death, which occurred in 1798, was still a minor, but probably soon after became of age as he and his brother, Barri, made provision, near the beginning of the 19th century for a home for their maiden sisters in the dwelling house of the family. This house was probably on the easterly side of that portion of Bridge Street which runs northerly from the end of the bridge to the present Grammar School building. Probably it was on the site of the latter.

William, son of Dr. Benjamin, had a wife, Lucy, and was living in Portland in September, 1814. He was by trade a cabinet maker. Barri Haskell had a wife Catherine who joins in relinquishing dower in a conveyance of land and mill property to Jonathan Webb, December 17, 1800. Included in this sale was a quarter interest in the Haskell grist-mill which was owned in common with Solomon Haskell, John Haskell, and William Cobb. Cobb was a son-in-law of Joseph Quimby and his wife Mary, a daughter of the elder Thomas Haskell.

John Haskell was another of the sons of the patriarch Thomas Haskell, and lived on a farm in Gorham immediately to the westward of the division of that town and Falmouth. A small clump of trees, still standing on the southerly side of the old road from Saccarappa to Gorham is said to mark the site of another of the Haskell burying ground, but if gravestones were ever erected they are no longer to be seen. The dwelling house in which he lived stood until fairly recent years in the rear of the store of Cressey and Graffam. It was a large two-storied structure, weather beaten and unattractive. It was removed from the Gorham site to Cumberland Mills many years ago. The wife of John Haskell was Abigail Libby of Scarborough. They had nine children. Of these Benjamin married Sally Berry and settled in Standish, and Reuben and Thomas lived in Portland. A daughter, Rachel, who married Michael Dyer, died in Pownal some years ago, about 100 years old.

William, another son of Thomas Haskell, was the ancestor of the Haskells of Windham.

Joseph Quimby and his wife, Mary Haskell, were the ancestors of the Quimby, Peter, Seal and Slemmons families of Stroudwater and vicinity. Of the elder Solomon Haskell much has already been said. His intentions of marriage with Mary White were filed September 24, 1749. She is said to have been a widow. By her he had two sons, Solomon, Jr. and Mark, to whom he left the "Tyng hundred acres," and daughters Anna, who married Daniel Conant, and Mary, who married William Lamb, Jr. of Deer Hill. Mr. Haskell was a deacon of the Congregational Church and is said to have been greatly exercised in spirit when the first Methodist minister held services in the town of his adoption. Since then, however, some of his own descendants have been useful and honorable members of that household of faith.

In spite of the difficulties between the Windham Proprietors and the town of Falmouth regarding a bridge over the Presumpscot River and the dividing line between the two towns, it is a fact worthy of notice that the early residents of Saccarappa attended divine worship in Windham where a church was gathered in 1743 under the ministry of Rev. John Wight who was ordained December 14 of that year. The church records in the handwriting of Mr. Wight show the names of several persons known to have lived in this town, notably Thomas Haskell and several members of his family. Haskell was dismissed from the First Parish of Falmouth (now Portland) to unite with the church in New Marblehead (Windham) and later in 1765 was again dismissed to join in the organization of The Fourth Congregational Society of Falmouth, now known as Capisic. Among the original members of the church long under the pastorate of the Rev. Thomas Browne and later under that of the famous Parson Bradley were the following persons who are known to have resided within the present limits of Westbrook: viz. Thomas Haskell, Nathaniel Knight, Solomon Haskell and Benjamin Haskell.

An early settler of Saccarappa was Daniel Godfrey, by trade a housewright. He was a personage of no small importance on the present Main Street of Westbrook, then recently "swamped out" for the passage of log and lumber teams. December 4, 1732, he had laid out to his thirty acres of land about ten rods above Saccarappa Falls. This was on the southwestern side of the river and probably included the tract of seven or eight acres lately owned by Mrs. Susan S. Conant. September 26, 1732, another tract of seventy acres adjoining the above tract was laid out to Godfrey. This tract included the present "old cellar field." November 24, 1738, one acre was laid out to him "for a house lot" at the corner of his thirty acre lot. Four days later there was laid out to him a lot of three acres "on the thirty acre lot" and December 27 of the same year he received four acres more. He is known to have been an owner in saw mills and water power, for on November 23,1761, "Benjamin Godfrey, shipwright sells to Robert Johnson "yeoman," one-eighth part of a double saw mill at a place called Saccarappa in Falmouth, together with one-eighth part of the stream thereunto belonging, where said double saw mill and stream which I purchased of Daniel Godfrey, late of Falmouth, housewright, deceased, being in common and undivided with other owners of said mill and streams."

Daniel Godfrey made a will which may be found in the volume of Maine wills published from the York records by the late William M. Sargent. It has date of December 25, 1750, and was witnessed by Thomas Haskell and John and Samuel Conant. It was admitted to probate the second of July, 1753, making it probable that Godfrey died in the early part of that year. The appraisers were Thomas Haskell, William Bucknam, and Charles Gerrish, and his estate was inventoried in English money as 437 pounds, 4 shillings, and 7 pence.

In the first item of the will he gave to his brother, Joseph Godfrey, 5 shillings; in the second item he gave to his sister, Sarah Godfrey, 5 shillings; and to his brother, Benjamin, all his real estate and appointed him as executor of his will.

Upon a tracing of land and water power of Saccarappa from a survey by William Pote, recorded in the York County Registry of Deeds, and dated April 28, 1742, a mill standing in nearly the same spot where Mill No.1 of the Dana Warp Mills now stands is indicated as the Godfrey mill. On the northerly side of the Island where the electrical building now is, is Bayley's mill with an open space, apparently much longer extent than can be found at the present day, indicated as the log yard. Only one dwelling house is given on this plan or survey, that of Mr. Knight which was a little northerly of the granite works of the late Charles T. Ames.

On the tenth of May, 1732, there was laid out a tract of land also shown on the above plan, whose central situation in what is now the most valuable part of our city will justify a full transcript of it description as the same appears in the Proprietors' records: "Laid out to the right of James Simpson's ten acres of land in the township of Falmouth, beginning at a stake at the southeast side of Daniel Godfrey's thirty acre lot and to run down Presumpscot River bounded upon Saccarappy mill yard till it meets with John Tyng's hundred acres at the lowermost part of ye Falls, and then to run back into the woods the same course of Tyng's and Godfrey's lots till ten acres be made up, it ye same be free from former grants." The record does not tell at whose instance the land was laid out bur seven acres thereof, with the road through it, were afterwards sold to Moses Pearson by the heirs of General Waldo. The "road through it" was doubtless the "forebear" of our present Main Street.

In a plan of the "Cooper claim" made by William Pote in 1748, a bridge across the river is laid down at a place apparently between the upper and lower Falls near where stood the bridge of the Westbrook Manufacturing Company which was carried away in the big freshet of 1896. This may have been the bridge about which the town had so much trouble with the good people of Windham and others by whom they were presented at court. A tract of land above Godfrey's and easterly of the division line between Falmouth and Gorham was laid out to one Moody who had purchased the right of Richard Powsland, an old proprietor in the first settlements. This land was purchased from Moody or his heirs by Moses Pearson, whose descendants hold some portion of it at the present time.

One hundred acres were granted by the Proprietors' committee to Daniel Ingersoll. It ran up the river to the Gorham line and the Pearson land was sold to John Ingersoll of Boston, shipwright, son of Daniel Ingersoll to George Johnson, Jr., the son of George, Sr., who lived on the well-known farm formerly occupied by the Hatch sisters and now by-----, and who went up the river to Mallison Falls where he was engaged in lumbering and farming. The Godfrey lands after the death of Godfrey were owned, in part at least, by Charles Gerrish. In 1762 Gerrish sold 20 acres with house, barn and outhouses thereof, to Major Enoch Freeman. This included the field west of the Conant place, now owned by William T. Hawkes who erected a fine set of farm buildings and with his son, Ferdinand Hawkes carries on a large milk business. Gerrish had previously (April 28, 1758) conveyed to

George Knight "the moiety of the twenty acres beginning at the northwest corner of thirty acres laid out by Daniel Godfrey" which he and Bartholomew had bought of the heirs of Josiah Plummer, then late of Falmouth, deceased. By this time Gerrish had removed to a place called Royallsborough, now the town of Durham, where he was the first settler. In 1787 he conveyed by quit claim deed to Major Enoch Freeman "all the rest of the farm at a place called Saccarappa." He appears to have received from Freeman a large tract or tracts of land in exchange for Saccarappa lands which thereafter passed in to the possession of Enoch Freeman, Jr., who resided in a large mansion house which formerly stood in the field already mentioned west of the Conant cemetery. This house was afterwards removed to the southerly side of Longfellow Street where it stood for many years, until it was taken down to make room for the large double house occupied for years by the late John W. and Albert F. Warren Enoch Freeman,Jr. died December 4, 1832, aged 82 years, and is buried in the Conant cemetery.

Chapter 6

There was a connection between the family of Enoch Freeman, Jr. and that of his second wife, whose parents were William and Hannah Atwood Freeman of Harwich, a town on Cape Cod. William Freeman's father and grandfather bother had the name of William, and like his grandfather, says the tradition of Cape Cod, he had only two children, William and Lydia. This last William was born March 22, 1791 and settled in or near Liverpool, Nova Scotia, where his descendants are numerous. Lydia Freeman was four years older than her brother, judging by the age given on the headstone mentioned several times; the inscription can no longer be read since it has been broken down nearly to the ground, but it was removed with the remains to Woodlawn Cemetery. Probably Thomas Haskell, the ancestor, was buried in the same burying ground, as was said, on Scotch Hill, a little to the rear of the present Bridge Street Grammar School building.

Benjamin Haskell had eleven children, nine of whom lived to maturity, and seven at least married and left children. By his first marriage with Abigail Parsons there was one son, Thomas, who on May 1, 1792 sold to his half-sisters, William and Barri, all his interest in the estate of his father, both real and personal. Of his subsequent career nothing is known.

The oldest child by his second marriage (with Lydia Freeman) was given the name of Benjamin. He doubtless died in childhood as his is one of the names given on the double headstone. William, the second of this marriage, was married to Lucy Neil of Portland, March 6, 1792, Elijah Kellogg, Sr. performing the ceremony. He was by trade a cabinet maker as has been previously stated. In 1797 he is described as of Portland in a conveyance of land at Saccarappa to Edmund March. The land is the same which for years was the homestead of the late David G. Hayes, at present the property of the Dana Warp Mills. February 1, 1804 he was living in Gray and sold to Benjamin Larrabee, Jr. of Falmouth the pew formerly owned by his father, Benjamin Haskell, in the Capisic church. That same year he sold lands in Gray to Moses Haskell of North Falmouth. In 1806 he was again in Portland, which appears to have remained his home for the rest of his life. Some of his descendants still reside there; in the city records of deaths, Lucy, wife of William Haskellis said to have died December 6, 1838.

Barri Haskell married Catherine Jordan, probably of Raymond, and settled in Limington. They had five children. Parsons, as was said, was a minor at the time of his mother's death; married Hannah Holt and settled in Albany, Maine. They had seven children. Mercy, daughter of Benjamin and Lydia Haskell, married Israel Swett of Portland, settled in East Limington, and had eight children. Lydia Parker died young. Hers is one of the names on the old headstone. Hannah, the seventh child by the second marriage, and one of the maiden sisters to whom the brothers, Barri and Parsons, allowed the "privilege of one room in the house at Saccarappy" as long as they should remain unmarried, did not marry but lived and died with the Shakers.

The deed of the room was dated March 8, 1799, and the same day by another deed Barri secured to Hannah one-sixteenth part of the income of the old Haskell grist mill for her support. Probably some different provision was made for her within the next year for the 17th of December, 1800, Barri and Parsons sold to Jonathan Webb 5 1/2 acres of land which they had purchased of their mother, Lydia Haskellanother tract of 13 acres between the above and land of Daniel Bailey and the Windham road; and an undivided fourth part of the Haskell grist mill. This was "all the land, buildings and privileges" which they had in Falmouth. The exact location of this dwelling house and land would be a matter of no small interest. The tract of 51 1/2 acres was without doubt one-half of the tract of 103 acres concerning which the elder Thomas Haskell had the contest with the Cloice heirs whose entire right in the township he had finally purchased and alter conveyed to his son, Dr. Benjamin Haskell.

Sarah, the ninth child of Benjamin and Lydia (Freeman) Haskell became the wife of Samuel Pike and had six children. This Samuel Pike should not be confounded with Samuel Beane Pike who married Mary, a daughter of Jonathan Webb, and was the father of the late Samuel G. Pike of Calais. Samuel Pike who is described as of Berwick, blacksmith, November 14, 1791 bought on acre of land at Saccarappa of Joseph Noyes "beginning at a stake north 80 degrees east, four rods from the easterly corner of the Haskell grist mill, with liberty to erect a building 30 feet square below the bridge with a running floom of water." This fixes the location of Pike's building and of the Haskell grist mill as on the former site of the Westbrook Manufacturing Company's property on the Lower Falls.

Pike's residence was on the acre which he bought of Noyes, which must have included the present site of the old Joshua Webb mansion, for many years used as a factory boarding house, but some years ago remodeled into an apartment house, as well as that of the agent's house on the corner of Brown and Bridge Streets, for many years occupied by the Hon. James Haskell, for years agent for the Westbrook Manufacturing Company.

Samuel Pike was one of the founders of the old Falmouth (afterwards Westbrook) Social Library in 1802. May 1, 1806 he sold one-half the land which he had purchased of Noyes to Elias Merrill, then a trader at Saccarappa, but afterwards for many years Register of Deeds of Cumberland County. Merrill had a dwelling house and resided on his purchase. July 28, 1806 Pike sold what appears to have been all the residue of his Falmouth property to Jonathan Webb. As none of his descendants are known to reside here, and not even tradition reaches back to him, it is likely that he soon after removed from town.

There is reason to suppose that he removed to Limington where his brother-in-law, Barri Haskell, finally settled. March 23, 1827 Samuel Pike of Limington, yeoman, sold to Archeleus Lewis of Westbrook, a small piece of land at Saccarappa bounded and described as follows, viz: "Beginning at the southwest corner of the Widow Freeman's garden and running westerly to the Windham road, or near the end of the bridge; thence by said road northerly to the land that leads in by the Widow Freeman's garden; thence by said lane to the northwest corner of the Widow Freeman's garden; thence southerly by said garden to the corner or place of beginning."

This conveyance was drawn by the late David Hayes, Esq. who subsequently owned and occupied the mansion house at the corner of Bridge and Brown Streets which was built by David Thompson. The house has already been mentioned as having been the residence of the late David G. Hayes, son of David Hayes, and now the property of the Dana Warp Mills.

At the date of this deed the large brick mansion of Joshua Webb had already been erected and had passed into other hands. From evidence obtained the site of the Haskell grist mill was in the vicinity of the Dana Warp Mill Dye-House, east of the so-called big Gingham Mill, now Dana Warp Mill No. 2, and the lane mentioned as leading to the Widow Freeman's garden subsequently became the passageway known as Mill Lane between the former Westbrook Manufacturing Company's office and the factory boarding house. It will be seen, therefore, that the Widow Freeman's garden was a part of the mill yard of the old Company's and that the land above described included the land where the company's office now stands. This is now occupied by the Westbrook Manufacturing District Nursing Association through the kindness of the Dana Warp Mill. This view is aided by the fact that the half acre which Samuel Pike had sold to Elias Merrill was conveyed by the latter to Captain Nathaniel Freeman (husband of Widow Freeman) with the buildings thereon, and accordingly became the home of the worthy couple whose daughter, Hannah, became the wife of John Stiles and the mother of our former townsman, Merritt W. Stiles, and therefore the grandmother of Dr. Fred W. Stiles of Waltham, Massachusetts, a prominent physician of that city for many years.

The conveyance by Merrill to Freeman was made in 1890 after the removal of the former to Portland to assume the duties of his office as Register of Deeds.

Mary, the tenth and youngest child of Benjamin and Lydia Haskell, will be remembered as one of the maiden sisters to whom was secured the privilege, during her unmarried life, of occupying a room with her sister Hannah, in the family dwelling house. She was born November 25, 1779 and, therefore, had not completed her sixth year on the death of her father. She did not long remain single after the considerate provision made in her behalf by her brothers, for on February 19, 1801 she became the wife of Nathaniel Hunt of Gray. She was the first lady school teacher in that town. She had eight children, one of the latter being the late Mrs. Sarah O'Brien of Deering (now Portland), widow of the late Colonel Thomas O'Brion.

Through their ancestress, Lydia Freeman, the family of Dr. Benjamin Haskell traces direct descent from Elder William Brewster of Mayflower fame. Several families having the name of

Freeman have lived in Westbrook, all of them, no doubt, more or less closely connected through their emigrant ancestors or some common progenitor on theother side of the Atlantic. The family of the Rev. Benjamin Freeman, whose death occurred some years since, is known to have sprung from the same American branch with Mrs. Lydia Haskell

    Of Captain Nathaniel and his wife Lydia, who after his death was called the "Widow Freeman," little is known, it being impossible to connect them with the other Freeman families in this vicinity. It is highly probable there was a connection between the family of Mrs. Lydia (Freeman) Haskell and that of Daniel Godfrey before mentioned. It will be remembered that the great grandfather of Mrs. Haskell was William Freeman who married Lydia Sparrow, and life his father he had but two children who bore the names of William and Lydia. This last named Lydia became the wife of Richard Godfrey of Chatham in 1701 and by him the mother of six daughters. This, it is true, brings us no nearer to finding out the parents of Daniel Godfrey then we were before, but it establishes the fact that there was a Cape Cod race of Godfreys, one individual of which intermarried with the Freemans. It is also known that in the emigration of Cape Cod families to Liverpool, Nova Scotia, which included William Freeman, the only brother of Lydia Haskell there were persons bearing the name of Godfrey whose descendants are found in that vicinity at the present time.

    In the first volume of the New England Family History in a magazine edited by Henry Cole Quimby, a son of Governor Quimby of New Hampshire, much information concerning the old families of Stroudwater and vicinity of great interest to the local historian is given. Thomas Haskell was first married to Hannah Freese of Newbury who died soon after 1718, and in 1719 he married Mary Parsons of Cape Ann. His first wife had one child, but which one of either of those given is not known. Hannah who married Hunnewell was born in 1720 according to the gravestone. She seems to have been named for her father's first wife. Solomon, born in 1724, married first Polly Partridge after whose death he, at the age of 84, married November 5, 1807 Eleanor Starboard Quimby, widow of Benjamin Quimby who had herself reached the age of 73. Mr. Quimby thinks five of Thomas Haskell's children were born in Gloucester and the others after he came to Old Falmouth. The two lines of Haskells whose descendants live in Westbrook and the numerous families of New Gloucester and North Yarmouth are doubtless sprung from a common ancestor in Roger Haskell, who was an early settler of Salem, who married Mary Tybbott, and whose son William born in 1760 was the first white child born in Gloucester. Mary (Tybbott) Haskell died in 1693 and her husband four days after her death. One of these children, Benjamin, born about 1648, married Mary, daughter of Thomas Riggs, and had sons; Josiah who married Mary Collins in 1715; and had among others a second Josiah who married in Gloucester Abigail Fellows before he was 18 years old; and had Dr. Benjamin Haskell a distinguished physician of his native town; and Hon. James Haskell, a senator in the general court of Massachusetts from Essex County who came with his family to Saccarappa a little prior to 1860, where as superintendent of the Westbrook Manufacturing Company, he took immediate rank as a leading citizen and man of affairs. The late Frank Haskell who succeeded his father in the management of the the Westbrook Manufacturing Company, and the late Edwin J. Haskell are his sons. And thus the connection is traced between these branches of Old Salem and Gloucester families.

In the active days of Hon. James Haskell in connection with the Westbrook Manufacturing Company, his brother, Alexander Haskell, the father of Lucy Haskell Raymond, was proprietor of a store near the northerly end of Saccarappa bridge. He later removed to Beverly, Massachusetts where he died. To James Haskelland his sons is due the credit of having established the industry known as the Haskell Silk Mill Company which was a flourishing industry for many years, of which more will be said later.

Chapter 7

A younger brother of the Joseph Conant, who is supposed to have made the first permanent settlement in Saccarappa, bore the Christian name of Samuel, and was also an early settler in what is now Westbrook. He was born in Beverly, Massachusetts November 18, 1717 and was, therefore, sixteen years the junior of his brother Joseph. It is probable, therefore, that he came here as a member of his brother's household. One of the early granters of land in our present limits, in the vicinity of Pride's bridge, was Timothy Worcester, whose daughter, Hannah, became the wife of Samuel Conant in 1741. She must have died within the next three for on the 9th of August, 1744, Conant was married to his second wife, Mary, daughter of Francis Peabody of Middleton, Massachusetts.

The old two-storied house on "Pork Hill" recently burned is said to have been owned and occupied by some of the Conant family. I have supposed that it might have been built by Joseph and his brother Samuel yet, although it was much out of repair it seems too modern for that, for Joseph Conant is known to have died near the end of 1764 (See note).

In a deed dated March 24, 1756 Samuel Conant describes himself as a millman and conveys to Joseph Noyes of Falmouth, gentleman, one-half of a grist mill "at a place called Saccarappa on the western side of the Presumpscot River, the other half belonging to my brother, Joseph Conant." Joseph Noyes will be remembered as the man who sold an acre of land on the northerly side of the river to Samuel Pike who married Sarah, a daughter of Dr. Benjamin Haskell the grist mill which is the subject of this conveyance is not to be confused with the Haskell which was on the opposite side of the river. Long after the first settlement of Gorham which is said to have been made in 1736, the only grist mill available to the inhabitants of that town was at Presumpscot Lower Falls, to and from which they were accustomed to transport their "grists" by boat, carrying both boat and cargo around the falls at Saccarappa and Ammoncongin. The inconvenience to which their neighboring townsmen were thus subjected could not fail to be noticed by the Conant brothers who were already domiciled at Saccarappa; and they no doubt had the wisdom and foresight to discover in this the opportunity for the beginning of a profitable industry. The cultivation of Indian corn which the white man had learned from the savage, whose methods he had improved upon, soon became of inestimable value to the former, and has so remained to the present time. The "Average" of corn planted in all the clearings soon became something immense affording sustenance for both man and animal. In the infant settlement, therefore, the grist mill followed close upon the saw mill, which it has always followed in the march of empire through the new world. The mill of the Conants at Saccarappa probably antedated that of the Haskells for on February 27, 1748, Parson Smith makes the following entry: "Went to Saccarappa. Mr. Conant tell me he has ground one thousand bushel of corn this winter, there being no other mills than his between North Yarmouth and Saco."

In 1760 Samuel Conant received one of the licenses from the Municipal Officers of Falmouth to keep a public house and sell spirituous liquors. It would be interesting at this day to know just where he lived at the time of keeping a public house. November 15, 1782, in a deed in which he is described as a miller he conveys to his son, Daniel Conant, one-half the house he lives in, together with the right he has to the mill privilege adjoining said house. This is the last time his name appears in the County records, and it is probable that his death occurred soon afterwards. He left three children who lived to marry and have families, viz.: Elizabeth, William and Daniel. The order in which the names are given is assumed on the strength of certain dates which would make them all the children of the second wife. But in this I may be in error regarding William since I find nothing from which to judge of the date of his birth except that of his marriage, which occurred nine years at least after his sister Elizabeth had married and became the mother of a family. Elizabeth, daughter of Samuel and Mary (Peabody) Conant was born in 1755 and was married previous to 1770 to William Babb. The latter was a son of James Babb, the ancestor of our former honored townsman of the same name, and was born "within a mile of a place called Saccarappa." The place of his birth was doubtless the farm formerly occupied by Mr. James Babb and his son Isaac G. Babb at the junction of Spring Street and the Buxton road. Of the family of William and Elizabeth Babb fuller details will be given in a future chapter.

William, son of Samuel and Mary Conant, was married to Ruth Chapman September 23, 1779 by Rev. Thomas Browne, first minister of the church at Capisic. He lived and died on a lot of land on the sport now occupied by the Warren Furniture Co., at the corner of Main and Bridge Streets in Saccarappa. This land, a comparatively small tract for the time, was purchased in 1780 from Daniel and Sarah Dole by Archelaus Lewis, afterwards the well known "Squire" Lewis, who built the house now occupied by Hon. Joseph A. Warren at Cumberland Mills. This house has been much changed outwardly as well as in the interior since Mr. Lewis' day. Mr. Lewis in early life a was tailor and had his hop on the land which he purchased from the Doles. I am not informed of the exact date when these premises came into the possession of William Conant, but it must have been during the latter part of the 18th century for it is known that his death occurred after 1803 and previous to 1808. Peter Thatcher, who for a short time was a practicing lawyer in Saccarappa, administered his estate. He left a widow, Ruth, and three children, Samuel, Lydia and Edward. Of Lydia and Edward nothing further is known. Samuel lived for many years in the family of his Uncle Daniel and that of his sons on the Conant place on Conant Street in this city, died there previous to 1870, and never married.

Besides the mills at Saccarappa and old Ammoncongin, there were saw mills erected in the last century at Stroudwater Falls, so-called, on Spring Street; at the outlet of the Duck Pond; and also upon Mill Brook a little north of the residence of the late Nathan W. Boody. The Haskell family and the Conant brothers, as we have already stated, had grist mills at Saccarappa which did a large and no doubt profitable business, and with 19 saw mills all in operation at one time, at night as well as day. Saccarappa must have presented the appearance of a busy and prosperous village.

In 1785 Benjamin Quimby from Somersworth, New Hampshire purchased water power on the Island, near where the electric power house now stands, of John Bailey and others, and erected a fulling mill, but he and his family did not confine their attention to the dressing of cloth only, for a saw mill standing near the fulling mill was known as the "Quimby mill." Benjamin Quimby had a numerous family and all the persons of the name now residing in Westbrook are supposed to be his descendants. But there were Quimbys here before his coming who were owners, or part owners, of mills and water power, undoubtedly the descendants of Joseph Quimby who married Mary, daughter of Thomas Haskell whose descendants reside at Stroudwater. The late Isaac Cobb gives inscriptions from the old cemetery at Stroudwater to Joseph Quimby who died April 14, 1776, aged 61 years, and to his widow, Mary, who died April 12, 1815, aged 93. Mr. Cobb thought Joseph Quimby was buried at Saccarappa but did not state his reasons for thinking so. The late William Willis was informed by old Mrs. Day who formerly lived on Elm Street, Portland, and was a granddaughter of Joseph Quimby, that her grandfather and his brother Benjamin (the last named being a weaver who settle at Saccarappa), came from Wales. But this family tradition was sadly misleading for according to other and more careful investigations the progenitor of the family in this country was Robert Quimby who settled in Salisbury, Massachusetts in 1653. Two of his sons are said to have removed to New Hampshire where their posterity's are numerous; and it was most likely one of those sons was the ancestor of Joseph and Benjamin who came to old Falmouth.

The foregoing paragraph embodies in condensed form the principal facts which I had been able to gather of the origin of the Quimby families of this vicinity at the time when it was written in 1895, but now with the assistance of the "New England Family History" already mentioned I am able to state that Joseph Quimby, son of Robert who himself was the son of Robert, immigrant ancestor of this line, had his first born in 1715, probably at Amesbury, Massachusetts, Joseph and Benjamin, twins. Joseph came quite early to old Falmouth where, as we have seen, he married Mary Haskell daughter of Thomas Haskell by whom he had several sons and at least one daughter who became the wife of William Cobb, who joined with Solomon and John Haskell in the conveyance of mills and water power to Jonathan Webb in 1800.

Benjamin Quimby, ancestor of the Saccarappa line, by trade a fuller, married at Rowley, Massachusetts Anne Plummer, November 4, 1742. After residing and carrying on business at several places he came, as already noticed, from Somersworth to Saccarappa in 1770 with a family of children and grandchildren, and here it is apparent that his first wife died, for November 6, 1779 he married Eleanor Starboard of the old Stroudwater Road family, and other children were born to this union. He died on February 26, 1807 and his widow, as we have already noticed, contracted a second marriage the same year with Solomon Haskell, Sr., the bridegroom being 84 and the bride 78. The children of Benjamin Quimby, the twin, but not in order of their births, so far as we are able to learn, were:

 1. Joseph who married Azuba Partridge. They were the grandparents of the late Captain Isaac F. Quimby.

 2. Benjamin, died in 1810, aged 64; buried in Saccarappa Cemetery.

 3. Nathan married Rosina Partridge. Their daughter Tamsin married Peter Libby and they were grandparents of the late Deacon Joseph P. Libby and of the late Daniel T. Quimby, son of their son. Simeon Abel Quimby, whose daughter Rhoda Babb lived on the spot where the Odd Fellows Block now stands, was also one of their sons.

 4. George was probably the father of "Esquire Ben Quimby" whose homestead was where Mrs. William F. Bettes (now deceased) formerly lived on Longfellow Street.

 5. I know nothing of him further.

 6. Moses, born in 1758, probably in Somerworth, married Abigail March. She was born in 1770 and died in 1818. He married second Mrs. Betsey Walker, born 1771, died 1849. The children of Moses and Abigail Quimby were: Moses who married Reliance Cloudman; Elizabeth who married James Proctor; another daughter married Fred Proctor; a third, Mary, married Daniel Larrabee of Scarboro; Aaron who married Esther Cloudman and whose sons Albion M. and George A. Quimby were well-known residents of Westbrook until their deaths some years ago.

 7. Simeon married Sarah Brackett and had children: Charles who lived on Main Street in the house next to the Ward 2 voting booth, long the residence of the late B. F. Roberts; Charlotte who died unmarried; and Nancy who married Charles Alden of Portland.

 "Esquire Ben" Quimby, already named according to the headstone in Saccarappa cemetery, was born in Somersworth July 13, 1786, and died in Saccarappa April 19, 1854, and nearby are buried his first wife, Elizabeth, who died October 27, 1821, aged 34, and his second wife, Sarah, who died August 2, 1850, aged 58. He was the father of the well-known Univeralist, Rev. George W. Quimby, D. D. of Augusta; Rev. Edward F. Quimby of Norway; Mrs. Levi Morrill of Morrill's Corner; and Mrs. Waters of Livermore.

One of the results of the contest with the mother country which made the unit of colonies an independent nation was the establishment in many of the New England towns of what were then called forges, for the production of iron that could be used for the various purposes for which it was then required from the "bog ore." That the production of iron form ores found in the vicinity was once a leading industry in Saccarappa's not even remembered at the present time by the oldest inhabitant, yet such is the fact. The forge stood on the northerly side of the river near the upper dam on a part of the site now covered by what is locally known as Dana Warp Mill No.2, on the same spot where W. K. Dana first began the business of manufacturing warps in Westbrook. The following document copied from the county records will be of interest as showing the names of persons engaged in this industry, and the proportion in which they owned: Falmouth, 17, April 1790

"An agreement mutually entered into by the subscribers witnesseth that they are owners of the Forge at Saccarappa just completed and owned as follows:

Aaron Burnham	1-6	65	8s	71-2d
Dennis Marr	1-6	65		
			8s	71-2d
Timothy Pike 1-31	130	17s		3d
Peleg Wadsworth	1-31	130	17s	3d

Peleg Wadsworth
Timothy Pike
Dennis Marr
Aaron Burnham

An account of the life and public services of General Peleg Wadsworth belongs to the history of the state and has often been written. He was the maternal grandfather of Henry Wadsworth Longfellow, the immortal poet, and his former residence in the city of Portland is the Wadsworth-Longfellow house, one of the first objects of interest pointed out to the stranger. Marr and Burnham were of Scarborough and men of energy and enterprise in their day and generation. The name of the other owner, too, is one that should not be forgotten, at least in Saccarappa, where, during the closing part of the 18th century and the beginning of the last century he was one of the foremost citizens.

Mr. Pike was the only son of Timothy Pike of Newbury. The older Timothy, by his will dated in 1767, gave to his son Timothy his "Negro man, Harry", his blacksmith tools, various household goods, his gun and sword, the family clock, 40 pounds in money, the whole of the land down in Windham, and a third of the house and land in Newbury after his wife's decease.

Timothy Pike the younger resided a while in Newbury where he married and had several children. His wife dying, he married Elizabeth, daughter of Ephraim Jones and granddaughter of the Hon. Moses Pearson of Falmouth, of whom a more extended account is reserved for a future chapter. Previous to his second marriage Mr. Pike seems to have removed to Falmouth Neck, in fact he came to what is now Portland in 1774. By the burning of the town by Mowatt in 1775 Mr. Pike was a heavy loser and soon after removed to Saccarappa where he died in 1818.

Whether his iron industry was successful we have no means of knowing. He was by trade a blacksmith, probably having learned the business from his father, and at Saccarappa he manufactured axes, scythes, shovels, and other implements useful in husbandry and about the mills, for which he could not have failed to find a ready sale.

For a year or two Mr. Pike resided in Windham where he served on the board of selectmen. The farm where he lived was near the Falmouth (now Westbrook) line, and is at present owned by Cornelius Small. Mr. Pike acted for many years as justice of the peace, in which capacity his name frequently appears in connection with real estate conveyances made during the first years of the last century. He was also the first subscriber to the old Falmouth (afterwards Westbrook) Social Library, later merged in the Walker Memorial Library, taking two shares.

One of his sons, Samuel Deane Pike, married Mary, a daughter of Jonathan and Mary (Coverly) Webb. They were the parents of the late Samuel G. Pike of Calais, who formerly owned the tract of land now the property of the S. D. Warren Co., and known during later years as "Scotch Hill." William, another son of Timothy Pike, was the father of the late Frederick A. Pike of Calais and James S. Pike, formerly the well-known correspondent of the New York Tribune. The wife of Frederick A. Pike, late of Calais, will be remembered as the author of a charming romance entitled "Ida May" which was popular in the days of anti-slavery agitation.

    I suspect that the building in which the iron industry had been carried on by Mr. Pike and his associates was suffered to stand for a long time after the business had ceased to be profitable, in a dismantled condition, for to the present day the term, "Old Iron Works" is applied to old buildings in Saccarappa, and for many years was the popular designation of the old meeting house which stood on Saco Street.

Chapter 8

All person in Westbrook bearing the name of Proctor--and at present they are not numerous--are descended from the John Proctor who lost his life in the heroic endeavor to stem the tide of fanaticism which swept over Old Salem, village, now Danvers, Massachusetts in 1692, known in history as the Salem Witchcraft Delusion. John Proctor was the son of the immigrant of the same name who came from Ipswich, Massachusetts from London in 1635 and subsequently settled in Salem. There is a tradition in the village where he lived that John Proctor, Jr. was a man of herculean mould as well as great force of character, traits which have been inherited both here and in the mother state by many succeeding generations of his descendents.

Samuel Proctor, a son of the martyr, came to Falmouth Neck between September 1707 and November 1719 and built his house on Fore Street between Market (formerly Lime) and Silber Street. He was born, no doubt, in Salem Village in 1680, and came hither from Lynn where he probably found his wife Sarah, daughter of Anthony Brackett. Whether this was the same Anthony Brackett who was killed by the Indians in 1689 cannot be learned. It was the union, however, of two hardy races and the offspring were well fitted by inheritance to cope with the hardships of pioneer life which awaited them from the cradle, and attended them to the end of what were, for the most part, long and eventful lives.

In the ledger of William Lunt, of which frequent use has been made before, several persons by the name of Proctor have been mentioned, thus showing that in the second half of the 18th century the name was quite common in the vicinity of the present Prides Corner. William, the fifth child of Samuel and Mary (Brackett) Proctor born August 31, 1724, married Charity Lunt in 1750 and Susannah Hall in 1760. There is a tradition among her descendants that the second wife had been left an orphan at a tender age by the killing of her parents by the Indians. In 1778 William Proctor isdescribed as then of Windham, but formerly of Falmouth, housewright. Prior to that date he had sold to Joseph Winslow one-eighth of a mill privilege on the Duck Pond stream, Mill Brook, about half a mile from the Presumpscot River, together with an eighth of three acres of land where the same would best "commode" said mill privilege. The privilege is further described in the deed as the same where the "Proctor Mill" had formerly stood. The site of this mill was the same mentioned in a preceding chapter as a little to the northward of the residence of the late Nathan W. Boody. A bridge once crossed the Presumpscot River in this vicinity about an eighth of a mile above Pride's Bridge and was called Proctor's Bridge. William Proctor died in Windham in 1806. He had a son, Willliam, Jr., who was a member of the New Gloucestor Society of Shakers, and a son, Anthony, who removed from Windham to Raymond, and was probably the ancestor of the Proctors in that town and Naples. An Anthony Proctor was among the original grantees of the township of New Marblehead (Windham) who may have been a son of Samuel of Portland. From William Proctor who joined the Shakers was descended the late John C. Proctor of Portland, the well-known real estate agent.

Samuel Proctor received from the Falmouth Proprietors several grants of land within the present limits of Westbrook, on which his eldest son John, who was born in Lynn, June 24, 1715, seems to have established his residence prior to 1773; for in that year he conveyed 35 acres from his homestead on the northerly side of the Presumpscot River in Falmouth to his son, John Proctor, Jr. The last named was the father of the later Frederick Proctor who resided for some time in Gray, and the late James Proctor who resided on Spring Street, Saccarappa. The wives of Frederick and James Proctor were daughters of Moses and Abigail (March) Quimby, and sisters of the late Hon. Aaron Quimby of Westbrook.

Nathaniel Proctor, a son of John and a grandson of Samuel, owned and occupied a large farm on both sides of the road now called East Bridge Street, a portion of which is now owned by the S. D. Warren Company. He left sons Samuel A., Richard, Charles Henry, and John, and several daughters, one of the latter having been the wife of Charles Babb.

The following plan accounts for its own origin and existence; to quote: "This is a Plan or description of Sundry lots of Land in the Township of Falmouth lying on the Northeasterly side of the Presumpscot River which I the subscriber with the assistance of Capt. George Berry and Thomas Brackett,

chairman, and by desire of Capt. John Waite and Mr. John snow have faithfully and impartially surveyed December 25, 1752.
"Attest John Small, surveyor."

On this plan a small tributary of the Presumpscot, presumably the present Mill Brook, is designed as "Proctor's Mill Stream" showing that the Proctors had already (1753) made a beginning of milling operations within our present limits. So much of the stream as is shown upon the plan is included in a tract of "Forty-three acres land out to John Cox, deceased." Cox was no doubt the same who married Sarah, a daughter of Samuel Proctor in 1739. According to the late Mr. Willis he had by her and two other wives a family of 20 children. In the Revolution he left this country for Nova Scotia where some of his descendents still reside. East of Cox's land, and adjacent thereto, is a tract of 43 acres which was laid out to Joseph Conant. This is probably the same land which Conant subsequently sold to John Webb "Taylor" and now known as the William Walker farm. Adjacent to Cox's land on the westerly side is a tunnel-shaped tract of 47 acres, also laid out to Joseph Conant; and immediately to the westward of this is a tract of 60 acres laid out to Ebenezer Cobb; while below Conant's tract of 43 acres is a lot of 13 acres laid out to Capt. Waite on the right of Isaac Sawyer. Below the last named is a tract of 60 acres which belonged to Mr. John Snow, he being "assign" of Timothy Worcester, deceased.

The lost above named all make their southerly boundary on the Presumpscot River. Northerly of these is another range of lots beginning on the westerly side, with 100 acres laid out to Joseph Pride. The next easterly is a tract of 33 acres laid out to (Thomas) Haskell. The remaining 4 lots purport to have been laid out to Mr. Snow and Capt. Waite, and it is evident from the ruthless cutting of corners that the original grants and surveys were made with a good deal of looseness.

John Snow appears to have been an early settler in the vicinity of Pride's Bridge, and an enterprising and active man of business in his time. It was probably his daughter Mary who married Thomas Brackett in 1743; and probably, too, Brackett was the same who served at the survey as one of the chairman.

"To ye selectmen of ye town of Falmouth:

According to ye vote of ye Town we the subscribers to choose ye stream lying between Persecataquis and Ammoncongin upon the N.E. side of Persumscot River as witness our hands. This our report to the selectmen of Falmouth. Dated at Falmouth July ye 12, 1728."

  Samuel Proctor   Edward Armstrong
  John Perry   Saml. McCausland

  This "report" was made to the selectmen the same day with that of Benjamin Ingersoll and others stating that they had chosen the falls at Saccarappa as a site for lumber mills. The stream selected by Proctor and his associates probably cared a much larger volume of water than that at the present time, for then all the back country was heavily wooded. Samuel Proctor who heads the list will be recognized as the first name in this vicinity. The stream which subsequently known as "Proctor's Mill Stream", it will be remembered had its outlet into the Presumpscot River upon land which is stated upon the plan, which was mentioned at such length above, as having been laid out to John Cox, deceased.

  The John Snow mentioned was by trade a ship carpenter, and had his home near Back Cove in the former city of Deering. Capt. George Berry, one of the chairmen at the survey of the lands near Pride's Bridge, was a brother of John Snow's wife, while the other chairman, Thomas Brackett, was his son-in-law. Brackett's home was in what is now Portland near Morrill's Corner, and the farm of snow embraced the land formerly owned and occupied by the late John Read as his homestead on Ocean Street.

  The 23rd of May, the Falmouth Proprietors grants to Samuel Proctor 154 acres of land at a place called Deer Hill in Falmouth. This place was probably in the rear of the present homestead of the late Marrett Lamb; at any rate it ran down to the Presumpscot River

  October 17, 1734 the same parties laid out to Proctor 43 acres on the northerly side of the Presumpscot River "beginning at the stake standing 14 rods north of the side of the small brook that empties itself into the Presumpscot River near John Cox's land." If the small brook mentioned here is identical with Proctor's Mill Stream, this grant might be shown upon the plan already mentioned, but in fact it is not there.

January 12, 1736-37 another tract of 30 acres is laid out to Proctor on the northerly side of the Presumpscot which also does not appear upon the plan. These omissions are not understandable, but certain it is that Proctor had grants of land in the present city of Westbrook, or purchased land from others on which John, one of his sons, had his home.

The mill stream was selected by Proctor and his associates in pursuance, as the "report" states, of a vote of the town; but he and his partners were less fortunate in their selection than their contemporaries Ingersoll and others, for the mill and dam erected on the Proctor stream have long since disappeared, and the land in that vicinity has little value except for agricultural purposes.

Among the names in the Lunt ledger is that of Peletiah March to whom two pages are accorded. The place of March's residence is not known but it was somewhere within our present city limits. The fact that he was one of Lunt's principal patrons does not prove that he lived in the vicinity of Prides Corner, for it is evident from the entries in his book that Lunt often went, after the fashion of the time I which he lived, from house to house, making or repairing boots and shoes of his customers and their families. Peletiah March was born April 7, 1741 in Amesbury, Massachusetts. In December 1772 he purchased a house lot in Portland of John Proctor. His transactions with Lunt began in October 1772 and continued until 1790. The last of the credit side throws light upon the business in which he was engaged, to wit: "By tanning one calf skin." It would seem, therefore, that he was a tanner. His first wife died in October 1775 and he married, second, September 15,1776, Mary, widow of John Brackett of Saccarappa. His children, 11 in all, were as follows:

By first wife:

1. Edmund, married ----Woodbury. In October 1802 he was a hotel keeper in Saccarappa. Of his after career nothing is known.

2. John married Mary Weare. She was the daughter of Joseph Weare, the famous Indian Scout, traditionally known as "old Joe Wyer."

3. Sally married Solomon Haskell, Jr. of Saccarappa. Her descendents in this city and vicinity are numerous.

4. Polly never married.

5. Abigail married Moses Quimby, son of Benjamin Quimby, who came from Somersworth, New Hampshire and was by occupation a clothier. They were the parents of the late Hon. Aaron Quimby and of Harriet and Elizabeth, who married respectively Frederick and James Proctor, sons of John Proctor, Jr.

6. Anna married Dean Frye who came to Saccarappa from Fryeburg. They were the parents of the late Col. John M. Frye of Lewiston and grandparents of the late William P. Fyre, United States Senator. Mrs. Anna (March) Frye is said to have been one week old at the burning of Portland by Mowatt.

By second wife:

7. Joseph. There seems to be nothing further of him.
8. Betsey married Johnson Knight of Otisfield.
9. Peletiah. Descendents of his are living in Hillsdale, Michigan, among them being Col. Edwin J. March of that place.
10. Jane married Stephen Swett of Portland
11. Dorothy (called Dolly) married Jacob Gerry of Falmouth. Their son, Peletiah Gerry, was formerly a merchant of Bath.

John March, son of Peletiah and his wife Mary Weare, were the ancestors of the late William M. Sargent who furnished most of the data given above.

Peletiah March the elder died in Falmouth in 1813. His first wife is thought by Sargent to have been Mary Gooding or Goodwin. John Brackett, whose widow became March's second wife, lived for some time and probably died in Saccarappa, on the old road to Gorham on the place owned and occupied by the late Mrs. Susan S. Conant. Several persons by the name of Brackett in the pages of Lunt's ledger, some of whom were his neighbors living within our present city limits, while others no doubt lived in Deering, and others still perhaps on the Neck, now Portland. Within a few years past a very excellent history of the Brackett families of this vicinity entitled, "Brackett Genealogy, Descendants of Anthony of Portland and Captain Richard of Braintree" by Herbert L. Brackett of Washington, D.C., has been published.

Chapter 9

No history of Westbrook, past or present, would be complete that did not devote more than a passing mention to Samuel Webb, the patriarch of a large family of that name in this and adjoining towns, and the first schoolmaster in New Marblehead, now Windham. According to one of his descendants he was born on Christmas day, 1696, at a place called Redrift, near London, England. The date, however, does not agree with that given in a letter from his son, Eli Webb of Gorham, to his half brother Samuel, written April 23, 1807, from which the following extract is made:

"My grandfather, Samuel Webb, was a native of the city of London. He followed the sea; was master of a ship. He was married and had five children, two sons and three daughters. My father, Samuel, was the second child. His children were Margaret, Samuel, Susanna, Elizabeth, and John or Hezkiah, I am not positive which. My father was born in the year 1697. After the death of his father he came to America and landed at Rhode Island in the year 1716 in the 19th year of his age. Finding himself in a strange land and no money to support him, he bound himself to a blacksmith and learned the trade. After your mother died he married the widow of Daniel Spear, late Bethiah Spear of Rhode Island, by whom he had ten children, seven sons and three daughters, David, John, Ezekial, Seth, Susanna, Eli, James, Josiah, Abigail, and Elizabeth, and removed from Rhode Island to New Marblehead, now Windham, in 1741 where he lived 23 years, and then removed to Deer Isle with brother Seth in the year 1767, where Seth and father both died, as I understand you know and I need not repeat. Concerning my brothers and sister, David married and lived in Falmouth and had five children, two sons and three daughters. Ezekial married his wife at Cape Cod and had one daughter. He followed the sea and went away and nobody knew what became of him; until the time of the American war he was at Bagaduce, commander of one of the English ships. After then I heard not from him until the year 1791. He came to Portland, master of an English merchantman, and stayed three days, and went away without my seeing him. Seth married in Windham and had nine children, and moved to Deer Isle. Susanna married Thomas Mayberry of

Windham and had two children, son and daughter, and died when young. And myself, I have had ten children, five sons and five daughters, and eight now live. James married in Windham and had two children, son and daughter. Josiah died at seven. Abigail died at five. Elizabeth married Jonathan Roberts and had nine children and lives in Buckfield, 40 miles from me. This being as accurate as my memory affords me of all from my grandfather. But I suppose all by the name of Webb in this country are akin, for I have heard my father say that his grandfather was the only one of the name that survived (accompanied with one brother) the Plague, 1666 A.D."

E. Webb

The descendants of Samuel Webb are not agreed respecting the name of his first wife. Seth Webb of Brooks states, presumably on the authority of family tradition, that Samuel Webb was apprenticed at Tiverton, Rhode Island to a Mr. McIntire, a blacksmith, whose daughter Mary he married on Christmas day, 1718; but others of the descendants say that the name of his first wife before marriage was Randall, and that she was not of Tiverton but of Weymouth, Massachusetts. Samuel Webb had two sons by his first marriage, Samuel and Thomas, who settled respectively in Weymouth and Hingham. From a letter written by a great grandson of the first Samuel who resided at the time of writing, some years ago, in Weymouth and bore the ancestral name, the following is an extract:

"Seth, his grandson always speaks of him (the first Samuel Webb) as moving into Maine from Tiverton, Rhode Island. Did he move to Tiverton after marrying his second wife? In 1740 he was certainly in Maine. Seth says "he removed from Tiverton in 1744 by land to Boston, by water to Falmouth (now Portland) and to Saccarappa. By this time the excitement had drawn so many into the place that no one could realize over $10 in any way whatever for a day's labor. He bitterly repented leaving Tiverton (or Weymouth) foreseeing that the lumbering business was going down; but he had sold his property at so great a sacrifice that he felt himself poor. He made the best of it and the next year moved to Windham, on his own land, where his wife's father lived."

Another extract from this letter is of interest as confirming the tradition respecting the location of the first graves in Windham. Seth Webb says: "My grandfather Farrow suffered extremely from the consequences of the (Indian) war, which so operated upon him and his wife that it shortened their lives. At their decease there was no public cemetery in town, and they were buried near their log house on the banks of the Presumpscot River. After their death their children sold the premises and went away, leaving no monument to mark the spot. The field grew over with saplings so no one can point out their resting place to this day."

"The sons, Samuel and Thomas," according to the letter, "were left in Weymouth by Samuel Webb with his first wife's father, Capt. John Randall, when he moved away. My father told me quite a pathetic story of these two boys, Samuel and Thomas, going down in Gorham to see their father after they had grown to be young men. They walked most of the way. They came to Gorham in the edge of the evening; one of their half brothers was driving up the cows from pasture and they inquired if that was Mr. Webb's house. Their father was standing in the doorway as they came up, and they stopped and talked with him, asked him about the farm, the town, etc., their father looking all the while in an inquiring sort of way from one to the other until one said, 'Well, you didn't know us', when he stopped quickly down and putting an arm around each, drew them to him saying, O', Samuel and Thomas'. But all this belongs to that silent sea of buried hearts which come to all ages and all hearts of individual life, and has nothing to do with the story of a country or a town."

It would seem that when Samuel Webb was drawn hither, Saccarappa was just recovering from its earlier "boom." In the decade preceding Ingersoll and his partners had built the first lumber mills on its still magnificent water power, and at the period of Webb's coming, 1744, Daniel Godfrey, Thomas Haskelland his sons, and the two Conants must have been the leading citizens and men of affairs in the then young and thriving village.

From Tiverton, according to one of Windham's early historians, came several of the early settlers of that town including John Farrar (or Farrow) whose daughter Bethiah, at the early age of 15 years, found herself the widow of one Capt.

David Spear, and mother of an infant daughter, also named Bethiah. This young widow soon dried her tears and entered a second time into the honorable estate of matrimony with Samuel Webb as we have already seen. It was Bethiah Spear, daughter of Mrs. Bethiah Webb by her first marriage, and not Susanna Webb (she, by the way, married William Maxfield of Windham) who became the wife of Thomas Mayberry. The eldest son of Samuel Webb by his second marriage was David, born according to some authorities in Tiverton, Rhode Island July 1, 1727. His marriage is thus recorded in the book of church records by Rev. John Wight, first minister of the church in Windham: "David Webb of this place and Mrs. Dorothy Peabody of Falmouth." The marriage took place November 16, 1749. the bride was designated as "Mrs." not because of a previous marriage, but in recognition of her eminent respectability, for in that age, especially in England, to speak of a single woman as "Miss", we are told, was to call in question her reputation of chastity. Dorothy Peabody was the daughter of Francis Peabody, Esq. and his wife Dorothy, of Middleton, Massachusetts, and sister of Mary Peabody who, previous to her own marriage, had become the wife of Samuel Conant of Saccarappa, as has been said.

She was born March 27, 1720, and was therefore a trifle of seven years older than her husband. A brother of hers, Samuel Peabody, lived for several years in the last century on the farm in Gorham now owned and occupied by M. Fred Fenderson.

Another brother, Francis Peabody, Jr., was the father of Joseph Peabody, formerly a distinguished merchant of Salem who passed several years of his early life with his relatives in Saccarappa, leaving here about 1785.

In the letter from which quotations have been made, David Webb is said to have resided in Falmouth, but this is probably not strictly true. His home was probably always in Gorham, not far from the Falmouth (now Westbrook) line, after he left Windham. On January 5, 1756, he bought of David Gorham of Barnstable "100 acres of land in Gorhamtown" on which he was living August 23, 1765. A daughter Dorothy, and a son David, children of David and Dorothy (Peabody) Webb were baptized by Rev. Mr. Wight. Of these children nothing further is known. Jonathan Webb, son of David and Dorothy, according to the inscription on the headstone in the old Conant cemetery, was born in Gorham November 25, 1756, and died (in Saccarappa) April 10, 1810. He was for years a leading citizen and manufacturer and dealer in lumber in Saccarappa, and also kept a public house in the same building (much modified, however) which was known for years as the Presumpscot house, and which was moved from the old site to make room for the Scates building. The Presumpscot house is still standing on Fitch Street. Bethiah, a daughter of David Webb, was married by Rev. Dr. Deane to Prince Hamblen of Gorham, March 22, 1781. David Webb is described in all conveyances as a blacksmith. August 25, 1763 he and one Thomas Jackson of Falmouth received a deed from Francis Peabody, Jr. of Middleton, who acted "by virtue of a power from his father, Francis Peabody of Middleton, gentleman, and Dorothy, his wife," of water power and mills at Saccarappa. David Webb conveys his interest in this purchase to Jackson on September 28, following, and from that time, as far as the records are in evidence, had no further interest in lands or water power in Saccarappa.

Jonathan Webb, I have little doubt, was employed about the saw mills of Saccarappa from his boyhood, for his maternal grandfather, Francis Peabody, was interested in mills and water power here as early as 1758; and Webb himself became interested in this class of property when he begun to buy up the interests of the Haskells and others about 1790 and during the two decades following. He was married to his first wife, Mary Coverly, March 4, 1781. The children by this marriage were:

    1. Joshua, born January 12, 1782, married --- Quimby. He like his father was at one time extensively engaged in manufacturing and dealing in lumber in Saccarappa, and in the zenith of his prosperity erected as his private residence the large brick mansion formerly used as a boarding house by the Westbrook Manufacturing Company, and more recently coming into the possession of W. K. Dana, and has been remodeled into an apartment house. One of his sons was recently living in Lowell.

    2. Mary, born September 26, 1784, married Samuel Deane Pike, one of the sons of Timothy and Elizabeth (Jones) Pike. She was the mother of Samuel G. Pike of Calais, and received by the division of her father's estate the well-known Pike field, now owned by the S. D. Warren Company and including the territory locally known as "Scotch Hill."

3. David, born November 30, 1786, married Jane Bailey. She died in 1848 and is buried in Saccarappa Cemetery. The date and place of his death are unknown.

4. Elizabeth, born January 21, 1791, married Capt. Henry Babb, at one time a well-known lumberman of Saccarappa. Mr. Babb died February 1, 1834 at the age of 49 years. He was a son of William and Elizabeth (Conant) Babb, and like his wife was in the fourth generation from Francis Peabody of Middleton.

5. Dorothy (usually abbreviated to Dolly) married Col. George Small of Westbrook. She was born November 9, 1800 and died in Deering in her 95th year.

Mrs. Mary (Coverly) Webb died in 1803, aged 38 years, and Mr. Webb married as his second wife Susanna Smith, one of the 12 daughters of Capt. John Smith of Stoughton, Massachusetts. By her he had two daughters of whom further mention will be made. After the death of Mr. Webb his widow married Capt. Nathaniel Partridge she married as her third husband the well-known Parson Bradley. She died in 1843 at the age of 62 years and is buried with her second husband in Saccarappa Cemetery.

Chapter 10

It would appear that at a date even earlier than previously mentioned Jonathan Webb began to acquire real estate in Saccarappa. March 5, 1786 he received a deed of "one-half of a saw mill and one-half of the Falls on which said mill stands" from Jesse Partridge.

This appears to have been the Bailey mill which stood where the electric plant now is, on the Island. Other fractional interests were afterwards acquired by him from members of the Bailey Family.

On May 3, 1793 he bought of General Peleg Wadsworth one-third of the "Forge which stood where stands Mill No.2 of the Dana Warp Mills. About this time he acquired by purchase of Mrs. Elizabeth Wise, one of the daughters of Judge Moses Pearson, one-fifth of Frye's Island in Sebago Lake. This purchase was doubtless made because of the timber growing upon this island, which subsequently became a famous resort for blackberry parties. September 24, 1787 Solomon Haskell and John Quimby sold him land on the southerly side of the present Main Street, adjoining land of Jesse Partridge "then occupied by said Webb." Probably Webb had previously built on Partridge's land the dwelling that he used as a hotel, which ever after remained his private residence and was the beginning of what was known for many years as the Presumpscot House. From a reservation which was inserted in a deed to his son Joshua, of a mill which stood on the lower dam on the westerly side of the river, it would seem that Mr. Webb had water for domestic uses brought to his house from the flume at this mill. For this to have been feasible the Main Street must have been at a lower grade than at the present time. Because of the freedom with which spirituous liquors could be retailed in those days, hotel keeping was much more lucrative than in the days of prohibition, and possibly than at the present day. A small annual license fee appears to have been the only restriction and Saccarappa, with a comparatively small population, could at least sustain more than one public house.

Jonathan Webb, in 1786, when he made his first recorded investment in saw mills, was about 31 years of age. It is fair to presume that he had already found inn-keeping lucrative in Saccarappa, and was now fairly embarked upon the high road to a prosperity which was promoted by the aqueduct that ran into his tap room. Had the supply of beverage from the mill pond been greater, and that from the West India market in exchange for "Jamaica" boards less, far better had it been for his thirsty customers, a fact, however, that few of them would have conceded at the time.

As has been stated, Bethiah, the only daughter of David Webb of whom we have any account, became the wife of Prince Hamblen of Gorham who, in the several conveyances of real estate where his name figures in the Cumberland Registry of Deeds, is invariably described as a "gentlemen." He never resided in Westbrook but as many of his descendants still live here, and he is remembered by some of our older residents, some notice of him may not be out of place. Like the other Hamblens of Gorham, he is said to have come of an old a family of Barnstable, Cape Cod. His father, Samuel Hamblen, is said to have married Temperance Lewis, also of a Cape Cod family. Samuel Hamblen was a deaf mute. The children of Prince and Bethiah Webb Hamblen are given as follows by the late Hon. Hugh D. McLellan of Gorham who, however, had fallen into one or two errors respecting names:

1. Dorothy married N. Rand in 1789.
2. Nancy married E. Bishop in 1804.
3. Joseph died in 1784.
4. Solomon died in 1785.
5. Fanny married Isaac Chesley 1803. She died in September in 1856, aged 70.
6. Sally married L. Wallace in 1808.
7. Katy married John Wallce in 1810. (This was probably an error for on the monument erected by her descendants her name is given as Dolly, born in 1782, which would make her the oldest child. It is probable, therefore, that the sister who married Rand must have borne some other Christian name. Possibly the error would be corrected by transposing the names.)
8. Bethiah married Nathaniel Watson in 1825. (They were probably the couple who long had their home on the old Townhouse road in that part of Portland, formerly Deering, near the crossing of the Portland, Nashua and Worcester Railroad.)

9. David died unmarried.

10. Dennis married Sally Crockett and lived in the town of Wilton, Maine.

Prince Hamblen was a Revolutionary pensioner and lived during the last year of his life in a small house on the old road from Saccarappa to Gorham, directly opposite the homestead of the late Capt. Daniel Mosher. It was afterwards used as a workshop by the late Merrill W. Mosher and is still well remembered by those who had occasion to pass that way a few years since, as standing in a condition of partial collapse during the same period that the various vehicles, machines, and other personal property of an ejected tenant were suffered to litter two sides of the highway in that region for a long distance.

In the last years of his life Prince Hamblen is said to have been in extreme poverty having little to subsist upon except his pension. In 1799 he leased from James Mosher a small tract of land where the dwelling house just described stood. This house, according to Colonel McLellan, had been previously occupied by a family named Thurrell, and had then stood on the spot where the large house of the late Freeman Richardson now stands. Having purchased this old structure, Hamblen removed it to the land which he had leased of Mosher and made it his home until the time of his death. The lease of the land terminated with his life and after his death the house, as had been said , was used as a workshop by members of the Mosher family until its final collapse.

David and Dorothy Peabody Webb had a son David who was baptized in infancy by the Rev. Mr. Wight of Windham on April 5, 1782. This second David was therefore some three of more years the senior of his brother, Jonathan Webb, the early hotel keeper and lumber king of Saccarappa. Of this David nothing is known beyond the fact that he was baptized, but on the strength of family tradition it would seem that he was the progenitor of certain Webbs who lived on Saco Street in the early years of the nineteenth century. These last named Webbs bore the names respectively of William and Kiah. But if father and son, which was which is not known. Possibly they were connected with the family of David Webb of Gorham and through him with the Samuel of Windham.

Another family of Webbs connected only remotely, if at all, with Samuel of Windham and Deer Isle, are still represented in Westbrook. They are descendants of John Webb who was brought to this country from England by his parents when he was four years old. He was born March 17, 1750. On coming to this country the family settled at Stroudwater where his father, who is said to have been a shipwright, no doubt found ready employment. The given names of his parents are unknown. November 6, 1781 this John Webb was described as John Webb,Jr. in a conveyance to him in Scarboro from one Knight. This land was near the present Coal Kiln Corner on the road leading from Buxton to Stroudwater. Here he took up his residence and lived for many years, and here most, if not all, of his children were born. He was married July 27, 1779 to Susanna Swett by Rev.Thomas Brown. Stephen Swett, a brother of Mrs. Susann Webb, lived at one time on the westerly side of the road from Ammoncongin to Portland near the residence of the late W. H. Holston. He was the father of Capt. Joshua Swett, once well-known in this part of Old Falmouth and subsequently a leading business man and land owner at Little Falls, Gorham. Mr. John Webb died in Windham December 17, 1835, and his wife Susanna, born December 15, 1755, died the last day of the year 1825. Children of this worthy couple are as follows:

    1. Thomas, born November 4, 1778, died November 1, 1829; married Lydia Bickford and lived in Epping, New Hampshire.

    2. Polly, born December 5, 1781, married John Goodell of Windham.

    3. John, born May 6, 1784, died March 23, 1880. He settled in Danville, now embraced in the city of Auburn. He had ten children. The name of his wife is not known.

    4. Betsey married Josiah Freeman and settled in Windham. Mr. Freeman was the son of Benjamin and Eunice (Seavey) Freeman of Scarborough and was born October 10, 1791 and died in Windham, March 28, 1868. Mrs. Freeman was born September 9, 1786 and died May 19, 1873. They had three sons and two daughters.

    5. Hannah, born October 22, 1789, died February 28, 1873; married Isaac Gibbs Walker. Mr. Walker was born in Hopkinson, Massachusetts January 12, 1786 and came to

Saccarappa when a young man, and was employed in the manufacturing of nails by Major William Valentine, also of Hopkinson and father of the late Hon. Leander Valentine. He was the son of Timothy and Lois (Gibbs) Walker. Isaac G. and Hannah (Webb) Walker had five children.
- a. Isaac, born February 16, 1810, died in infancy.
- b. Lois, born February 25, 1811, married James Babb of Westbrook; died April 10, 1889.
- c. Moses B. Walker, the veteran teacher, born April 1, 1813, married Caroline, daughter of Major William Valentine.
- d. Isaac N. Walker, born November 2, 1815.
- e. Lowell N. Walker, born January 6, 1818, died in Portland August 29, 1882, a well-known locomotive engineer.

6. Stephen, born April 10, 1792, married Mary Padden. He first lived on the farm in Scarborough which his father bought of a Mr. Knight, but subsequently removed to Windham where he died May 13, 1868. He left one son, John, father of the late ex-mayor Mahlon H. Webb of Westbrook, and two daughters, Betsey, who married Mark H. Stevens, and Hannahette who died August 2, 1840 at the age of 16.

7. Joshua, born May 30, 1796, died September 4, 1801.

In 1777 the following Webbs were taxed in Falmouth, which then included all of the old town except Cape Elizabeth which had received separate incorporation in 1765, viz.: John Webb, Jr., John Webb, 3rd, William Webb, William Webb, Jr., James Webb, Henry Webb. It may be that the father of John Webb who married Susanna Swett, also bore the name of John, but be that as it may, form information obtained some years ago from an aged member of the family who has since died, James Webb and Henry Webb named in the above list were brothers of the John whose children have just been given.

James Webb and Henry Webb both lived at Stroudwater. James is described in real estate transactions as a trader, and was at one time in possession of large tracts of land in Bakerstown, now Poland. But he subsequently met with financial reverses and his real estate at Stroudwater was levied upon by Samuel Parkman and Edward Blake of Boston, who went to the length of setting out a part of the dwelling house in which he lived to satisfy their demand. Samuel Parkman was a wealthy merchant of Boston, and the father of Dr. George Parkman of tragic memory, and the father of Francis Parkman, Jr., the distinguished historian, lately deceased. Samuel Parkman was the original proprietor of the town of Parkman in Piscataquis County which, on its incorporation, was named in honor of himself. It is probable that James Webb had bought his merchandise from him at wholesale with the disastrous result above noticed.

Henry Webb is described in old deeds as a mariner. He was married on March 20, 1778 to Anne Riggs by Rev. Thomas Browne.

Chapter 11

Intentions of marriage between John Webb and Catherine Randall were entered upon the Falmouth records in 1762. This could not have been the John Webb who married Susanna Swett, for in 1762 he would have been about 12 years old; nor could it have been John Webb the (Taylor), who bought land near Pride's Bridge of Joseph Conant, on which he seems to have resided at the time of his decease, which occurred between January 25 and February 22, 1766. John Webb "Taylor" as he is called in the conveyance from Conant, was one of the numerous sons of Samuel and Bethiah Webb of Windham. He is thus mentioned in Eli Webb's letter to his half brother: "John lived in Falmouth and had eight children, three sons and five daughters." He was married in 1753 to Elizabeth, daughter of Benjamin and Amy Pride Larrabee. She was born in 1732 and lived until 1827. Her father, Benjamin Larrabee, was doubtless the same who was one of the grantees 1728 of the water power at Saccarappa. He was born in 1700 at Falmouth Neck, the son of Captain Benjamin and Deborah (Ingersoll) Larrabee. The first Benjamin was a native, probably, of old North Yarmouth. He had been second in command the Casco Fort, as it was commonly called, near the mouth of the Presumpscot River, and when the Fort was dismantled, had come to Falmouth Neck with Major Moody and had engaged in business pursuits. His wife, Deborah, was a daughter of John Ingersoll, an ancient proprietor of Falmouth lands. The Larrabee family, in every generation of which, from 1666 to the present time, there has been a Benjamin, has always been more or less prominent in the affairs of the old town and its numerous divisions, and will receive especial attention later. John and Elizabeth (Larrabee) Webb probably had ten children instead of eight, as stated by his brother, Eli Webb. The following seems to be, according to authorities, a correct list, although not in the order in which they were born:

1. John, Jr. born May 19, 1754, married Sarah Leighton in 1777.
Their children were:
    a. Dorothy married Andrew Hunnewell of Durham.
    b. Elizabeth married Brackett Sawyer.

    c. Abigail married John Lord of Falmouth. They were the parents of the late Elbridge Lord, formerly of this city, and who served on the board of County Commissioners.

    d. Seth, who emigrated to Penobscot County where his descendants are numerous.

    e. Lucy married James Lord of North Yarmouth.

    f. Eunice married William Tobin of Durham.

    g. Bethany, the second wife of Charles Jameson of Westbrook.

    h. Phoebe married Simeon Libby of Richmond, Maine.

    i. Ruth, the first wife of Charles Jameson.

    j. Mary, twice married; more concerning her is given in Chapter 18.

2. Anna

3. Betsey

4. Abigail married Ebenezer Cross of Portland. The late Hon. William

    W. Cross of Bridgton was their grandson.

5. Mary married Green Hannaford of Cape Elizabeth.

6. William was a successful sea captain and resided in Portland on Congress Street, near the head of India. He married a daughter of ----Moody.

7. Susan

    There were also sons, Benjamin and Thomas. Benjamin was married but left no children. He resided on the farm in Westbrook, near Pride's Bridge on the westerly side of the County Road. The farm buildings, in a ruinous condition, stood in the field away from the public road until a few years since. Thomas Webb was never married, but lived with Benjamin in Westbrook. John, Jr. died July 8, 1846. He lived near the Duck Pond on a farm subsequently occupied by his son-in-law, Jameson.

    As has been already noticed, Mrs. Elizabeth Larrabee Webb, born in 1732, survived her husband many years, dying in 1827. One of her granddaughters, who remembered her well, says that in her grandmother's girlhood she was accustomed to attend divine worship at he First Parish Church in Portland, then under the pastoral care of Parson Thomas Smith, and was present at the dedication of the wooden structure about 1750, being then a young woman some eighteen years of age and unmarried; and that she was again present, when upwards of four score and ten, at the dedication of the present stone edifice which had been erected on the same spot. On this last occasion, as was natural, she received much attention from ministers and people, and was invited to dinner by the pastor, Rev. Ed. Nichols, but was obliged to decline the invitation because of the infirmities of age.

    Before he settled at Pride's Bridge, John Webb appears to have been engaged in the business of a tailor in that part of Falmouth then called The Neck, now Portland. October 10, 1763 he sold to Joseph Bayley "mariner", "a certain small lot or parcel of land containing 10 square rods the northeasterly side of Love Lane, so-called, (now Center Street), beginning in the westerly corner of a lot of land belonging to Nathaniel Ingersoll whereon he now liveth." Ingersoll was probably a kinsman of Webb's wife. Previous to this time Webb had built a on the Neck on land belonging to Benjamin Larrabee, probably the father of his wife. This land Larrabee sold to Ebenezer Mayo by deed dated January 25, 1766. Larrabee's wife who is mentioned in this deed as having a right of dower in his land, was Catherine, who may have been his second wife. In 1763 a Benjamin Larrabee of Falmouth married Catherine Tibbetts; and the previous year, 1762, Benjamin Larrabee, also of Falmouth, married Lydia Bayley. The land thus conveyed to Mayo by Larrabee is described as "a certain small lot of land lying and being in that part of Falmouth called the Neck, on the northeasterly side of Middle Street, on which is a house lately built by John Webb in which he lately dwelt." This land was adjacent to land of Joseph Bayley but the task of its definite location is not known. On the same day that Larrabee sold the land on which Webb's house was standing today, Webb conveyed the house to the same, but it appears that Webb's deed was not acknowledged until March 25 of the same year, two months after the deed was made. From the fact that Mayo conveyed to Webb's wife and children on February 22, 1766, the same lands at Pride's Bridge which Webb had conveyed to him the previous year, 1765, it has been assumed that Webb had deceased just previous to the former date. But against this we have the magistrate's certificate of acknowledgment just noticed; the time of his death, therefore, becomes uncertain, but it is probable that he did not survive many years after this period. The late Hon William W. Cross his great grandson, writing sometime in the "eighties," of the 19th century, said that he had been dead over a hundred years.

The deed of the house given by Mayo is witnessed by Joshua Moody and "Mary Letherbee, her mark." This fact is interesting as showing an old pronunciation of the name of the Larrabee family, who were called "Letherbee" by many persons as late as the early part of the 19th century.

Mrs. Elizabeth (Larrabee) Webb took part in the division of the estate of her father, the second Benjamin Larrabee, in 1792, at which time she appears to have been a widow. The heirs at this time were Benjamin Larrabee, John Larrabee, Mary Tuckfield, Elizabeth Webb, David Ross and Amy, his wife, and Abigail Larrabee.

To Benjamin Larrabee was assigned in this division a tract of 60 acres of land at Deer Hill at a valuation of 36 shillings per acre. At this time Benjamin was of Portland, but he probably soon afterwards took up his residence here, on the same spot where the large house built by the late C. P. Maxwell now stands, in a house which had been built by David Small, an early settler. The Small house, which was a one-storied structure, was subsequently removed to make room for the large house, long the home of the several generations of the Larrabee family, which now forms two stories of the Westbrook Inn, at one time called the "White House" at Cumberland Mills. Benjamin Larrabee who shared in this division was the third to bear the name in a direct line. He married Sarah, a daughter of Joshua Brackett of Portland, and through their mother, his children and their descendants inherited a large tract of land from Congress Street to the Back Bay, some of which is still (or was recently) held in the family name. Mr. Larrabee was born in 1735 and died in 1809. He received from Joseph Noyes a conveyance of a large tract of land near his Deer Hill inheritance and in the definite location on the road from Capisic to Saccarappa, made December 1803, mention is made of Larrabee's 60-acre lot on which "he now resides."

Benjamin Larrabee, who was the fourth of the name in the direct line, son of Benjamin and Sarah (Brackett) Larrabee, married Jane Cobbey, and second, Sarah Lamb, a sister of the late John and Samuel Lamb. He owned large tracts of land inherited from his father, from Deer Hill in Westbrook to near

Harper's Hill in the Deering district, and including the present Portland City Home. With his son, Benjamin, who died a few years since in Portland, leaving three daughters and no son, the direct line of Benjamin ceased, but the name is still borne in the family by one of his grandsons.

And although persons bearing the name have never been very numerous in Westbrook, the posterity of the second Benjamin Larrabee is still well represented in each of the cities that have been craved out of a portion of the territory of ancient Falmouth.

The time when Joshua Webb, the oldest son of Jonathan Webb, died, and the place where he was buried have been matters of uncertainty, but are settled by the following entry in Parson Bradley's journal, having been furnished by a friend, and which I give in all the quaintness of the original, as follows:

"June 1, 1841, I set out for Saccarappa Village on foot, one half past 12 at Mr. Foster's where I took dinner and stayed until 2 P.M.; then called at James Merrill's and spent an hour, then at Henry Stevens, 1/2 hour, then called at the home of mourning, Mrs. Plummer's, who father, Joshua Webb, a corpse, aged 59, he wishing me to attend his funeral and perform the religious ceremony, making the request while alive as well as his children. I asked a blessing at the house, then at 4 P.M. proceeded to the Congregational Meeting House where I preached a funeral sermon, sung the 90th psalm S. M. road the 14th chapter of Job, made some remarks, then prayed, sung again 90th psalm S.M. then the blessing, then to the grave where was deposited the body of Joshua Webb, there to remain till the trumpet of God shall awaken his sleeping dust."

It is "in evidence" therefore, that on the first day of June 1841, Joshua Webb was buried in the Conant cemetery near the grave of his father, Jonathan Webb.

Chapter 12

I have before me, as I write, an original deed given by the elder Joseph Conant, the alleged first settler in Saccarappa, to Benjamin Sweetser and John Marston, both of Falmouth, "gentlemen," bearing date of March 17, 1756, and conveying "a certain tract or parcel of land, lying and being in the township of Falmouth, and on the northerly side of Presumpscot River, containing 47 acres bounded as follows: Beginning at the lower bounds on said Presumpscot River of 60 acres of land laid out to the heirs of Ebenezer Cobb, late of said Falmouth, deceased, thence running down said river east 23 degrees north 19 rods, thence north and by west, 140 rods and one-half rod to a stake, thence west 23 degrees south, 100 rods and thence southeast 40 rods, and one-half rod to the bounds first mentioned; being a lot of land laid out to me by ye proprietors of the said town of Falmouth, February 1, 1736-7 as by said proprietors records may more fully appear." This deed is in the handwriting of Major Enoch Freeman, the founder of the distinguished family of that name prominent for so many years in the affairs of the old town, and was acknowledged by the maker before him. Deeds at that time required two subscribing witnesses, and this one was signed in the presence of Mr. Freeman and Jonathan Webb. As the transaction took place in March, 1756, when Jonathan Webb, afterwards a leasing business man and boniface in Saccarappa, was not yet 6 months old, it is evident that he could not have been a witness on this occasion. The question has been asked how to account for the fact that there were two Jonathan Webbs. Mr. Willis answers the question in a marginal note to Parson Smith's journal as follows:

Jonathan Webb from Boston graduated from Harvard College in 1754, and came here (to Falmouth Neck now Portland) to take charge of a school. He was not very popular. The boys called him "Pithy Webb" from his habit of putting the pith of the quill in his mouth when he made the pens. Edward Preble, afterwards the commodore, who was always ready for a joke, once made the pith a little too unpalatable for the dominie, which brought down his vengeance on the offender's head. Mr. Webb married Lucy, eldest daughter of Brigadier Preble, in 1736, but had no issue by her. He lived in the house subsequently the

Casco House on Middle Street (the same spot in the rear now occupied by the Casco Bank) at the breaking out of the Revolution and kept boarders. President John Adams boarded with him when he attended court here, which he was in the habit of doing before the War. He died soon after the war commenced. He is not know to have been connected with any other person of the name in this vicinity.

The land described in the above mentioned conveyance was one of the grants laid down which was noticed in Chapter 8, and according to the scale given upon the same the starting point was on the northerly bank of the Presumpscot River about 70 rods above the mouth of Mill Brook, or "Proctor's Mill Stream" as it was formerly called, near the residence of the late Nathan W. Boody. Beginning at the mouth of Mill Brook and extending about 60 rods down the northerly bank of the Presumpscot, was a grant of 43 acres which Joseph Conant conveyed in 1761 to John Webb, the tailor. No highways or town ways are indicated upon the plan in question, and probably at the time when it was made December 25, 1753, none had been formally laid out in its vicinity. The last named grant is now, and has been for many years, crossed diagonally by the County Road from Portland to Bridgton; while the same and the grants above it bordering on the river are traversed by an old road, now called West Bridge Street. The heirs of Ebenezer Cobb, to whom the 60-acre grant was made which formed the westerly boundary of Conant's 47 acres, I assume, for the want of better information, were the progenitors of a part, if not all, of the Cobbs now resident in Westbrook, Deering and Windham. The westerly boundary of the Conant and Cobb grants, as was noticed, is upon the 100 acres laid out to Joseph Pride and 30 acres laid out to Haskell

The Joseph Pride to whom this tract of 100 acres was granted, was most likely the first person of the name in the old town. He is noticed by William Willis in the history of Portland as follows: "Isaac Savage and Joseph Pride, the first immigrants of the name, also came with their families." This was in 1726. Pride is said to have lived at Back Cove. On April 12, 1728, Joseph and Sarah Pride had a son, Joseph, born in Falmouth, and it was probably their daughter, Amy, born before they came here, was married Benjamin Larrabee, whose daughter Elizabeth, born in 1732, married John Webb. There is no evidence that the elder Joseph Pride ever occupied the grant of 100 acres, but on or near it persons of that name still reside, having acquired their homes by inheritance from ancestors who had long been domiciled with our present town limits. The elder Joseph Pride was probably in middle life when he "emigrated" to this vicinity, and it was no doubt his death which was noticed in 1747 among those of the persons who had died that year, by Parson Smith as that "old Mr. Pride."

Another ancient document of interest, now in my possession, bears the autograph of Moses Pearson, a man who held numerous high positions during a long and useful life, among which were those of high sheriff of the County of Cumberland and judge of the Court of Common Pleas. It is a deed from Pearson to Joseph Conant, Sr. under date of March 5, 1754, and conveys land near the Duck Pond, in Falmouth, probably the same premises which Conant conveyed shortly before his death in November, 1764, to his sons, Joseph, Jr. and Bartholomew. The deed is in the handwriting of the maker, except the certificate of acknowledgment, which was written by the magistrate as appears from their customary phraseology "Coram Enoch Freeman, Jus. Pacis." The land which the deed conveyed is now the property of the Gowen family. The subscribing witnesses are Jesse Stephenson and Benjamin Titcomb.

Of the first name witness, Jesse Stephenson, nothing further is known. Benjamin Titcomb was the ancestor of most of the persons of the name in this vicinity. He was doubtless connect-ed with Pearson, being at once his son-in-law and the nephew of his wife. Moses Pearson never lived in Westbrook, but many of his descendants have resided and still reside here, and some of them have been among our most enterprising and useful citizens. No history of the town, therefore, can be complete that does not give a sketch of his long and eventful life, at least in an abbreviated form. He was born in Newbury in 1797 and emigrated to Falmouth Neck in 1728, which ever afterwards remained his home. He as by trade a Joiner, but being a man of intelligence and great capacity for business, he was soon elected to positions of responsibility and trust in the young town, serving town clerk, selectman and treasurer in the first years after settling here. In 1737, '40 and '49 he was representative in the General Court. In 1745, having raised a company in this vicinity, he joined the army in the memorable and important expedition against Louisburg. After the capture of that strong-hold of the French King, he was made treasurer of the regiments which had been engaged in the siege, and appointed to receive and distribute the spoils of victory. The principal part of what is now the town of Standish was granted to Pearson and others as a remuneration for their sufferings in the Louisburg expedition, and was called Pearstown until its incorporation by its present name in 1785. In 1760, on the establishment of the County of Cumberland, Pearson was appointed the first Sheriff and served until 1768 when he was succeeded by Col. William Tyng. Although not a lawyer he was made Judge of the Court of Common Pleas and continued in office till the War of Independence. He died June 5, 1778, aged 81 years. He married Sarah Titcomb, daughter of William Titcomb of Newbury, and sister of Col. Moses Titcomb, who killed at Ticonderoga on September 8, 1755. She was born in 1693 and her death on November 2, 1766 is thus noticed by Rev. Dr. Deane who was her son-in-law: "Mrs. Pearson died about 9 o'clock in the morning." Moses and Sarah Pearson had six daughters and no son. The daughters, all of whom married, were:

    1. Mary, born December 8, 1720, married Ephraim Jones in 1739, and died in 1775. Their daughter Elizabeth married Timothy Pike of Saccarappa, already noticed, and was the mother of his children. The descendants are quite numerous.

    2. Elizabeth, born February 20, 1722, married Joseph Birney 1745, and second, Joseph Wise 1749. Her descendants by the second marriage are somewhat numerous in Westbrook.

    3. Sarah, born November 27, 1723, married Daniel Dole, and died in 1785. Their descendants reside in Stroudwater.

    4. Eunice, born January 25, 1727, married Rev. Samuel Deane, D.D., second pastor of the First Parish Church of Falmouth (now Portland), April 2, 1766, and died in 1812. They had no children.

    5. Anne, born January 19, 1729, married 1753 her cousin, Benjamin Titcomb, subscribing witness of the deed of Pearson to Conant, as we have seen. She died in 1800.

    6. Lois, born August 11, 1733, married Joshua Freeman in 1750, and died March 21, 1818.

The father of Joshua Freeman bore the same name. He came from Barnstable, Cape Cod, to Portland previous to 1740 and kept a store and tavern on the same spot where the First National Bank now stands. He bought the land for 80 pounds O.T. which was equal to $90 in silver. Mr. Willis says: "It may show something of the style of our early day to describe the dress of Joshua Freeman when he went to court Lois Pearson in 1750, as given by himself to Mr. Isaac Ilsley. He said he wore a full bottomed wig and cocked hat, scarlet coat and small clothes, white vest and stocking, shoes and buckles, and two watches, one on each side." He was then 20 years old. Think of any man of sound mind, young or old, of American birth, appearing in the streets of Portland at the present day in such attire.

Benjamin Titcomb, who married his cousin Anne Pearson, was long a prominent man in the affairs of the old town, and acquired a large estate for his time. He came to Falmouth in 1746, after the capture of Louisburg, having been persuaded to settle here by his kinsman, Moses Pearson, whose daughter, as we have seen, he subsequently married. He was by trade a blacksmith and had a shop on the breastwork, from which Central Wharf was extended before the filling of the flats and the construction of the present Commercial Street. He was long a deacon of the First Parish Church, served the old town on the board of selectmen, and in 1784 was one of the representatives to the General Court. He died October 15, 1794, aged 72, and his widow died in 1800 at the same age.

The eldest son of Benjamin and Anne Titcomb, who is called Willia Andrews Phillips, but who appears in recorded conveyances without the middle name, married his cousin Mary, daughter of Daniel and Sarah (Pearson) Dole, and settled in that part of Falmouth, which is now Westbrook, where he died in 1818. The following persons participated in the division of his real estate on July 23, 1819, viz." Sarah Titcomb; Moses Quimby and Anne, his wife; Levi Quimby and Mary, his wife; Luther Fitch and Almira, his wife.

Among his Saccarappa possessions mention is made of a saw mill called the Titcomb Mill, which was upon the land now owned in part by W.K. Dana & Co. To Luther Fitch, and Almira, his wife, who was Andrew Titcomb's daughter, was assigned the water power and land between Main Street and the river, now in the possession of the S. D. Warren Co., large tract of land formerly owned by Jeremiah Johnson, the westerly boundary being the road to Scarboro, now called Saco Street. This was the well-known Fitch property now traversed by Mechanic and Central Streets, as laid out by Capt. Isaac F. Quimby, who purchased it from the late Judge Fitch.

Chapter 13

Frequent references have been made in these chapters to the ledger of William Lunt, who built his home and resided upon the farm at Prides Corner, formerly owned and occupied by the late Henry B. Walker. For the use of this book, as well as the deeds and other documents, from which I have already made extracts, I am indebted to Mr. Walker. The most valuable from an historical point of view, perhaps, is a leather pocketbook about six inches in length, fastened with what was once a somewhat eleborate and substantail brass clasp, and bearing on its exterior the unmistakable indications of age and severe usage. In it are two compartments for the reception of papers and such currency as was in use in the days when it was new; and inside the pocketbook itself, but outside of one of these compartments, a bold and not unpracticed hand wrote, many years ago, the following legend indicative of ownership;

"Daniel Lunt
In Colonel Tupper's Regt.
General Patterson's Brigade
Bought of Nathaniel Dearing
of Falmouth 1777"

That which gives the chief historic interest to this mouldy relic, however, is the manuscript diary which it contains, portions of which were written amid scenes which have long since become the tourist's mecca, and events the most thrilling in the history of the great struggle which gave our Country its independence. This document consists of 28 pages of what in its day was white letter paper, stitched together at the back, probably by hand of some affectionate wife or sister, and with the scissors reduced to a size to fit the space where it was ever after to be carried. At the very beginning it introduces us to historic ground.

"Valey Forge May 1778 Sargt. small pr. stockings lent."

This is the first entry, and fortunate, indeed, was he who made it, in that he had, in the poorly clad and poorly fed army of our patriotic forefathers, a pair of stockings to lend, when many a poor fellow, forsooth, had no stockings or shoes for that matter, to cover his bleeding and lacerated feet. The entries which follow are generally brief and to the point.

"Sargt. Nowel, one coat 3-10-0. aug.18 arrived at Camp Orange town, 23 marched to Tenneck very hot weather on front guard.

September 4, marched to Stren rophia one man died in my company.

September 8, General Poor died in the night.

September 10, Sunday, this day General Poor was buried.

September 11, on duty officer of day.

September 12, one man was hanged for meroding the inhabitants.

September 13, the hole army was revued by his excellency and a number of the Indian Cheffs, no provisions. September 14, and no provisions this day and that has been the case half this month."

No better evidence is needed than the private journals of the soldiers, of the obstacles that were met and overcome in the mighty conflict.

This class of writings, too, is characterized by a vigor and directness for which one looks in vain in the works of the professional author. Even the bad orthography, the misplacing of capitals and the absence of punctuation, add to, rather than detract from, their value and give them a charm which all the studied methods of the rhetorician are powerless to attain. But before we proceed farther with extracts from this interesting diary, the reader will naturally wish to know more of the one who wrote it.

Three brothers, William, Daniel and John, sons of Samuel Lunt, came from Kittery about 1760. William, born September 19, 1742, by trade a shoemaker, settled as we have said, in that part of old Falmouth known as Prides Corner, within our corporate limits, where he died March 21, 1806. John, who was born July 5, 1754, and died July 3, 1809, settled in Gray. Daniel, born November 19, 1749, settled in what is now Westbrook, on the farm formerly owned and occupied by Deering Colley. His first wife was Molly Frink whom he married about 1770, and who died Christmas day 1787. She was probably the daughter of John Frink, an early settler in that part of the old town, the father, if I mistake not, of Samuel Frink, who died in the "fifties" of the ninetieth century at the home of his son, John, at Little Falls, Gorham. Mr. Lunt married, as his second wife, Eunice, a daughter of Bartholomew Conant, who survived him many years, dying on February 19, 1841, aged 77.

Mr. Lunt was a large real estate owner in old Falmouth, having extensive tracts of land on both sides of the Presumpscot River, as well as at Duck Pond and Blackstrap. In the war of the Revolution he served till the close of hostilities as a lieutenant in 1778, and as a captain in 1780 and subsequently; and after the war received a pension. He purchased of the Massachusetts committee a large territory in No.1, now the town of Peru, in the county of Oxford, and thither several of his children removed and made for themselves homes. Portions of the original town were known as "Lunt's upper and lower grants."

Captain Lunt died in Westbrook on November 27, 1823. Descendants of his are still living in Westbrook, or were quite recently.

Captain Lunt, as a commissioned officer in the Revolution, took part in founding the Society of the Cincinnatithe idea of which is said to have originated with General Knox whose last days, as is well known, were spent at Thomaston, Maine. In memorials of the Massachusetts Society (of the Cincinnati) by , Francis S. Drake, page 392, is found the following:

"Daniel Lunt. He was of Falmouth, a member of Brackett's Co. of minute men in April 1775. Sergeant of same company in Phinney's reg. 10, May 1775; in Skillings Co. of Francis' reg. 1776; com., 2nd lieut. of Francis' reg. 3 feb. 1777; capt. in Tupper's (11) reg. 18. mar. 1780; in Voses (1st.) reg.1783. He was living in Westbrook, Me. in 1819 aged 69, an invalid."

"16 Sept. 1780. this day marched to Mountain Meeting House and put up at Revd. Doctor Chapman's.

20. this day received orders to march back of the New Work (Newark?) Mountains and bring off what fat cattle, sheep, oxen and cows would do for beef."

Mr. Lunt, as we have noticed, was commissioned a captain in Tupper's regiment March 18, 1780. It is probable that he had command of this expedition to bring off cattle for the use of the army.

"24. This day wrote home a letter to Captain White."

The next entry is made with more than usual care, and betokens the deep interest which the writer took in the events then passing.

"25. (Sept.1780) This night at twelve o'clock the whole army was under marching orders on account of the filliny (villainy) that had been carried on betwixt Genl. Arnold and the Adjutany Genl. of the British Army--the Adjutant Genl. was made prisoner the 23 instant, 25 Arnold deserted to the enemy before he was able to carry his hellish plot into execution."

The Adjutant General whose capture is referred to here, was no other than the brave, but unfortunate Major Andre, whose tragic fate, although it gave him a monument and final resting place in Westminster Abbey, will never cease to moisten the eye that read s the account thereof even in the plain narrative of a private diary like that now before us.

"27. this day cold wett wether, 2nd of October. This day Major Andree (Andre) was executed.

26. This day the army was revued by his excellency and the Embassador from France. I left camp. Lodged in cokitat."

Capt. Lunt now seems to have set out for his home in Falmouth, on a furlough that lasted till the following spring. The stages of the homeward journey are of interest when compared with the modern facilities for traveling over the same route.

"27. This day crest at King's Ferry and lodged at West Point.

28. This day rany wether. Lodged at the widow Sutherds.

29. This day showers. Lodged at Colo Mowhouses.

30. This day pleasant wether. Lodged at Mr. Baldwin's at herinto.

31. This day rany wether. put up at Mr.Co-es Simsbury.
1st. November, This day did not travel.
2. This day cold lodged at Springfield parsols (Pearsol's?).
3. This day lodged at Lincoln's in Brookfield.
4. This day lodged at Baldwin's in Shresbury.
5. This day lodged at Mr. Livermores Waltham.
6. This day lodged in Boston cold wether.
7. This day lodged at Capt. Clark's Chalcy (Chelsea).
8. This day lodged at Beverly, Capt. Francis.
9. This day lodged at Hampton.
10. This day lodged at Colo Littlefield's (Wells)
11. This day arrived home."

The return home seems to have been for the purpose of attending to his private business while the army was in winter quarters.

16. (same month) Thursday. Began to work on my house. Mr. Thomas Brackett, Mr. Walker, Mr. Frink, William Lunt, Wm. Brackett, Sam'l. Hicks, helped me."

There is no hint in the diary to indicate where this house was located. Possibly it was on the farm owned by the late Mr. Colley in this city. The entries through the winter are few. The 12th of December he states that he removed to Jacob Merrill's at pursuma (Presumpscot ?). He borrows five hundred dollars of Lt. Buxton, four hundred dollars of Capt. Partridge, and four hundred and fifty-nine dollars of Capt. Starbird. Over each of the entries relating to these transactions is a significant cross, indicating that the money was subsequently paid.

The 12th of March he set sail for Boston arriving there the next day, and the 14th met with Col. Tupper, Capt. Abbott and Capt. Emerson. The 19th he returned by ship to Falmouth. The 9th of April one Wm. Cressey began work for six months.

"23. Capt. Starbird, Thos. Starbird, Wm. Pride, and John Proctor worked on my house.

30. This day sowed by Ry and a peck of Sybami wheat.
May 7. this day sowed two pecks and 1/2 wheat."

That he expected an abundant harvest is evident from the fact that on the same day of this last entry he made a contract with Adam Barbour "for a Barn frame sixty dollars and to Bord and shingle it for $15."

And with a house either completed or under way, a new barn contracted for, his wheat and rye in the ground, and a man hired to work on the farm for six months, he was ready to return to his post in the army.

"22. (May) Tuesday sat out on my Jorny to camp and got to LeCriek and Returned home.

23. Wednesday this day set out for camp and put up at Capt. Bradbury's (probably at Kennebunk.)

24. Thurdsay put up at Goodwin's York.

25. Friday Rainy put up at Greenland house.

26. Saturday, put up at Capt. Greenleaf's Newburyport.

27. Sunday put up at Doctor Jones. Lodged with Lieyt. Shaw."

This was probably Dr. Benjamin Jones, Beverly, whose daughter Lydia married Parson Thomas Lancaster of Scarborough. Mary, another daughter of Dr. Jones became the wife of Major Billy Porter of Wenham of Revolutionary fame and was the mother of Dr. Benjamin Jones Porter of Topsham.

"28. Monday put up in Boston Mr. Tuffts.

7. (June) Thursday stormy went to the tresury.

8. Fryday Received from the treasury 85:15:"

This was doubtless his pay as a soldier, and was received from the treasury of Massachusetts.

9. Saturday paid Mis Tuffts for Board thirty-one dollars N. (?) omition.

10. Sunday sot out for Camp Dind, at W.Town (Watertown?) Jones, Lodged Colo Hawes Sudbury.

11. Monday Brex Lawene (?) Moubrought (Marlboro?)

17. Sunday arrived at Camp West Point.

25. this day we celebrated the day of St. Johns.

30. Saturday the division was revued by his excellency on Callus Hill."

As this was not the hill in Salem where the witches were hanged in 1692, it must have received its name from some other act or acts of legalized strangulation. Possibly it was the place where Major Andre had met an ignominious death in the previous year.

"1 July 4 o'clock in the morning marched from Peeks Hill and on Monday morning 7 o'clock halted on Valentine's Hill, the

10 men we killed was ____ no wounded ____ the enemy's los was killed ____ wounded 6 ."

The blanks seem to have been left to be filled whenever accurate information could be obtained, and remain blank to the present time. No account of this engagement is given in any of the histories of the Revolutionary war that I have met with; but Valentine's Hill became famous from being occupied, alternately, by the English and American according as one or the other was in the ascendant. On its summit entrenchment's were thrown up in the summer of 1776, and here Washington encamped a few days before the battle of White Plains. In a book entitled "The Valentines of America" is given a picture of the old Valentine house which was occupied by Washington as his headquarters at this time, and perhaps at other times during the war; and it may have been to this very same house that Capt. Lunt was invited to dine with the great commander who honored him with the yellow and time-stained missive, which he thought worthy of preservation, and which is one of the treasures in the collection kindly loaned me by Mr. Walker. "General Washington presents his Compliments to Cap. Lunt and requests the favor of his Company at Dinner tomorrow at 3 o'clock. Thursday. Answer if you please."

The missive is without date and was doubtless one of several written by the General's private secretary in a peculiarly elegant hand except the words of Cap. Lunt and Thursday which may have been filled in the "Father of his Country" himself, thus making the honor of the invitation all the more distinguished.

Mention is made in the diary of the death and burial of Gen. Enoch Poor, who entered the service from New Hampshire. He was born in 1736 in Andover, Massachusetts, and died in fever near Hackensack, New Jersey on September 8, 1780. He was in several of the principal battles of the war where he displayed great courage and ability. He was alluded to by Lafayette, during his farewell visit to this Country, as "Light Infantry Poor."

Washington mentioned him after his death as "an officer of distinguished merit who as a citizen and a soldier had every claim to the esteem of his Country."

Less conspicuous than that of Gen. Poor was the career of Capt. Lunt, but now less useful in its way, and the encomium which the great captain bestowed upon one of his generals he would not have withheld from the worthy commander of a company who he honored with an invitation to partake at his own board, of the humble fare upon which officers alike and privates were compelled to subsist in those days of privation and hardship.

Chapter 14

The first Bracketts in old Falmouth were Anthony and Thomas, sons of Anthony of Portsmouth, "Selectman." Concerning them the late Hon. William Willis writes as follows: "We first meet with Anthony's name in 1662, as witness to the delivery of the Bramhall farm to Hope Allen, June 3 of that year. He married Ann, the daughter of Michael Mitton, and occupied the 100 acres granted her by her grandfather, George Cleve, at Back Cove. He subsequently enlarged his farm to 400 acres." These were the lands now occupied in part by the well-known Deering mansion in Portland and the pleasant suburb of Oakdale. Mr. Willis continues: "His brother Thomas married Mary, another daughter of Michael Mitton, and occupied the homestead on Clark's Point. Thomas Brackett was killed near his dwelling house in 1676 by the Indians, and Anthony by the same enemy on his farm at Back Cove in 1689." All the Brackett families who settled in what is now Westbrook were descendants of these two brothers, and their descendants, as well as the descendants of the Proctors and Larrabees now residing in this city, are also the descendants of Portland's first settler, George Cleve. From Thomas Brackett, the distinguished statesman, the Hon. Thomas Brackett Reed, was a direct descendant. The line given me by Mr. Reed himself is as follows: Anthony Brackett (killed by the Indians in Portland), Joshua Brackett, Anthony Brackett, Thomas Brackett, Mary Brackett married Joseph Reed, Thomas B. Reed, Sr., Thomas B. Reed, Jr.

Zachariah Brackett, whose father, Anthony, was killed by the Indians in 1689, returned to the Back Cove farm in 1720. He sold the farm about 1740, and moved to Ipswich, where he died in 1751. His children were as follows:

1. Sarah, born March 1, 1709, married first Isaac Sawyer of Back Cove; second Jonathan Morse.

2. Jane, born January 13, 1711, married Daniel Mosher of Gorham.

3. Anthony, born August 25, 1712, married first Abigail Chapman; second, Abigail, a daughter of Joshua Brackett. He died in 1775.

4. Abraham, born July 3, 1714, married Joanna Springer 1743, died in 1806.

The foregoing were born in Hampton, New Hampshire. Those who follow were born in Falmouth.

5. Zachariah, born November 30, 1716, married Judith Sawyer in 1742, died in 1776. He lived at or near Stevens Plains.

6. Thomas married Mary Snow. He probably settled near Prides Corner in Westbrook and it is probable that John Snow Brackett, whose name occurs in William Lunt's ledger, was his son.

7. Susannah, born February 13, 1720, married John Baker in 1740.

8. Joshua, born June 7, 1722.

9. Abigail, born June 7, 1727, married James Merrill, third, of Falmouth. The name of James Merrill occurs in Lunt's ledger and it is probable that he also lived in the vicinity of Prides Corner, or perhaps in the present town of Falmouth.

Joshua Brackett (8) above named, who was born in 1723, married Esther Cox, a daughter of John Cox, commonly called "the old Ranger." It will be remembered that Cox had a grant of land on the northerly side of the Presumpscot, which included the Proctor Mill privilege within its limits. The Cox, Proctor and Brackett families were all connected by intermarriages and it is probably that several of the name settled as neighbors, on that account, near Pride's Bridge and vicinity. Joshua Brackett lived probably on the farm lately owned by Alton C. Brackett who appears to have been his descendant. He was captain of a company of minute men in the war of the Revolution and marched with them to Cambridge in 1775. It was in this company that Daniel Lunt, afterwards Captain Lunt, first served. According to Willis, Captain Brackett who died in Westbrook in 1816 had by his wife, Esther Cox, children as follows:

1. Anthony who lived in Westbrook where the family of the late Alton C. Brackett made their home.
2. James, who lived in Westbrook.
3. Abraham, who lived and died in Limington.
4. Joshua, who also lived and died in Limington.
5. Tabitha, married --- Tobey.
6. Mary, married Benjamin Lunt.
7. Samuel, died in the army of the Revolution.
8. Joshua, died in Westbrook.

The first Bracketts who settled in Portland married a daughter of Michael Mitton. According to Mr. Willis there were two families of Bracketts among the early settlers of New England, on in Boston and one in Portsmouth. The first of the name found in New Hampshire was William, who was sent to Piscataqua in 1631 by Captain John Mason among "his stewards and servants." Anthony Brackett who is supposed to have been the father of Anthony and Thomas who came to Old Falmouth, is known to have been in Portsmouth in 1740 in which year he gave a deed of "globe lands" to the church wardens for a parsonage. It is probable from this that Brackett, like most of the early settlers in Portsmouth, was an Episcopalian; in fact, this town seems to have afforded refuge for Thomas Walford and other Episcopalians who the Puritans found in possession and at once proceeded to exile from Charlestown and other Massachusetts towns. Walford, here mentioned, I suspect of being the maternal grandfather of Col. Thomas Westbrook, a native of Portsmouth probably, and not of England as Mr. Willis supposes, for whom this city was named.

Thomas Brackett, who, as we have seen, married Mary Mitton and was killed by the Indians in 1676, is known to have had a son, Joshua, who likewise had a son Joshua, born in Greenland, New Hampshire (whither the family had fled during the Indian Wars) in 1701. This second Joshua and his brother Anthony, born in Greenland in 1707, returned to Portland upon the resettlement of the town, and became large land holders. Joshua died in March, 1794, aged 93 years. Anthony married first Sarah Knight in 1733, and second, Widow Kerenhappuck Hicks in 1756. I have not learned whether there were any children by the first marriage as the dates of his children's births I have been unable thus far to find. His second wife, who was the daughter of Samuel and Sarah (Brackett) Proctor seems to have been his cousin. He died in 1784, aged 77 years. After his death a large tract of land was set out to his widow from his possessions in the upper part of Portland, which was long known as the "Brackett Dower." His children, ten in number, were:

1. John, who married Mary Fabyan of Scarborough. He lived in Saccarappa on the same land formerly owned by Mrs. Susan S. Conant on old Gorham road. His son, John, Jr., married Jane Warren, daughter of John and Jane (Johnson) Warren, and

sister of the well-known lumber merchants, John and Nathaniel Warren. He lived at one time on the farm in Gorham later owned by Mr. Fred Fenderson, but subsequently removed with his family to Parsonfield.

    1a. John Brackett, Sr. had other children as follows: Mary, married Eleazer Burbank; Lucy married Asahel Foster of Harrison; and Sally who married first Simeon Quimby, and second, Thomas Mayberry. She was the mother of the late Charles Quimby who lived on Main Street where B. F. Roberts formerly lived, and of Simeon Mayberry who lived on the Windham road in the house later occupied by the late Abner L. Hawkes.

    2. Thomas, whose daughter Mary was the great grandmother of Hon. Thomas B. Reed.

    3. James.

    4. Mary, whose second husband was James Smith. It was at the house of her grandson, James Smith of Gorham, that the widow Kerrenhappuck, who usually wrote her name "Happy Brackett" died in 1822 at the age of 93.

    5. Joshua settled in Gorham near South Windham, formerly known as the "Factory Village." Most of the name in that vicinity and several in Portland are believed to be his descendants.

    6. Elizabeth, married Dr. James Brackett of Lee, New Hampshire.

    7. Keziah, married -- Bancroft.

    8. Samuel, who appears to have died unmarried in Portland.

    9. Nathaniel of Portland followed the sea.

    10. Sarah, married Joshua Fabyan of Scarborough. I have the impression that she was left a widow by the death of Fabyan, and subsequently married Solomon Haskell, Jr. as his second wife, his wife who died May 17, 1805 at the age of 40, being a daughter of Peletiah March, who has already been noticed, married as his second wife, the widow of the elder John Brackett.

    It was by March and his second wife, Mary, and the children of Brackett, that the homestead on the Gorham road was conveyed to Daniel Conant, Sr. from who it passed by descent and conveyance to Mrs. Susan S. Conant and heirs.

Brackett Street in Saccarappa took its name from Zachariah Bangs Brackett who built the brick block of stores and the double house adjoining at the corner of Main and Brackett Streets in the first half of the last century. Mr. Brackett came to Saccarappa from Prides Corner where he had previously owned and occupied a farm. He was the son of Joseph and Sarah Bangs Brackett and is said to have been born in Cumberland February 12, 1789. Sometime during his early life his family joined the Shakers and moved from Gorham to New Gloucester, where his brother Joseph became and always remained a prominent member and businessman of the community. Another brother, Barnabas, lived and was a large owner in Denmark in this state. He married Polly Howard, a sister of the late Judge Howard of Portland. Our late fellow townsman Sewall Brackett, was a son of Z. B. and Abigail (Reed) Brackett. In the early fifties, before Deering was taken off, Sewall Brackett represented Westbrook in the State Legislature. Two of his granddaughters still reside in Westbrook, Misses Alice and Lindette Stackpole, who are still living in the brick house built by Zachariah B. Brackett.

Chapter 15

We have noticed in a former chapter the ownership of extensive tracts of land southerly of Deer Hill and both sides of the road from old Ammoncongin to Portland by Benjamin Larrabee, father and son, and their descendants. Connected with the Larrabees by intermarriages were the Lamb families, descended from William Lamb who first resided at Stroudwater, subsequently purchased and lived upon the old homestead now owned and occupied by William M. Lamb, a little northwesterly from the crest of Deer Hill. February 17, 1767, this William Lamb purchased of Ichabod Hunt and John Wilson "a tract of land at a place called Deer Hill near Ammoncongin containing 40 acres and bounded as follows: Beginning at a stake standing twenty-seven rods northwest from a pitch pine marked 'P' on Deer Hill aforesaid, said tree being the westerly corner of a tract of land Mr. Samuel Proctor formerly sold to Moses Goold; from said stake running north, northwest ninety-six rods toward Ammoncongan at a stake; thence east northeast, one hundred and thirteen and one half rods to a stake; thence south twenty degrees west, one hundred eight rods to a stake; then south forty-five rods to the stake first mentioned, the said northwest course, or westerly sideline of said forty acres is bounded on the easterly side of a rod road from said tree down to Edward Gilman's house, said forty acres being one half of eighty acres we this day had a deed of from said Gilman."

There is reason to believe that the land which Proctor conveyed to Goold extended from the northeasterly boundary of the present farm of William M. Lamb, to the river; but from the perishable nature of the land marks used in those early days it is no longer possible to follow any of the ancient boundaries with any satisfactory degree of accuracy. All we really know is that from the corner of Goold's land a rod road led to Gilman's house which was nearer to Ammoncongan. From other investigations in the county records we are able to state that Gilman's farm was the same recently owned in part by the late Harlan M. Raymond at Cumberland Mills. It is described as beginning at Deer Hill and extending north, northwest two hundred and fifty-six rods to Presumpscot River, and down said river until one hundred and fifty-four acres are completed. The 25th day of

January, 1804 the farm was sold to Nathan Winslow by Ebenezer Gilman of Standish, John Gilman of Falmouth, Zachariah Small and Jermina, his wife, of Falmouth, in his right, Paul Leighton and Phebe, his wife, of Falmouth, her right, and Edward Gilman of Bolton in Lower Canada. The grantors describe themselves as grandchildren of Edward Gilman who purchased the farm as they tell us in their deed of Edward Gilman of Exeter, New Hampshire. We have no information respecting this family of Gilmans except the Zachariah Small whose wife was Jermina Gilman, was one of the sons of "prophet" John Small, and lived on the farm owned by the late Simon H. Mayberry in a house that formerly stood on the westerly side of the Windham road, now called Pierce Street, at the curve near the Maine Central Railroad. April 16, 1770 William Lamb, Jr., son of the William Lamb above named, bought of David Small twelve acres of land at Deer Hill "adjoining Edward Gilman's land." I do not know whether this Small was connected with Zachariah Small just mentioned. He is said to have lived part of the year in a house which stood where the "White House" formerly stood, and at other times in a house which stood near the Presumpscot River. It would seem from this that he was a man of peculiar habits, perhaps somewhat eccentric. I do not find that he held title to any land except the twelve acres which he conveyed to Lamb. I suspect, therefore, that he was a tenant of Benjamin Larrabee who owned the land where his house stood, and as Larrabee resided at Falmouth Neck, he may have been employed by him to guard his timber lands which were doubtless of considerable value, and offered great temptations to trespassers.

  William Lamb, Jr. married one of the daughters of the elder Solomon Haskell and left a numerous family. Of his five sons, Solomon settled in Naples; Nathaniel in Otisfield; John succeeded to the family homestead on Deer Hill; Samuel who married a daughter of Benjamin Larrabee settled on land inherited by his wife from her father, now a part of the Portland City Farm; and Mark lived and died unmarried at the home of his brother John. One of his daughters was the wife of Capt. John Warren of Saccarappa and the mother of our late townsmen, George and Lewis P. Warren. The late William W. and

Marrett Lamb of Cumberland Mills were grandsons of William Lamb, Jr., being sons of his son John.

In 1767 Edward Gilman sells 80 acres of land at Deer Hill to Ichabod Hunt, shipwright, and John Wilson, cordwainer, both of Falmouth. Previously in 1742, Gilman had conveyed to these parties the same land and had received a reconveyance for some reason that after the lapse of years is no longer apparent. Through this tract Gilman reserved the "rod road" leading down to his dwelling house. I am at a loss to determine the locality of this road, but think it was easterly from the present Maine Street, or Portland road from Cumberland Mills. It was probably only a wood road at the time of the reservation. June 29, 1779, Edward Gilman, Jr. gave a bond to William Lamb,Jr., in which he came under obligation to sell to the latter land adjoining his own. Gilman died probably at Falmouth, intestate. Chase Stevens of Windham, a somewhat noted land surveyor in his time, was his administrator. It is not clear whether Edward Gilman and Edward Gilman, Jr. are on and the same person or not, but it is most probable that they were father and son, and that the former returned to Exeter, New Hampshire, having come hither from that place, leaving the son in possession of his lands there. One of the Gilmans sold about two acres near the Falls at Ammoncongan to Waite and Moody, who were probably engaged in the lumber business upon the river. He also sold land at the same place to Ebenezer Mayo in 1779.

The following grant of land made by the Falmouth Proprietors' committee may still be of interest to those living in the vicinity of Cumberland Mills, viz: "Laid out to the right of Edward Shrove at the request of Joseph Quinby, 30 acres of land in the township of Falmouth, and bounded beginning at a point of rocks 12 rods up the river from the lowermost part of Ammoncongan Falls, said point of rocks being the most norther-ly corner of 70 acres of land laid out to said Shove June ye 1st. 1832, thence joining said 70 acres lot to a stake in the line of 60 acres laid out to William Hide, thence south 67 degrees and 30 minutes each one hundred and 46 rods to a stake in the line of 60 acres in the line of 60 acres laid out to Benjamin Larraby, Jr., thence north northwest one hundred and thirty rods to the river, thence southwest up the river to the first bounds provided the same be free from former grants, etc.

Approved by the proprietors May 5, 1774.
                    Enoch Freeman
                    Stephen Longfellow
                    Benjamin Winslow
                    Joseph Noyes
                                    Committee"

William Hide who is mentioned in the grant to Joseph Quinby was an early grantee of lands in this part of the old town. The grant which was made to him on August 26, 1734, is the one referred to in the grant to Quinby nearly forty years later and appears to be all the land he ever owned in town. This tract is described in the Proprietor's records as follows: "On the southerly side of Presumpscot River, beginning at the west, northwest corner of one hundred and fifty acres of land laid out to Henry Wheeler and from thence to run west northwest one hundred and sixty rods to a stake and from thence south southwest sixty rods to a stake standing on said Wheeler's line and from said stake southeast sixty rods to the first bounds." The committee for laying out lands at this time were Edmund Mountfort, John East and Joshua Moody.

Henry Wheeler at whose "west northwest corner" this grant was made to begin was, according to the late Mr.Willis, admitted an inhabitant of Falmouth in 1729. He came from Charlestown, Massachusetts. His first wife, Sarah, died in 1736. The same year he married Mary, the widow of John East, and occupied the house which had previously been East's on King (now India) Street,Portland. He was by trade a blacksmith and a very active and useful man in the affairs of the old town. There was a connection between the family of Wheeler and the Riggs family of Capisic. It is not probable that Wheeler ever resided within the present limits of Westbrook, although the grant of land above mentioned, or a part of the same, was laid out September 29, 1731 as follows: "laid out to Henry Wheeler a certain tract of one hundred and two acres, bounded beginning at a pitch pint tree marked on the north sided of Birch Hill, and to run S.S.W. one hundred and sixty-four rods to a stake; thence N.N.E. one hundred and sixty-four rods to a stake; then to the first bounds mentioned. - - - said Wheeler to leave a four rod way through said lot most convenient for the town's use." The

Proprietor's Committee at this time were John Tyng, Thomas Haskell and Moses Pearson. By Birch Hill was probably meant the eminence northeast of the present Stroudwater road now occupied in part as the Catholic Cemetery, and assuming that the four rod way which Wheeler was obliged to leave through his lot was identical with the above mentioned Stroudwater road, the grant in question would have embraced the lands formerly owned by the late Alonzo Libby, Smith Babb and others, while Hide's grant may have included the lands on the present Haskell Street near Cumberland Mills.

In the grant to Quinby mention is made of a former grant to Edward Shove on June 1, 1732. This grant according to the Proprietor's records was a follows: "Laid out to Edward Shove 70 acres - - - - bounded as follows, beginning at the upper side of Nathaniel Winslow's 60 acre lot at Presumpscot River near Ammoncongin Falls and to run up said river 70 rods and to run back into the woods the same width bounded upon said Winslow's land until 70 acres be competed - - - -said Shove to leave a convenient highway through said land where it will be most convenient for the town's use.

                Dated in Falmouth June 1st 1732.
                          John East
                          Thomas Haskell
                          James Winslow
                          Moses Pearson
                                  Committee"

I am at a loss to determine the exact location of this grant, but I think it embraced within its limits the farm near Cumberland Mills, known as the Dexter Haskell farm, while the land intermediate and extending westward between the same and the Tyng hundred acres was laid out by the Proprietors to the great land owner, General Waldo. The highway reserved would, therefore, be the present Main Street from Saccarappa to Cumberland Mills. Thus the great antiquity is established of two of our principal roads, viz.: Main and Stroudwater Streets. The latter may have been originally a mast road used by Col. Westbrook and subsequently in the establishment of saw mills at Saccarappa by the ox teams which drew the manufactured lumber to Stroudwater for shipment to the West Indian ports.

After the resettlement of Falmouth more of the wealthy and well-to-do citizens of the Neck had grants of land made them in the then wilderness portions of the town. Edward Shove was evidently one of this class of citizens, it not rich, possessed of a competency for the time in which he lived. He was admitted an inhabitant at the time of the contention between the old and new proprietors and had a house lot granted him at the foot of Center Street where he lived for some years. He was the son of Rev. George Shrove, minister at Taunton, and was born in 1690. He had a family of nine children. He came here from Dighton, Massachusetts and probably returned thither before his death. In 1766 his sons were Theophilus, Edward and Nathaniel, and he had daughters, Mary Smith, wife of John Smith; Ruth Southwick, wife of Paul Southwick; Elizabeth Osborne, wife of Paul Osborne; and Lydia Chase, wife of George Chase, all residing in Massachusetts and New York.

Chapter 16

Parson Smith writing in the now famous journal under date of May 4, 1759, makes the following entry: "Gov. Pownal came in here in Capt. Saunders." Again on the 8th of the same month he writes: "He sailed today with 400 men for Penobscot to build a fort there," and on the 31st he continues: "We hear that Brigadier Waldo died suddenly at Penobscot on Wednesday last."

In a magazine not to the journal Mr. Willis tell us that "the fort was built in Prospect near Penobscot River, on Fort Point, and was called Fort Pownal. - - - General Waldo accompanied the Governor and took great interest in the erection of the fortification as promotive of the interest of the proprietors of the WaldoPatent, whose boundary extended to this spot. While viewing the location with the Governor, May 23rd, he exclaimed in reference to his patent 'here is my bound' and instantly fell in an apoplectic fit, and expired on the spot."

The Governor, to commemorate the melancholy event, caused a leaden plate, with an inscription upon it, to be buried in the place. General Waldo was 63 years old, and left four children, viz.: Samuel and Francis of Portland; Lucy, married to Isaac Winslow of Roxbury; and Hannah, who married Thomas Flucker of Boston, and was the mother of General Knox's wife.

The elder Williamson in his "History of Maine" published many years ago, says that General Waldo was born in England, and was "a man personable, tall of stature, and of light complexion." For aught that appears to the contrary, the personal description is correct, but the historian was in error respecting the place of General Waldo's birth, and the error is repeated by the younger Williamson. Instead of being of foreign birth, Waldo was born on New England soil, probably in Boston, where his father, Jonathan Waldo, was a distinguished merchant. General Samuel Waldoappears always to have had his principal residence in Boston, although the care of his large estates brought him frequently to the District of Maine. The high social standing of the family is shown by the position of the names of his sons in their respective classes at Harvard. In 1743 when the names of students were arranged according to the social rank of their parents, and not alphabetically as at the present day, Samuel Waldo's was the fourteenth in a class of thirty, and in 1747, four years later, that of his brother, Francis, was second in a class numbering twenty-eight, a fact which indicated the high and ever increasing importance of the family in the province. By the time General Waldo, who had been second in command in the memorable expedition against Louisburg in 1745, had gained a foothold in almost every habitable part of Maine. In old Falmouth, prior to the Louisburg expedition, after extending his possession in connection with Col. Thomas Westbrook, everywhere that lands could be purchased, he had swooped down upon the latter with an execution for a very large amount, seizing his possessions wherever they could be found and leaving him to die soon after, in disappointment and destitution, at his home in Stroudwater. In what is now the city of Westbrook, Waldo acquired title to the Simpson tract of ten acres through which the Main Street of Saccarappa is now located; the Tyng tract of one hundred acres, next below the Simpson tract; a tract of one hundred and sixty acres below the "hundred acres"; a tract of eight hundred acres extending up the Stroudwater River to the Gorham and Scarboro lines; and the Munjoy Hill Square, otherwise called the Cooper claim, on the north side of the Presumpscot River.

Col. Samuel Waldo, son of General Waldo, was the first Judge of Probate of Cumberland County, which was taken from York in 1760. He settled in Portland soon after leaving college in 1743.

He was twice married and left several children, some of whose descendants are believed to be still living. He died in 1770. In 1753 he went to Germany in the interests of his father, and brought over a company of immigrants who settled in the town of Waldoboro upon the Waldo Patent. The history of this enterprise, especially in the misrepresentations made to the poor colonists, and the manner in which they were treated after reaching the shores of Maine, is alike discreditable to father and son.

Francis, the second son of General Waldo was never married, having been jilted in an early love affair. When the collection district at Falmouth Neck was established he received the first appointment as Collector of Customs. Like most holders of office at the breaking out of the Revolutionary struggle, he took sides with the mother country and accordingly went to England and never returned.

From the college triennial we learn that he died in 1784.

Lucy Flucker, daughter of Thomas Flucker, secretary of the Province of Massachusetts Bay, and his wife, Hannah Waldo, became the wife of Henry Knox, a young man who, at the time of their marriage plied the plebeian handicraft of a book binder in the town of Boston. This alliance was anything but agreeable to the high-born and aristocratic kindred of the bride. But the humble mechanic, who was a worthy representative of the young democracy of the time, lived to be one of the most distinguished of the Revolutionary generals and Secretary of War under President Washington; and it was the last named office which he resigned in 1795 for the purpose of indulging tastes not altogether republican. Mrs. Knox, by inheritance from her mother, was the owner of a large undivided interest in the Waldo patent. To this General Knox added by purchased till he found himself in possession of what is now the larger part of Knox County. Laying down the duties and responsibilities of public life, he betook himself thither while still in his prime, and selecting an eligible situation overlooking a bay of the Georges River, in the present town of Thomaston, he erected himself thereon the famous mansion house flanked on either hand by long rows of barns and outhouses.

This palatial residence was named "Montpelier" by Mrs. Knox who, notwithstanding she had had the temerity to marry below the station of her family, was at no pains to conceal the pride that she felt in the rise of her husband to the high position which he now occupied in the young republic and the spirit which she had displayed from her girlhood was an inheritance which she had received from her mother, Hannah Waldo. The latter, when a girl, had been engaged to young Andrew Pepperell, son and prospective heir of the Kittery baronet who had led the land forces of New England in the siege of Louisburg. Young Pepperell had been the class mate of her brother Samuel at Harvard, and the inclination which the young people manifested for each other had been a matter of no little gratification to the parents on both sides, who at this time were among the foremost people of the land. A day was set for the nuptials, but young Pepperell, for some reason which is not recorded, notified the bride elect that a delay of three years would be necessary. To this the young woman consented and waited with all patience for the three years to go by; but when the phlegmatic suitor notified her that still another delay was necessary, she promptly broke off the engagement, and was led to the alter six weeks later by the province secretary, Thomas Flucker, to who she seems to have been a model wife. Young Pepperell died a few months after this, and it may have been the consciousness that he was laboring under an incurable malady that occasioned his singular conduct in relation to what would have seemed so flattering marriage prospects. General Knox was the warm person friend of Washington, and although his human foibles and frailties are lost sight of with the lapse of years, it is probable that his daily conversation did not lack for the spice that history also accords to that of the first President.

An anecdote that is vouched for as true by high authority is worth recording. At one of these elegant dinners given by Washington after he had come to the Presidency, and which were presided over by his estimable wife, the pickled olives, now so common, but at that time almost unknown, were passed to General Knox. The first trial of the new relish was quite enough for the valiant Secretary of War, who quickly taking the obnoxious fruit from his mouth, thus addressed himself to his hostess, "Please Madam, may I put this damned thing on the floor?"

Lucy Waldo, one of the daughters of General Samuel Waldo, married, as we have seen, Isaac Winslow of Roxbury. I have not learned to what branch of the famous family of the old colony Isaac Winslow belonged. The first ones of the name who settled in old Plymouth were Nathaniel and James. The former who had the "sixty-acre" lot below the grant made to Edward Shore at old Ammoncongan in 1732 is not known to have left any descendants. All of the name in this and adjacent towns are supposed to be descendants of James, who was a great grandson of Kenelm Winslow, son of Edward, and brother of Governor Edward of the Plymouth colony. The members of one branch of the family of this vicinity have traced and recorded their descent from Kenelm Winslow of Wincelow and to this record I am indebted for the following facts: Kenelm Winslow of Wincelow, born in England, arrived in Plymouth in 1629. In 1634 he married , Eleanor Newton, the widow of John Adams, and settled in Marshfield. Job Winslow, son of Kenelm and Eleanor, settled in Freetown. James, the son of Job, born May 9, 1687, came to Falmouth, Maine about 1728 and was granted lands at Back Cove, but subsequently settled near the Presumpscot River in the present town of Falmouth. He had a wife, Elizabeth (?), and sons: Nathan, in 1713, married Charity Hall; Job, born 1715, married Margaret Barbour; Benjamin, born 1717, married Hope Cobb; James, born 1725, married Annie Huston. He also had two daughters who married respectively Hate-evil Hall and David Torrey.

James Winslow and his family were the first persons to unite with the Quakers in Falmouth, which act of sacrilege (according to the views of good Parson Smith) they committed about 1743. three years before July 30, 1740, the parson tells us that: "the church kept a day of fasting and prayer on account of the spread of Quakerism." The heresy that had been thought deserving of a halter a century earlier in Salem, had by this time broken out anew, but it does not seem to have found many converts in old Falmouth till the ministers and other rulers of the then dominant parish, had taken active measures to prevent it from taking root. It is probable, as Mr. Willis observes, that our pious ancestors were shocked at the idea of any person attempting to be more Puritan than they were themselves. In fact, the medium course which they had chosen they thought the only fit one to be pursued by others; therefore, when Mr. Wiswell, who had begun his ministry as a Congregationalist, became a Churchman in 1764, and immediately departed for England to receive ordination by apostolic succession "with the laying on of hands," Parson Smith, his deacons and the more zealous of his church members, were again sorely afflicted in spirit. Useful to an eminent degree, and eventful was the long life of Mr. Smith, but thorny at times like that of every man who concedes only with reluctance the same rights to others which he claims for himself, especially in matters of opinion; and there is not imagining what the good man would say could he be advised of the lapse of his ancient church from the faith and creed of his day; and yet there is no spot on earth where his name and memory are more revered than within the somber stone edifice that stands upon the place where he so long and so earnestly ministered.

Many of the descendants of James Winslow still adhere to the simple faith he imbibed from the broad brimmed propagandists of his time, but not all of them have exhibited the most pacific spirit under strong provocation. It is related of one of them that being challenged to a personal encounter by one with whom he differed in some matter of business, he promptly threw aside his drab coat with the injunction: "lie there Quaker" and soon proved to his antagonist that he had found a foreman worthy of his brawn.

Nathan Winslow, a son of Nathan and grandson of James, was the last clerk of the Falmouth Proprietors. He was born in 1743 and died in Westbrook in 1826. James Winslow, the immigrant, died I 1773; to Nathan Winslow, long a leading business man in Portland, belongs the credit of having inaugurated what is now a colossal industry in most parts of the United States and Canada, the preservation of food products in cans by what is known as the process of hermetically sealing. In this connection it its worthy of mention that the first sweet corn ever canned for the market, was so canned for Mr. Winslow in what was then a woodshed at Cumberland Mills, and that the building is still standing in a greatly modified form, having been incorporated into the dwelling house of the late Alfred H. Larrabee.

Chapter 17

The Babbs are an old New England family whose founder came over with the first settlers of "Strawberry Bank", now Portsmouth, New Hampshire. In a list of emigrants from England to America and the ships which brought them over covering the entire 17th century under date of July 28, 1635, we meet with the name for the first time as follows: "These persons herein under expressed are to be transported to New England embarked in the Hopewell of London, Thomas Babb, master, per certificate from the master of St. Giles Cripplegate that they are confortable to the Church of England. The members have taken the oath of allegiance and supremacy." The passengers were: "A smith, Thomas Treadwill, 30 years; Mary Treadwill, 30 years, Thomas Blackley, 20 years; Thomas Treadwill, one year."

The fact that these people were required to be members of the Church of England renders it certain that their destination was not Plymouth or the Massachusetts colony, but rather New Hampshire or the neighboring shores of Maine, possibly our first incorporated city of Gorgeana.

There is recorded evidence that as early as 1652 a Philip Babb lived upon one of the Isles of Shoales, where he held the office of constable, and that Mary Babb, daughter of Peter Babb, was baptized in 1713; and the church records of Greenland, original a part of Portsmouth, show baptism of children of Philip Babb as follows: Peter 1730; Nathaniel 1732; and Judith 1735. Persons of the name were among the early inhabitants of that part of Scarboro known as Dunston, having come hither, I suspect, in the employment of Col. Westbrook, who was by this time fully established in business in Maine.

Southgate mentions John and Nathaniel Babb among the Dunstan settlers, and says that Nathaniel was one of the Scarborough colony who settled in Machias where he and one Munson won as a wager a barrel of rum for moving a stick of timber after a pair of oxen had failed to start it.

The first of the name of whom we find any mention in Westbrook was James Babb, who purchased land of Colonel Westbrook and his partner Gen. Waldo in March 1735-36. This was doubtless the same land since owned in part by his namesake and probable descendant, the late James Babb, at the corner of Spring Street and the Buxton Road, where the buildings were burned but have been rebuilt.

William Babb, a son of this first James, has been already mentioned. He was born, as he informs in a deposition recorded in the Cumberland Registry of Deeds "within a mile of Saccarappa." In 1805, when the deposition was taken, he was 63 years old, thus making it evident that the year of his birth was 1742. In a deed dated March 3, 1807, he conveys to his son Henry, doubtless the well-known lumberman, his interest in the land, one hundred acres, which his father, James Babb, had bought of Westbrook and WaldoWilliam Babb married before 1770 Elizabeth, daughter of Samuel and Mary (Peabody) Conant, who according to a deposition given at the same time with that of her husband, was three years his junior.

William and Elizabeth (Conant) Babb had six sons and two daughters (but we do not attempt to give them in the order of their birth), as follows:

1. Solomon, born 1770, died in 1854; married Joanna Roberts, born 1778, died 1850. They had sons, Stephen, born in 1802, died in 1881; married Emily, daughter of William Babb, Jr., born in 1807, died in 1896. They were the grandparents of Mrs. Oscar Fick of Monroe Aveune, this city, and Mrs. Edwin Sutermeister of Main Street, this city; Oren married Melissa Libby who died on the home place occupied until recently by their daughter, Mrs. Alton N. Files, whose death occurred in the spring of 1939; George, born in 1800, died in 1826; Solomon, Jr., born in 1811, died at seas in 1832; Lewis, born in 1816 and died 1837; and daughters, Betsey, born in 1811 and died in 1842; Mary Ann married Ebenezer G. Sturgis; Joanna married D. D. Shackford; and Caroline, wife of the late Sargent S. Files. Stephen and Emily Babb were the parents of Adeline, wife of the late Dr. J. L. Horr and Louise T. of this city and W.Scott, now deceased.

2. Alexander lived on the farm of Stroudwater Street adjoining his brother Solomon's, where his two sons, Smith and Samuel C. afterwards lived and died. He was born in 1780 and died 1862. His wife, Esther Wescott, born in 1786, died in 1881. They had sons, Daniel, born in 1810, died in 1872; Samuel C., born in 1813, died in 1886; Smith, born in 1824, died in 1902; and daughters, among whom were Elizabeth, married Levi Wescott of Standish; Maria, wife of Henry F. Sands; Mary W.

married John Proctor, Jr.; and Ellen, wife of Joshua Roberts; Sarah F., wife of Enoch B. Cobb, all now deceased. They had 12 children in all.

    3. Henry, born in ---, died in 1884; married Elizabeth, daughter of Jonathan and Mary (Connely) Webb. He was extensively engaged in lumbering. His residence was on Bridge Street at the entrance to Winslow Street. There were several children, all now deceased.

    4. George, born ---, died in 1830. He married Almira Jordan who came to Saccarappa from Naples with the family of Jonathan Webb. Their son, David Webster Babb, was the father of the late Howard S. Babb, Mrs. Edwin J. Haskell, Mrs. Mabel Weymouth, and Harlan P. and Fred W. Babb. Harlan P. and Fred W. are now deceased. another son, John, who lived in Windham, married Mary, a daughter of Horatio Gates Winslow. They were the parents of Edward Babb, mayor several years of Minneapolis.

    5. William, Jr. married Elizabeth Wescott May 10, 1792 and had Sarah, who married Samuel Cox March 17, 1812. They were the parents of the late William Cox of Saccarappa. Captain Solomon Babb,Jr. married Sarah Small and died January 24, 1829 (?). Emily, born in 1807, died in 1896. She married Stephen, son of Solomon Babb, Sr.. Nelson Babb was also their son. He married Sarah, daughter of Benjamin Goold, and lived at North Gorham. William Babb, Jr. sold March 22, 1833 to Henry B. Plummer the place on Bridge Street which he then occupied and "had occupied for 36 years."

    6. Daniel drowned July 22, 1828 aet. 45. Married Abigail, daughter of Enoch, Jr. and Mehitable (Cushing) Freeman, who is still remembered as "Aunt Mabby."

    7. Lucy, married Samuel Plummer from Scarboro, February 9, 1789. They had sons, Major (by name), Henry B., married a daughter of Joshua Webb; and a daughter, Jane, who married Gardner Bacon November 27, 1828.

    8. Elizabeth, married Hugh Woodbury. He died in 1816, aged 50; his widow March 9, 1853, aged 92. They were the parents of the late Edmund M. Woodbury, and of Mrs. Henry Pratt, mother of the late Joseph P. Pratt, and several other sons of whom John is still living with in Chelsea, Massachusetts.

The ancestor of the other Babbs of Westbrook has always baffled me, was possibly a brother of James, the father of William, who married Elizabeth Conant and left a numerous posterity, as we have seen. He married a Wescott who was doubtless a descendant of the famous "Post" Wescott, and had seven sons, viz.: although possibly not in order:

1. Peter, who married Lucy, daughter of David Bailey and had:

    a. Charles, born October 24, 1793, died May 20, 1821; married Rebecca, daughter of Nathaniel Proctor, born January 1798, died April 4, 1882. Their only child Charlotte married Benjamin J. Woodman, and was the mother of the late Charles B. Woodman.

    b. Peter Babb, Jr. I think he was married and had a family.

    c. Bailey Babb (otherwise Jesse B.) born in 1807, died 1839; married Hannah Thurlow of Windham, born in 1808, died 1899. One of their sons was drowned in the Presumpscot below the bridge at Saccarappa before 1850.

    d. Apphia married James Frost.

    e. Jane married Gardner Waterhouse of Windham. She died about 1851.

    f. Mary L. married Nathan Libby. They were the parents of the late David B. Libby.

    g. - - - married Joseph Whittier.

    h. Harriet married in Connecticut.

2. Joseph drowned at Saccarappa April 15, 1819, aged 47. Margaret, his wife, died September 8, 1841, aged 65. They had sons:

    a. Henry C. died in Portland, November 16, 1864, aged 69 years. He married Harriet Farmer, January 6, 1820. The had daughters, Sarah Smith, wife of Hon. P. J. Carlton of Camden, and Adaline P., and a son Cyrus K. who was formerly in business in the Fluent Block, now the Union Mutual, at the corner of Congress and Exchange Streets.

    b. Elias married Betsey Hawkes of Windham, in which town he lived and died on the farm afterwards owned by Joshua S. Roberts. He left one son, the late Joseph H. Babb, the father of Mrs. Edward Harding, and two daughters, both of whom died unmarried.

 c. Lemuel married Eliza Jones of Gorham, aunt of Paul Akers, the sculptor. They had sons, Joseph, William A., Isaac W., Henry S., and several daughters.
 d. John married Rhoda, daughter of Abel and Eunice Akers Quinby. They were the parents of late John R. and Marshall L. Babb, and several daughters.
 e. Joseph married Tabitha Darling of Gorham and had several daughters, one of whom was the second wife of the late F. A. Bettes. The last years of his life he resided in Portland.
 3. Zebulon. I have not ascertained whom he married, but he had at least one son, the late Warren P. Babb of Prides Corner, and a daughter, Sally, wife of Montgomery Anderson; William C. Mayberry married Philene, daughter of Zebulon; Mary, wife of David Dyer; and Susan, the first wife of Josiah Cloudman.
 4. Nathaniel married Joanna Libby. He died August 6, 1812, aet.34, and his widow in 1844 aet.72. They lived on the place now occupied by Thaddeau L. Dodgeon, Spring Street. A son, Josiah, died some years ago in California, and a daughter Miriam married Tritten Best and was the mother of John L. Best and Martin W. Best.
 5. Mark married Anna, daughter of Daniel and Anna Haskell Conant and settled in the town of Harmony where he had a family.
 6. Captain John married Rebecca Skillings. She died December 30, 1848; he, May 10, 1862 aet. 80. Captain John Babb occupied the farm at the corner of Spring Street and the Buxton Road afterward owned and occupied by his son, the late James Babb. The late Samuel S. Babb was also a son of Captain and Rebecca Skillings Babb.
 7. James died young June 24, 1760. A Peter Babb was married in Falmouth to Anna Haskell. The bride is reported to have been one of the ten children of the old patriarch, Thomas Haskell, and was born April 22, 1737. It is possible, chronologically, that this Peter Babb was the son of Philip of the Isle of Shoals, and the same who was baptized in Greenland, New Hampshire in 1730, but it seems that the name of the great apostle was long much in favor in the Babb family for in 1770, a Peter Babb of Falmouth, bought land of Nathaniel Jose of Scarboro, and in 1788 and '90 Rhoda Babb, his probable widow, was living in Windham near Great Falls, and August 26, 1841,

Peter Babb of Westbrook and went with his father to Great Falls when he was 16 years old. It would seem, therefore, that he was born in 1770 and went to Great Falls in 1786, and was probably the same Peter Babb mentioned above who married Lucy Bailey.

Other Babb families have been early settlers in Gorham, Limington, Sebago, and other Cumberland and York County towns, where their descendants still live.

Chapter 18

There is reason to believe that most of the Johnson name who settled in this region were of one kindred. Persons of the name were among the early settlers of York County, but I have suspected that the progenitor or progenitors of those settling in old Falmouth came with the Scotch-Irish immigrants who landed at Cape Elizabeth in 1718, and after a winter of great hardship and privation departed for Londerry, New Hampshire where they in time found comfortable homes and helped to establish what eventually became a flouring town. In the family, at least, of the Johnsons of Westbrook, there was a tradition that their ancestors came from Ireland. This was the family, several generations of which lived on the farm lately owned by Rufus and Gardner Johnson, now deceased, sons of Jeremiah and Hannah Hatch Johnson.

James Johnson, the first of this line of whom we find any mention, was in Falmouth as early as 1767, in which year he conveyed to his son, George Johnson, the father of Jeremiah above mentioned, 100 acres of land near Stroudwater, which he had bought of General Waldo. James Johnson is described in this conveyance as a weaver. Afterwards George Johnson conveys the same to John Johnson, Jr., which makes it evident that there must have been a John Johnson, Sr. The land conveyed began at the corner of Porterfield's land, which was the same, in part at least, now embraced in the farm of Elmer Randall, formerly owned by the late Edward Trickey on Stroudwater Street this city. The farm on the same road, formerly the homestead of Cushing Pratt and that of his son, the late Asa W. Pratt, was sold in 1791 to Samuel Butts of Portland by a James Johnson, who describes it as the land which he had purchased of Waldo and Flucker and William Porterfield. On this farm was born, according to tradition, the late Charles Johnson, Esq. of Windham Hill, the well-known trial magistrate for local lawyers, the father of Mrs. Ann Johnson Walker of Portland, wife of Joseph Walker, who gave to Westbrook the Memorial Library. Most of the Johnsons seems to have bought their farms of Waldo or his heirs. In 1765 John Johnson of Falmouth sells to his son, Robert Johnson, one moiety of the farm where he lived, which he had purchased of Samuel Waldo. At a still earlier date lands at

"Birch Hill" in the same vicinity were owned jointly by Benjamin Johnson and John Bodge. Bodge is supposed to have been the person of the same name who soon after went to New Marblehead, now Windham, where he married Rebecca, the daughter of Thomas Chute, the first settler in that town, and thus became the ancestor of most person of the Bodge name and many others in this vicinity. A Robert Johnson purchased one-eighth of a double saw mill at Saccarappa in 1761 of Benjamin Godfrey, it being the same which Benjamin had purchased of Daniel Godfrey, the first of the name in old Saccarappa. George Johnson, son of James, the weaver, is known to have had sons, George, Jr., Francis, and Jeremiah, and a daughter, Anne Sinnet. Jeremiah, as we have seen, married Hannah, a daughter of Capt. Nathaniel Hatch, and succeeded to the homestead of his father, the well-known Johnson farm on Saco Street, as previously mentioned. George Johnson, Jr. married Anna (or Nancy) Quinby, a daughter of Benjamin Quinby, who came to Saccarappa from Somersworth, New Hampshire about 1770. Francis died unmarried. Nancy, a daughter of George Johnson, Jr., who had settled at Mallison Falls, then called Horsebeef Falls, married Nathaniel Knight of Windham, and was drowned February 22, 1807, by reason of the horse attached to the sleigh in which she was riding running off the unrailed bridge at Little Falls, now known as South Windham. It was the occasion of her death that inspired one Thomas Shaw, a famous rhymester of his day, to drop into the wretched doggerel ascribed in the "Poets of Maine" to Nathaniel Hawthorne.

The late Thomas Laurens Smith, in his very able address delivered at the centennial of the first settlement of Windham, on the 4th day of July, 1840, tells us that John Farrar was the third settler of that town, that he came from Tiverton, Rhode Island and located on home lot No. 31, a few rods from the river on the farm owned at the time of the delivery of the address, by Col. Edward Anderson, the younger. In the same connection he tells us that on No. 32, the adjacent lot, Mr. Farrar himself, his sister who was the first wife of Stephen Manchester, and a child were buried, being the first burials in the town. "After their death," writes a kinsman in a private letter in a passage already quoted in a former chapter, "their children sold the premises and went away, leaving no monument to mark the spot. The field grew over with saplings so no one can point out their resting place to this day."

After breaking up of the family in Windham the survivors are said to have gone to the town of Bristol, from which their descendants removed to Bangor and Islesborough. Of the Bangor branch came Isaac Farrar, the well-known mason, who removed to California from this town a few years ago.

The Isleborough branch, who with the name Farrow are quite numerous, are for the most part followers of the sea. One of them, Capt. John Pendleton Farrow, is the author of a very creditable history of Isleborough, although he himself was born in Boston.

The late col. Joseph Porter of Bangor, who was himself a descendant of old Samuel Webb by the latter's first marriage, traces the Farrars back to Massachusetts, to Hingham, and tells us that John Farrar who died July 7, 1687, was an early settler of that town, and that his grandson John, son of the same name, who came to New Marblehead, after living in several other places, had April 30, 1696, married Persis, daughter of Capt. William Holbrook of Weymouth. His children, according to the list given by Col. Porter, were nine in number. Bethiah, the fifth of these, born in Hingham November 29, 1704, was the ancestor of many persons in this and other parts of Maine. At the age of 14 she became the wife of Capt. David
Spear of Braintree, who left her a widow and mother at the age of 15. The child, a daughter, who was thus orphaned in the first year of her life, was given the name of Bethiah for her mother. It would seem that after the death of her first husband Mrs. Bethiah Spear had gone back to the household of her father, who now lived in Tiverton, Rhode Island, but subsequently helped to form the colony from that town which had joined the first settlers in New Marblehead, now Windham, where they took up their abode on one of the home lots then recently acquired by Samuel Webb, whom she had married Arpil 10, 1723, and by whom she already had a considerable family of sons and daughters, and through whom, by the marriage of her daughter, Bethiah Spear, with Thomas, the second son of Windham's second settler, William Mayberry, her posterity is well nigh innumerable.

John Farrar, born in Hingham, who came to New Marblehead with his father, married in 1741, Hannah, daughter of

Timothy Worcester. The latter had come to old Falmouth from Bradford, where he was born December 6, 1693, and had settled on the northerly side of the Presumpscot River, below what was formerly Riverton Park, and I suspect by comparison of dates and ages that Hannah Worcester Farrar was the same person whose intentions of marriage with Samuel Conant of Falmouth had been filed in 1741, sometime previous to her marriage with Farrar, the engagement for some reason having been broken off as the result of a lover's quarrel, the details of which tradition has failed to preserve.

This John Farrar removed with his family to Bristol, as we have seen, but his mother, Persis (Holbrook) Farrar, died in Windham May 12, 1785.

Windham was incorporating as a town, having previously been the plantation of New Marblehead, 1762. The first town meeting was held at the old fort by virtue of a warrant granted by Stephen Longfellow, great grandfather of the poet, as a justice of the peace on the 5th day of July 1762, at which meeting Caleb Graffam, William Mayberry, and John Farrar were elected selectmen; but the board of the following year does not include John Farrar, he having probably by that time removed from the town.

Mary Webb, of who mention was previously made in Chapter 11, was born in Falmouth, now Westbrook, on April 1, 1801, and died November 1, 1837; was married March 5, 1818 to Daniel Beverlywho died the same year leaving one child, Elizabeth, born September 20, 1819. On the 10th of July, 1822, the young widow contracted a second marriage with Ebenezer Hodgkins who was born in Minot, March 27, 1800, and died May 17, 1865. Ebenezer and Mary Webb Hodgkins had nine children as follows:

John Webb, Sarah Webb, twins, born in Westbrook February 17, 1824, both married and died at a good old age, leaving descendants; Deborah Crandell, born July 30, 1825; Maria Webb, born July 15, 1827; William H. Tobey, born January 13, 1829, married Harriet L. Bunker, and settled in Durham; Charles Edwin, born December 9, 1831, in township No. 1, now Newfield in Penebscot County; George Freeland, born July 15, 1833, died young; Leonard Franklin, born November 20,

1835, died at Gettysburg; Freeland D., born in Passadum-keag, died young.

The only survivor of this numerous family was the late Charles E. Hodgkins so well known to his fellow citizens in Westbrook, among whom he lived for many years, yet much of his life was spent on the water. He began in the engineering department of the steamers plying between Portland, New York and Boston and New Brunswick 1852, continuing until about the beginning of the present century. By a fortunate chance he escaped going down in the ill-fated Portland with the ten who had been his companions on previous occasions.

Old Ironworks
First Church in Westbrook

It may seem strange that so enterprising a hamlet as Saccarappa had become by the middle of the 18th century, with its many saw mills and vast lumbering operations engaged both night and day in rendering the pine trees into boards for the market, strangely said, that the village had no place of public worship.

But there was a reason of course and that was that the territory where we now live was still a part of Old Falmouth, and property owners were compelled, under the then union of Church and State, to pay rates for the support of the one legalized church, now the First Parish of Portland, then under ministerial charge of the Rev. Thomas Smith.

In Smith's Journal we are informed that Thomas Haskell, the ancestor of many of the older Westbrook families, in 1743 was dismissed from the First Parish in Falmouth, now Portland, to become connected with a new society just gathered in the village of Marblehead, subsequently Windham, under the ministry of Rev. John Wight, the first Congregational minister of that town. Other Saccarappa settlers, including Conants and Peabodys, appear to have become members of Mr. Wight's church and to have so remained under his successor, the Rev. Peter T. Smith (son of the Rev. Thomas Smith of Portland), whose large and interesting dwelling house is still standing on River Road, so-called, and is the home of Mrs. Louise Goodell and her sister Miss Mary Goodell, also their brother Reginald Goodell, descendants of Rev. Peter Smith. For the Saccarappa people the journey thither through circuitous roads must have been toilsome, and for a portion of these early years worship was held in the Fort in what was later the garden of the Smith house.

But when the Fourth Parish in Falmouth was organized on the 8th day of April, 1765 the Saccarappa people were for the most part dismissed from the Windham Society to attend the new church whose house of worship was erected on the spot near Capisic now occupied by the Eunice Frye home.

In a list of members of this society, which had now become the First Congregational Church of Westbrook under the pastoral care of the Rev. Henry C. Jewett who had been ordained in 1829, and settled as the successor of the famous Parson Bradley. At this time Esquire Archeleaus Lewis, whose home at Old Congin, built by him about 1808, and now the residence of ex-mayor Joseph A. Warren, was one of the three deacons, and among the members are found the well-known names of Akers, Brackett, Barbour, Webb, Edwards, Freeman, Hayes, Lamb, undoubtedly belonging to this part of the town. In the small pamphlet in which the list of members is printed, together with the Covenant and Confession of Faith, are a few times of an historical nature telling us that this church was organized in 1765, and that the original members were John Bailey, Thomas Haskell, Nathaniel Knight, James Johnson, Henry Knight, Jeremiah Riggs, James Merrill, Clement Pennell, Anthony Morse, Solomon Haskell, and Benjamin Haskell. The Haskells were of Saccarappa, Thomas being the father and the others his sons, Solomon, Solomon, Jr., who died in 1816 leaving to his sons, Solomon, Jr. and Mark, one hundred acres of land beginning a little above the present Saccarappa bridge and extending down the river to the present city lot, and including much of the most valuable territory in the present municipality of Westbrook.

    The moral condition of the people of Saccarappa from the first settlement in 1726 or '27 would seem not to have been of a very high order, but only the Congregational form of worship was tolerated until the missionaries of Rev. Jessee Lee had found their way thither in 1793 and the following years, and even then they were not received with favor by the "standing order" as the Congregationalists were called. Tradition has it that when a Methodist preacher had obtained liberty to preach in a home in Saccarappa, an over-zealous deacon of the Congregationalists was with difficulty dissuaded from taking along his musket to intimidate and possibly drive out the intruder. But from this time a marked and somewhat speedy change seems to have come over the spirit of the prevailing intolerance, for on the 20th day of May, 1806, we find Daniel Conant conveying to Nathaniel Hatch, Joshua Webb, James Grant, and Jotham Partridge, proprietors, a tract of land on the present Saco Street measuring 6 rods on the road and 5 rods back for "building a meeting house at Saccarappa."

    The rapidity with which the intolerance of the early Congregationalists had yielded to better counsels is apparent from the fact that Nathaniel Hatch, whose name head the proprietors from having been a master mariner, had by this time, or not long afterwards, been a well-known Methodist preacher. He was born in Gorham September 27, 1749, and died in Westbrook in 1832. After following the sea until he became commander of a vessel, he settled in Falmouth, now Westbrook, where he erected the brick house, still standing on Saco Street on the farm still known as the Hatch place, although it is now owned and occupied by Mayor Roscoe F. Libby and family.

But after the obtaining of the lot, the matter of building the meeting house was allowed to slumber for eleven years before any definite action was taken for the erection of the edifice; so it was not until October 6, 1817 that Nathaniel Hatch and his co-owners conveyed to Nathaniel Partridge and forty-six well-known citizens of Westbrook and adjacent towns the lot which they had purchased of Conant on condition that they should erect thereon the meeting house, so long in contemplation, and finish the lower floor entirely in pews, reserving eleven pews on the back side wall on each side of the pulpit for the use of the Methodist Episcopal members and aged persons of other denominations; the gallery with one tier of pews on the wall and the remainder thereof in seats for those not otherwise provided for, excepting four seats in the front of the gallery for the singers. All the remainder of the pews were the property of the grantees and were to be assigned and divided in such manner as the majority might determine, having regard to the amount of the subscription; the pulpit to be occupied "each other Sunday by the Methodists and other Sunday by the Congregationalists, "especial provision being made for the Methodist love feast.

But although the Methodists by their zeal and perseverance had succeeded in causing the meeting house to be built, they soon had a vestry all their own which was later enlarged and called Wesley Chapel. It was situated on the same lot of land on Main Street in Saccarappa proper where now stands the pleasant residence of Edwin Sutermeister.

This structure is still remembered by some of our older residents as being converted into a block of dwelling houses which stood for many years on the corner of Warren Avenue and Cumberland Street at Cumberland Mills, but quite recently removed and converted into separate houses on the land north of the White House, so-called. The chapel was drawn to the corner of Warren Avenue and Cumberland Street in the Winter of 1859 and 60 by several strings of sturdy oxen.

This Saco Street "meeting house" was doubtless occupied quite regularly in its early years, especially by the local preachers of the Methodist persuasion, "Capt." Hatch and Elder James Lewis, and even by ministers of more liberal views, and it was here that the Rev. John Greenleaf Adams, subsequently a distinguished clergyman of the Universalist persuasion, delivered his first sermon on the 29th of January, 1832.

But the career of this old edifice was in the end inglorious, for although it had stood 30 years or more it was for quite a period without doors or glazed windows; in which condition it was derisively known as the Old Iron Works, and was finally destroyed by fire in the Autumn if 1847, no doubt by vandals.

The First Baptist Church Westbrook

In 1888 there was quite a body of people who were of the Baptist faith in Westbrook, and were desirous for a church to be organized here. Rev. A. T. Dunn of Portland, who was the secretary of the State of Maine of the Baptist organization and a most zealous worker, was keenly interested in the project. Stipulated by his interest and help, and assisted financially by a denominational fund from the state organization, the project became a living issue.

To that end a small story and a half house, which stood where the present church edifice now stands, was purchased of the occupants, a Mrs. Stevens and the family of a Mr. Cobb, and moved to Cloudman Street where it is still doing duty as a residence, to make room for the church.

On October 28, 1888, the church was dedicated, Rev. A.T.Dunn preaching the dedicatory sermon.

Letters of dismissal were asked and granted the following persons who made up the first body of members of the new church. They were: Roger Hilton, Mrs. Margaret Hilton, Mrs. Robert Bryson, Mrs. Elizabeth Bryson, James Boyd, Mrs. Agnes Boyd, William Thompson, Mrs. Annie Thompson, Robert Patten, Mrs. Elizabeth Patten, Mary McKay, Maggie McKay, Agnes Ferris, Lizzie Bryson, Isabella Forrest, Lizzie Mason, Mrs. Mary Cummings, Mrs. June Murray, Maggie Brown, Mrs. Mary Murray, Letitia McKay, Mrs. Harriet Chatham, Rev. Albert N. Dary, Mrs. Carrie E. Dary, Mrs. Mary F. Lincoln, these last three from the Baptist Church of Dighton, Massachusetts; the others from the Free Street Baptist Church of Portland. Also Dr. Noah R. Martin from the First Baptist Church, Portland; C. A. C. Treadwell from The Buxton Church; and J. C. Morton of Clinton, Massachusetts.

Mr. Dary was invited to become pastor.

The first officers chosen were:

Clerk	C. A. C. Treadwell
Deacons	Roger Hilton
Treasurer	James Boyd
Superintendent of Sunday School	Rev. A. N. Dary
Secretary of Sunday School	Mary McKay.

The Sunday School prospered and in June 1889 a most successful Children's Sunday was held. In September of that year the annual business meeting of the church was held with an attendance of over 50.

September 8, 1890 showed a membership of 77. The next year was prosperous, but uneventful, as most years are when things are going smoothly.

In 1892 Donald Wight and Joseph Eaton were chosen deacons to fill the places of Dr. Martin who had removed to Newark, New Jersey, and Roger Hilton who had been killed in an accident at the Westbrook Manufacturing Company's Plant.

The year 1893 showed a membership of 83. That year the church welcomed to its fold James H. Tolman and family who had come to reside in the town. For a quarter of a century Judge Tolman was a prominent figure in the affairs of the church and Sunday School, as were also his wife and daughters, the last named to whom I am indebted for a record of some of the years very hard to find.

The next year was a prosperous one, but 1895 saw hard times in several ways. Several members left the town; the church was in debt which was a source of woriment.

In May of 1896 the Baptist Association met with the church. The general financial depression was much felt by the church. In October of 1896 Rev. Mr. Dary resigned to accept the pastorate of the Baptist Church in Skowhegan.

Joel B. Slocum was called to become pastor of the church. Mr. Slocum came from Roxbury, Massachusetts. In May 1897 Mr. Slocum resigned.

From the resignation of Mr. Slocum on May 15, 1897 to October 7, 1900 when Dr. George B. Ilsley began his long pastorate with the Baptists, was a trying time for the church and parish. To quote from a pamphlet pertaining to the history of the church: "During the past three years it has been a severe trial to uphold the regular services (the shutting down of the Westbrook Manufacturing Company's gingham mills and the hard times caused many to move away from the town, so not only the financial but the spiritual life of the church was greatly diminished.) Among the various ones who have supplied the pulpit Sunday afternoons mention must be made of the theological students A. E. Isaac and W. B. Whitney from Newton

Theological Seminary, J. B. Bryant of Deering Center, Missionary Nathan Hunt, Harvey Bishop, Jr. of Paris, Maine; pastors Wilson Ayres, Green and V. R. Foss of Portland, and also the Westbrook pastors. In the Spring of 1900 Evangelist J. W. Hatch encouraged the members to repair the meeting house and secure a new pastor."

This they did and a call was given Dr. George B. Ilsley on September 16, 1900. He began a long and most profitable pastorate during which much was accomplished, and as always happens many changes took place.

In 1903 the church was saddened by the death of its good friend, Dr. A. T. Dunn, who, as has been said, was largely instrumental in helping to establish this Baptist church in Westbrook.

In 1905 the Christian Endeavor Society was instituted which was a flourishing organization for years. This year a membership of 109 was reported at the annual meeting.

The Baptist Association was entertained by the church in 1906. This year is the first mention of the Farther Lights Circle which is still in a floushing condition.

The next year was a critical one financially, so the record says; however, toward the end of the year things were much improved.

In 1908 the church was much interested in the evangelical campaign of Chapman and Alexander, as were also all the churches in Westbrook

In 1911 James H. Tolman resigned as superintendent of the Sunday School having served most faithfully for eighteen years. Many member were lost by death and removal to other places.

During the next two years the financial condition was not as good as could be wished. Dr. Ilsley tendered his letter of resignation which it was voted not to accept. However, the next year, 1913, Dr. Ilsley resigned and Rev. Adrian T. June was hired as minister in October, 1913.

In 1915 the annual meeting of the Cumberland Baptist Association was held with this church, September 22 and 23.

In the year 1916 an association known as the Baptist Brotherhood, which has flourished for many years, was formed. The next year society gave letters of dismissal to Mr. and Mrs.

George S. Wilson, who had been most zealous workers, to unite with the Warren Congregational Church of Cumberland Mills, this city, as they had moved to that section of the city.

On April 18, 1919 Rev. A. T. June resigned his pastorate. This was accepted and Rev. A. A. Walsh became pastor in May of that same year.

The year 1920 saw the church and parish in a prosperous condition.

The next year mention is made in the records of the Philathea Class which has done, and is still doing, such very good work.

In 1922 the growth of the church in number was rapid. Mr. Walsh resigned April 12, 1923; that year also the church was incorporated under the name of "the First Baptist Church of Westbrook, Maine." May 20, 1923 the present pastor, Rev. Burton H. Tilton was called. This year was a very prosperous one; there was a large Sunday School and a Young Peoples Society or Christian Endeavor was formed. The matter of buying a parsonage was agitated. To that end a house was bought on Stroudwater Street which is still occupied for the same purpose.

In 1924 the church had long wanted a bell and this wish was gratified by a gift from Mr. Luther Dana of the bell which had for years called the operatives of the Dana Warp Mills to their daily toil.

The next several years were uneventful, like all churches, some years prosperous and some less so.

In 1933, in line with most churches, choir robes were used adding much to the dignity of the service. The annual roll calls for these following years showed an increase in attendance.

As the church attendance of all of our churches has a marked tendency to fall off very much during vacation months, the Baptists and Methodist churches have united in several years for the Sunday services, which has seemed wise, thus insuring a larger summer attendance to greet the minister of the day, the pastors taking turns in preaching.

For the past several years this church, like all churches, has felt the so-called "depression", nevertheless, it is a living, growing condition and that it has many more years of usefulness ahead is the hope and prophecy of its many well-wishers.

The Westbrook Congregational Church

Records of the Congregational Church in Saccarappa, January 17, 1832; so says an old battered book. The first entry is as follows, I in rather quaint language we of today would doubtless say: "In consequence of letters missive issued by a committee of the First Congregational Church in Westbrook, an ecclesiastical council convened in Saccarappa village January 3rd, Tuesday."

Right here it should be said the first church of Westbrook was at Capisic, Stroudwater, and was on the spot where the Eunice Frye Home now stands. At the right stands a small building called a chapel, which was originally a schoolhouse situated near the meeting house, and after the taking down of the church, was moved back to its present position. It is a most interesting place to visit, containing as it does many things of the vintage of a hundred years ago and more.

It must be kept in mind that Westbrook was, at that day, a large town, extending as it did from the Gorham line as its western boundary to the Portland line which was about where the old power house stands on Forest Avenue, nearly to Kennebec Street.

In consequence of the absence of several pastors and delegates it was deemed best to adjourn from January 3rd to Tuesday, January 17th, 1832, which was done. This meeting was held and there was, evidently, a large attendance. The record states that representatives were present from Yarmouth, Gorham, Portland, North Yarmouth, Scarboro, and Falmouth, to act on the request of 23 members of the First Congregational Church of Westbrook to be dismissed and form a new church. This request was granted after an extended examination of the persons proposing to form the new church.

Rev. Caleb Bradley, whose name is so familiar to many of us who have listened with interest to the many humorous and witty sayings and doings of this noted man, is given as one taking a prominent part in the proceedings of the council.

The new church was made up of the following persons, many of whose descendants still live in Westbrook: two men and twenty-one women. Possibly quality rather than quantity our forefathers had in mind:

William Akers	Betsy Babb
Brice M. Edwards	Nancy Hayes
Ann Senate	Elizabeth Babb
Mehitable Freeman	Sally Adams
Hannah Johnson	Lydia Pease
Rebecca Foster	Joanna Babb
Nancy Murch	Sally Akers
Ruth Merrill	Sally Quinby
Mary Freeman	Dorcas Brown
Ann V. Wise	Elizabeth Johnson
Charlotte Quinby	Betsey Clements

Certainly no more upright or Godfearing men could have been found than these two, William Akers and Brice M. Edwards. The former was the father of the well-known sculptor, Paul Akers, whose famous Pearl diver is in the Portland Public Library, it should be in Westbrook, and who was born here on what is now Park Hill, known to old residents as Pork Hill. The latter was the father of the late Lewis W. Edwards and grandfather of Miss Carrie McCann and Frank H. McCann.

In November of that same year the record goes on to say: "the church met in the hall and David Hayes was chosen clerk, "an office which he filled for nearly 38 years or until a few years before his death.

Among the first to be admitted to membership were James and Lucinda Walker. Mrs. Walker, or as she was generally called, Auntie Walker, was a most patriotic woman. Before there was a general observance of Memorial Day she decorated all the soldiers' graves in the Saccarappa Cemetery, and after her death the Grand Army each Decoration Day placed a wreath on her grave, and I think the custom is still kept up by those on whom the G. A. R. mantle has fallen. She lived for many years on the corner of Main and Ash Streets, where now is a brick block.

After going through the regular form of procedure Rev. Joseph Seale was duly installed as first pastor of the new church, known as the Second Congregational Church of Westbrook. Clerk David Hayes records the event as follows: "Pursuant to letters missive from the church of Christ in Saccarappa Village, an ecclesiastical council was convened in hall opposite Barker's

Tavern on Wednesday, April 2, 1833." This places the hall where meeting were held definitely. This hall was in the store which many of us remember as the L.W. Edwards store. It was a large wooden block on the corner of Main and Bridge Streets, on the spot where Mr. Edwards afterwards erected the brick block now occupied by the Warren Furniture Store. The hall was in the second story fronting on Bridge Street and was known as Small's Hall. It was later used as a stock room by Mr. Edwards. Traces of the arched doorway and broad staircase remained for years. The Baptists and Episcopalians occupied it at different times. Barker's Tavern was the old Presumpscot House situated where now stands the Scates Block. This building was built by Jonathan Webb as a public house very early in the 19th century, perhaps in 1820-22. This hotel was moved on to Fitch Street where it now stands, and has been used as a boarding house. The old Edwards Block was moved farther down on Bridge Street to make room for the brick block, and was used as a store and later as a laundry, finally being taken down to make room for the Duclos Block.

The account of this first installation contains the names of many whose descendants are known to us. The first church to be represented is the third Congregational Church of Portland, Rev. M. T. Dwight, pastor, Rev. Israel Waterhouse, del.; High St., Portland, Rev. George C. Beckwith, pastor, Bro. M. G. Greenwood, del.; Saco, Rev. Sam.Johnson, pastor, Bro. Dominicus Jordan, del.; First Church of Westbrook, Rev. Henry C. Jewett, pastor, Rev. William Graves, del.; Gorham, Rev. Thaddeus Pomeroy, pastor, Bro. Tappan Robie, del.; (he was the father of the late Gov. Frederick Robie); Standish, Rev. Thomas Tenney, pastor, Deacon Enoch Higgins, del.; Windham, Rev. J. L. Hale, pastor, Bro. John Waterman, del.; Rev. Caleb Bradley gave the charge to the new pastor.

Such a unique personality as that of Parson Bradley requires more than a passing notice, which will be accorded later.

The rules for governing the church and the covenant make interesting reading. Matters of discipline were of a strict nature. The first case was that of an erring sister for the too frequent imbibing of ardent spirits. Not being convinced of the error of her ways after being dealt with, her name was dropped from the records. A few years later the records show her to be a member in good and regular standing, so evidently she had seen the light.

The following will explain itself: "The undersigned having been appointed a committee by a vote of the parish at a legal meeting held March 21, 1833, to superintend the erection of a meeting house agreeable to a plan previously adopted, having attended to that duty and succeeded in the good providence of God in the erection and completion of said house, would report the following of expense, viz.:

Nathan Holden, bill as per contract	$1,950.00
Extra work done by Holden	50.00
Marrett Cobb, bill for underpinning	120.00
Benja. Boody, bill for underpinning	50.00
Benja. Boody, bill for stone posts	11.25
Pulpit Furniture, lamp, chimney	115.80
Charles Patrick, bill for whitewashing	3.25
Westbrook, Sept. 25th. 1834	$2,300.30

> David Hayes
> Wm. Akers
> J.B. Walker

The building was modeled after the meeting house at Capisic. The late Deacon Edwin J. Haskell is authority for the following story of how the meeting house was built as told him by Aunt Mary Murch, using her own words as nearly as possible: "Well, you know in those days we had no meeting house in Saccarappa, and we used to go down to Parson Bradley's to meeting. In good weather we would walk down there. When we got outside of the village (Saccarappa) we would take off our shoes and stockings so as to keep them clean and put them on just before we got there."

"We would be sure to go if one of the girls we knew was to be read out in meeting. There was a little box out in the entry of the meeting house where the fellow who was going to be married would put the name of the girl and himself. When the minister came in he would take the slip of paper with the names and read them from the pulpit. On these times we used to get a seat where we could see the girl and see her blush when her name was read."

"It was quite a walk to go so far to meeting so we decided to form a church in Saccarappa. So we took letters from the First church in Westbrook, as parson Bradley's church was called, called a council what was called the Second Congregational Church of Westbrook. We called the Rev. Joseph Searle to be out pastor, and hired a hall over North and Pierce's Store to hold our meetings. (This was the store L. W. Edwards purchased of North and Pierce.) We were getting along nicely when one Sunday we found the door of the hall locked. One of the men went for the key and he brought back word that the man who owned the hall (who was a Universalist) said he was not going to let the Orthodox have the hall any more as he didn't want them to hold meetings then and there, right on the sidewalk, Mr. Searle began to talk to us about a church of our own. So we began to plan and work. A lot was got from Deacon Haskell, we went round to the mills and as lumber was plenty in Saccarappa in those days we got a lot. The men put in the stone foundation. When lumber gave out we would stop work and go to the mills and buy some more. Then the nails or something else would give out and we would raise some more money. We girls who worked in the cotton mill gave and gave. That winter Mr. Searle went to Massachusetts and gave a course of lectures and gave all the money he received for the house. We kept on and at last got the pews and stoves in place, then we had the dedication. We felt pretty good to have a meeting house of our own, I can tell you.

"This meeting house was about the same size as the present church. There was no cellar. It was a plain building with a platform in front of the two doors; a belfry in which in the late thirties was the same bell (which does duty still.) There was a wood stove in each corner near the doors, the smoke pipes running the length of the church to the chimneys. The pews were box pews with a door with a button. They were painted green inside and the outside was white. There was a little rail on the top painted red, but the paint never dried hard, and in warm weather ladies would get a mark of red across their backs if they did not take the precaution to put a hymn book between their backs and the rail.

"In 1858 there were two deacons, David Hayes and Brice M. Edwards. There were wing pews each side of the pulpit, the people sitting there faced the minister and side to the congregation. Deacon Edwards sat in one of the wing pews, and Deacon Hayes sat in the second seat from the front facing the minister. During the long prayer both deacons would stand.

"The choir was in what was called the singing seats in the rear of the house and the congregation would stand and turn around with their backs to the minister during the singing. There was a pipe organ in the singing seats that was built by Mr. Rufus Johnson, who was a member of the church and quite a musician. Some of the wooden pipes of the old organ were used in the organ installed in 1881.

"The pews in the old meeting house were sold generally to those who attended church there, but some to people who bought them as an investment and let them to those who worshipped there. When the house was remodeled all holding deeds to pews were asked to give them up. Some held out but I think some settlement was made with them."

In 1836 the membership had grown to 76. In 1837 Mr. Searle resigned, the reason being for lack of financial support. Evidently the church was in financial straits and the burden of support fell on a few who could no longer keep the task.

Just when the bell which today hangs in the belfry was purchased is not stated in the records; however, March 14, 1837, mention is made of paying for the care of the bell. This bell was obtained by the efforts of Deacon Brice M. Edwards who went about collecting from everyone so minded, whatever he could get. That it is a Paul Revere bell is evidenced by the inscription cast with the bell. It reads "Revere, Boston, 1821."

After the resignation of Mr. Searle in 1837 there was no settled until 1840, when a call was given Rev. John H. Mordough, which was accepted. Right here in the records are one or two pages of baptisms, many of them being such familiar names as Babb, Johnson, Murch, Marrett, Hayes, Bacon, Edwards, and others.

It is amusing to read that at a proposed meeting to revise the articles of faith, only men should be present, too weighty for the female mind evidently.

In 1843 a meeting was held to consider the matter of several members straying from the fold and going after false Gods, so to speak. One or two members had been interested in

Univeralism, also some in Swedenborganism, and others in spiritualism.

In 1848 Mr. Mordough resigned. In 1845 Rev. Calvin Chapman was to become pastor at a salary of $500 with the hope of increase in the year to come, also the privilege of two or three Sabbaths' absence during the year.

In the previous year the first mention of electing deacons is made, and David Hayes and Dr. Wm. Marrett were chosen.

Mr. Joseph Walker who gave to Westbrook the Memorial Library had been a resident of the village some little time, and a church attendant, although he never became a member, and in 1848 Mrs. Walker united with the church. Later they removed to Portland, but they always retained a warm place in their hearts for this community and visited her frequently.

Finances gradually became a little easier. But in the Fall of 1848 Mr. Chapman resigned and the society was without a settled pastor until October, 1851, when Rev. John L. Ashby became the pastor at a salary of $600, and two Sabbaths out, as the record says. Mr. Ashby remained in Westbrook until September 1858 when he resigned, giving as his reason the cry so familiar to us all "the high cost of living."

An entry that excites no little conjecture is as follows, to quote: "October 2nd 1858, at an adjourned regular meeting of the church held in the meeting house at 7:30 o'clock____on motion ____ voted unanimously that the clerk is hereby instructed and directed to make no record of the doings of the church at the church meetings held on the 27th and 29th of September and 1st of October." Just enough is said to excite curiosity.

During the next three years the records are of little moment. The church then numbered 18 men and 42 women. Mr. Ashby finished his work with the church May 10, 1865.

In 1865 Rev. Joseph Danielson of Killingly, Connecticut became pastor. In 1866 several prominent members asked to be dismissed as their views had changed and they had become spiritualists. During Mr. Danielson's pastorate the church grew largely in numbers and was in a most flourishing condition.

In 1869, owing to ill health, Mr. Danielson resigned, much to the regret of his parish. The church numbered at that time 115.

In July 1869 the services of Rev. E.P.Thwing were secured for one year.

September 2, 1869 the following were dismissed to form a new church at Cumberland Mills, which is known as The Warren Church:

Elisha Newcomb	Jane McFarland
Phoebe Newcomb	James Graham
Geo. W. Hammond	Annie Foye
S. A. Cordwell	George Millions
Lucretia Cordwell	Ellen R. Millions
Peter W. Files	John Wheeler
A. G. Bickford	Susan R. Wheeler
Salome Bickford	Isabel Gladhill
Julia E. Libby	Lizzie J. Graham
Nancy M. Andrews	

Nineteen from our church, four from Portland, 23 in all, same as the mother church started with.

In 1869 Harlan P. Murch was made deacon, an office which he held for over 50 years.

Deacon David Hayes had acted as clerk since the Fall of 1832, and in 1872 illness and the infirmities of age led him to resign. He was held in most affectionate regard by all of the parish. He died three weeks later, March 25, 1870.

In 1870 Joseph Libby, so well remembered as Deacon Libby and whose deep bass voice is recalled in "I love thy church, O Lord," was made deacon. Mr. Thwing resigned in 1871. Rev. S.L. Bowler became pastor. This year the church sustained a keenly felt loss in the death of Deacon Brice M. Edwards. Always the foremost in everything beneficial to the church and community, thrifty but with always an open purse where real need was to be met, his likeness was indeed hard to find.

In 1872 the first mention of a yearly get-together of the church members is notes. This years, also, began the talk of building a chapel or vestry on the lot of land given tot he parish some years ago by Nathaniel Haskell.

Up to this time there had been two preaching services and it was voted to have Sunday School in the forenoon to take the place of the morning service.

In 1874 the church edifice, no longer called the meeting house, was renovated. The record says "It was rebuilt from the foundations throughout." In this year of our Lord, 1941, it is being thoroughly renovated as regards the auditorium.

While the church was being rebuilt and a chapel built, the Sunday School met in the upper part of the building, until quite recently Graf's Meat Market. The lower part was the drug store of the late Charles B. Woodman, the father of Dr. George M. Woodman.

The total cost of the chapel was $1,236.46, that of the renovated church $12,241.59; the debt on both chapel and church was $7,662.77.

The clock was placed in the position this year at a cost around $600.

A great event was the dedication of the remodeled building.

The exercises were as follows:
    Invocation, Rev. H. Whitcher, Freewill Baptist, Saccarappa.
    Anthem Scripture, Rev. S. F. Strout, Methodist, Saccarappa
    Prayer, Rev. Addison Blanchard, Warren Church
    Historical Sketch, Woodbury K. Dana
    Hymn, composed for the occasion by Rev. E. P. Thwing, a former pastor.
    Sermon, Rev. Jos. Danielson, Saugerties, N.Y.
    Benediction, Rev. S. L. Bowler.

September 6 of this year it was voted at a church meeting "that no notices unless of a religious nature to be read from the pulpit."

Mr. Bowler closed his labors September 14, 1874. Rev. Henry B. Mead was installed as pastor February 10, 1875. He was the possessor of a very fine tenor voice. During his pastorate a rather remarkable male quartet flourished. It was composed of Mr. Mead, Temple H. Snow, E. B. Phinney, and W. W. Cutter; George F. Mariner also substituted. Owing to trouble with his throat Mr. Mead could not stand our harsh climate and resigned June 15, 1880.

Rev. Edward E. Bacon was called that same year in October. He was installed January 11, 1881. Rev. E. C. Ingalls supplied the pulpit from October to January and so well did he like Westbrook and the people that when he left he took with him as his wife one of our most zealous workers among the young people, Miss Ella Cloudman. Mr. and Mrs. Ingalls were most successful in their chosen field of work. Both are now dead.

The need of an organ being very great, Mr. Bacon interested himself to such good purpose that an organ was obtained which has served the church for fifty years. It was not new when purchased and in 1941 has been replaced by a much more expensive instrument, being a memorial organ given by four of the church members in memory of their deceased wives: Harry F. G. Hay, Harry W. Saunders, Rufus K. Jordan, and Hiram B. Rich. The installation of this instrument made necessary many renovations as well as renovations sadly needed and repairs sadly needed, which at this writing, 1841, are in progress. The organ of 1881 cost $1,000 second hand, originally $1,800; the organ of 1941 approximately $5,000; this of course is now.

During the next ten years the church was most prosperous and grew in numbers, although the years took toll of many of our older members.

It became apparent that a new vestry was sadly needed; it was called parish by our up-to-date members. So in May 1891 it was voted to build a new one from the ground up.

In 1892, after considerable discussion, the declaration of faith was revised to conform more nearly to that of other churches of the same denomination.

June 19, 1892 the first Children's Day was observed. The church was literally filled with flowers and many canaries were brought in whose songs at times almost drowned the children's voices.

A board of deacons was organized that year consisting of four members to serve one, two, three and four years, and that the clerk and treasurer should be one of the members.

In 1893 Mr. Bacon resigned after 12 years pastorate. During these the church and parish had gone steadily forward. Mr. Bacon introduced weekly offerings. In 1893 the church was electrified and in this the parish, which had been known as the Saccarappa Congregational Parish, became the Westbrook Congregational Parish.

In 1893 Rev. Silas N. Adams became pastor, coming here from South Gardiner. The new parish house was dedicated October 25, 1894.

In 1897 Edwin J. Haskell became deacon and remained so for 35 years. Mr. Haskell's death was a great loss to the church.

In 1898 a memorial service was held for Rev. Joseph Danielson, a former pastor, intercourse with his family having been kept up for years.

The two notable things to record in 1898 seem to be the using of individual communion cups for the first time, and that Sunday, July 3, the heat was so intense that the preaching service was postponed until 7 p.m.

On April 1 a disastrous fire occurred with much damage by smoke and water. Services were held in the parish house while repairs were made.

In 1900 the membership had risen to 188. Mr. Ashley Small was elected deacon to fill the vacant caused by the resignation of Mr. George T. Springer. The first mention of deaconesses was this year when the following were chosen: Mrs. George H. Raymond, Mrs. Ashley Small, Mrs. James W. Morris, and Mrs. Alice B. Libby.

In 1902 Mr. Adams resigned. During the rest of the year the pulpit was supplied.

Rev. Eugene Webster became pastor in February of 1903 and in June he asked to be released from his engagement which was granted at once.

January 3, 1904 Rev. Lee Maltbie Dean preached his first sermon as pastor. The first mention of a union Thanksgiving service was this year.

January 15, 1905 John R. Lowell died of pneumonia, having served the Sunday School for 33 years and a half as recording secretary. This was a wonderful record as he lived over two miles away at his post.

The first rally day mentioned is that of October 15, 1905.

This note occurs: "Mr. Dean introduced the boy choir, 15 boys wearing black gowns and white surplices, at the Easter service. This unheard of innovation caused much comment, both for and against, some fearing we were being made Episcopalians, however, we are still Congregationalists. Mr. Dean resigned October 7, 1907. Rev. Freelan Bolster was asked to preach for three months, and he remained until 1909. Rev. W. G. Mann was engaged to supply until a minister was called. Late that year Rev. Dorr A. Hudson of North Chelmsford was invited to become the pastor. He accepted and began his long and successful work here in March, 1910. That year Mr. Woodbury K. Dana was chosen deacon."

There was very little to record in 1914 aside from this: January 14th, 1914--this was the coldest day for 40 years, only 33 at the morning service."

Temple H. Snow died November 29, 1915. He sang for over 30 years in the church quartet without pay. During those years up to 1920 a large number were admitted to the church and a most prosperous condition prevailed.

In 1920 Deacon Murch celebrated a half century as clerk and was given a purse of gold containing $50. The pastor's salary was raised to $2,000.

Walter F. Haskell was elected deacon in 1920 and in 1922 clerk and treasurer.

In 1923 it was voted to hold the morning service at 11 o'clock, a custom which has since prevailed.

Deacon Murch died August 20, 1923 and Leon E. Waterhouse was chosen to fill the vacancy.

March 9, 1923 Charles M. Waterhouse was taken into church memberhsip from the pew in which he had worshipped for nearly two score years. It was an impressive ceremony. Deacon Smalldied in April and Deacon Dana in May of this year. Harry F.G. Hay was chosen deacon this year.

April 5, 1925 Mr. Hudson resigned after 15 years of most faithful service, the longest pastorate in the history of the church. Mr. Hudson received and accepted a call to Charlement, Massachusetts.

Rev. J. Albert Hammond of Closter, New Jersey became pastor in September, 1925. January 26, 1926 a bad fire wrecked the parish house. As the place could not be heated the Methodist people most kindly offered their church, and as their pastor had recently resigned, Mr. Hammond held union services until March when the building was repaired. In February 1927 Mr. Hammond resigned owing to the serious illness of Mrs.

Hammond. The time of the annual meeting was changed to April, the church membership being the largest in its history.

In May of 1928 a call was given Rev. Ray Gibbons of New York. Mr. Gibbons began his pastorate in September of that year. That same year was built the parsonage on Monroe Avenue, which was sponsored by the Ladies' Guild and entirely paid for by that organization.

The annual meeting of the church was the largest in its history in 1929, and at the annual meeting in 1930 the name of the church was change to the Westbrook Second Congregational Church as the first no longer existed, meaning the one at Capisic.

The united of the church and parish had long been considered and it now became a fact, and the church and parish were incorporated as one April 21, 1931.At the beginning of 1935 Rev. Ray Gibbons left to become pastor of a church at Northampton, Massachusetts.

April 1935 Rev. Edwin R. Carter accepted the pastorate of the church. He came from a flourishing church in Ashtabula, Ohio. He is still pastor while serving as chaplain of the- - - - in Portland Harbor, the world, as well as a small piece of it, namely, Westbrook, being in a most unstable condition.

Warren Congregational Church

Previous to the year 1865 no religious services were held regularly at Cumberland Mills. In that year Rev. Joseph Danielson, pastor of the Congregational Church at Saccarappa, now known as the Westbrook Congregational church, and Rev. J. H. Mordough, then residing for a time in this community, began holding prayer meetings. These meetings were held from house to house, or at times in a room rented for the occasion. Following these house to house meeting, (the people had heretofore gone to Saccarappa for Sunday services and often times for the weekly prayer meeting), the people realized the need of a place of worship and steps were taken which led to a church organization. In July 1868 the Warren Parish came into existence. The lot on which the present church stands was given by the late Samuel Dennis Warren, a member for many years of the Mt. Vernon church of Boston, and the owner of the S. D. Warren Paper Mills of Westbrook. Mr. Warren also subscribed $5,000, which amount was thought in the beginning would cover one-half the cost of the church, but as it was found inadequate Mr. Warren generously again contributed liberally to the debt. The church was dedicated July 8, 1869, the Rev. Elnathan Strong of Waltham, Massachusetts preaching the dedicatory sermon. The parish had already secured the services of the Rev. Elijah Kellogg of Harpswell, so well known as the author of "Good Old Times" (a story of early Gorham), and many boys' books, who preached his first sermon in the unfinished vestry of the church in May 1869. Warren Church was organized on September 30 of this same year with 19 members from the Congregational Church at Saccarappa, 4 from the Central Church of Portland, and 10 new members added during Mr. Kellogg's pastorate and ministry. In 1880 a parsonage was built by S. D. Warren, the minister of the parish being given the use of the house without cost. The church was enlarged. Mr. Warren and his partner, Mr. M. B. Mason, a member of the Old South Church of Boston, shared equally with the parish in the debt of $6,000. Mr. Warren was always most helpful in the church during his life, hence the two organizations bear his name.

Mr. Warren thought his own interests were closely bound up with the mental, moral and spiritual development of the community, of which a large part of the population was in his employ. His death took place in Boston in 1888 to the universal regret and sorrow of this entire community.

Two other prominent supporters of this church in its early days were Deacon George W. Hammond, afterwards a member of Trinity Church, Boston, and Deacon Elisha Newcomb, whose house was what is now the residence of Dr. Frank Smith.

The church clock was purchased by a subscription of citizens and placed in the steeple in 1872. The next year the organ was bought through the efforts of the women of the church In 1877 the chandelier was purchased by the Ladies' Society. At a later date when the church was repaired, a heavier and better bell was procured and pealed forth on Tuesday, November 16, 1886. The old bell was given to the chapel at Sebago Lake.

In 1884 the first Young People's Society was formed with the late Frank H. Cloudman as president. In 1869 a Sunday School was formed with George Hammond as superintendent; William H. Holston holding the combined offices of secretary, librarian and treasurer, which he held for over 50 years.

In 1886, the congregation being too large for the auditorium, a vestry with sliding partitions opening into the church proper was added. This provided for a room on the second floor for the Sunday School and for social purposes. There is now a commodious kitchen and dining room with all the modern helps as improvements, in the basements. June 12, 1887 is recorded as the first Children's Day.

During the pastorate of the Rev. Edgar M. Cousins, the 25th anniversary was celebrated with special services and observances. Again the church was remodeled with a cost of $12,000, the Warren Avenue entrances being done away with; two entrances were made opposite each other, both on Cumberland Street, the space formerly used as the Warren Avenue entrance being used as a rest room; two other rest rooms were also added to the lower vestry. The grounds were relaid with curved walks and shrubbery and flowers planted effectively.

The charter members were: Elisha Newcomb, Mrs. Phoebe J. Newcomb, George W. Hammond, Stephen A. Cordwell, George Millions, Mrs. Ellen R. Millions, James Graham, Mrs. Elizabeth Graham, Abner G. Bickford, Mrs. Salome Bickford, Mrs. Jane McFarland, Peter W. Files, Mrs. Isabella

Gladhill, Miss Nancy M. Andrews, Miss Julia Libby, John Wheeler, Mrs. Susie R. Wheeler, Mrs. Annie Foye, George D. Brown, Mrs. Melissa Brown, Isaiah Manchester, and Mrs. Margaret S. Manchester.

There have been only ten pastors in the history of the Warren Congregational Church in the more than seventy years of its life,

viz.:

	Rev. Elijah Kellogg	1869 - 1870
	Rev. Jeremiah E. Fullerton	1870 - 1872
	Rev. Addison Blanchard	1872 - 1877
	Rev. Edward S. Tead	1877 - 1884
	Rev. Edgar M. Cousins	1884 - 1893
	Rev. David Martin	1893 - 1895
	Rev. William G. Mann	1895 - 1903
	Rev. Edward E. Keedy	1903 - 1915
	Rev. Jonas Taylor	1915 - 1921
	Rev. Roderick A. MacDonald	1921 -

The first infant to be baptized was Stephen E. Cordwell, son of the late Stephen a. Cordwell, a charter member of the church.

Methodist Episcopal Church

It is a well-known fact that the numerous and ever increasing denomination known in the United States as Methodist and in England as Weslayan was founded by John Wesley. He was born the 28th of June, 1703 in England, probably at Epworth. He graduated from Oxford and after serving several years as curate with his father, Rev. Samuel Wesley, a priest of the established church B. H. Oxford 1688, and without doubt poor on a moderate living, since he had ten children, three of whom were educated at Oxford, viz.. Samuel, a somewhat famous political writer; John, above named; and Charles, the composer of hymns, who may be compared to the later Samkey, leader of the music for his greater brother's evangelical work, both in the home country and the colonies, as we were then termed.

After giving up his office as John retired to Oxford in 1729 where he took pupils, and with his brother Charles and some kindred spirits entered upon a systematic course of religious living that led these young men to be called Methodists. This was about 100 years after Richard Gibson, Trelawney's chaplain, had instituted Episcopal worship and built a chapel at Richmond's Island, within the limits of ancient Falmouth.

The Wesley were of an old ecclesiastical family bearing the name before the coming of the Normans of DeWellesley, whose home was in Somersetshire. It may be of interest to know that a descendant of a lateral branch was Arthur Wesley, later by a slight change of the family name, Sir Arthur and Viscount Wellesley, and later best known to history as victor in one of the world's greatest battles, the famous Duke of Wellington.

Although John Never ceased to consider himself as a priest of the English church, it seems never to have been his purpose to found a new sect, although such was the result of his labors, and to make his work more effective he found it best to employ lay preachers, which in his own way he ordained. He made frequent trips to America, everywhere ministering to large audiences and making many converts. One of the men whom he sent to America was Francis Ashbury who had been consecrated to the work by Bishop Thomas Coke who, as a minister of the English church had himself been made a bishop of the established church, and was thus able to pass along the authority that comes, or is supposed to, by apostolic succession through the laying on of hands.

A quite remarkable coincidence is that Wesley, to make a place for the assembling of those who came to hear him and were denied accommodation in the regular church, acquired an old building in Mooresfield called "the foundry" and transformed it into a meeting house.

To those of us who remember the union church built on Saco Street under the leadership of zealous Methodist preachers, especially Capt. N. Hatch, this coincidence of the "Old Ironworks" is rather remarkable.

On the 10th day of September, 1793 Rev. Jesse Lee, born in Virginia in 1758, whose parents were of the same sect, preached the first Methodist sermon to a Maine audience in Saco, and two days later in Portland in the house of Theophilus Boynton, on the spot where is now 169 Newbury Street. Mr. Lee had been sent out to do missionary work in Maine and went as far as Castine. There is no tradition of his preaching in Saccarappa, but he must have passed through the village in order to reach Fort Hill, Gorham, where he preached several times in January 1794.

There is a tradition that services were held in the barn of one named Conant, an early settler.

But Methodism had made its beginning in the old mill hamlet and the work was carried forward by such famous local echorters as Elder James Lewis of Gorham and Capt. Nathaniel Hatch of Westbrook, who discoursed their faith as a charity while tilling the soil and a means of support by the sweat of their brows.

From the names found enrolled in the first organized society or class it is probable that the substantial citizens lent not only their presence but pecuniary aid to the new society, and helped in the construction of a vestry on the lot of land occupied by the consent of Mark Haskell on the spot where Mr. Edwin Sutermeister's house stands today.

In 1833 it was enlarged and called Wesley Chapel until a later date when an ample church structure was built on the present Church Street (which thus acquired its name) on land acquired from Nathaniel Haskell, Jr., who was a brother of Mark Haskell.

The chapel, as it was called, now passed to a society of Freewill Baptists whose career seems to have been neither long nor prosperous, and was often used for amateur theatricals, and as has been said, finally in the Winter of 1859 and 1860 was moved to Cumberland Mills by the late Albion P. Ayer who had lately been burned out in the Nathan Harris store, which stood where the Cumberland Block now stands. The chapel remodeled into a tenement block did duty at the corner of Warren Ave. and Cumberland Street, but a few years since was cut up into small houses and moved farther up the street to he vicinity of what was known for years as the White House.

Meanwhile, as was said, the new lot on Church Street had been acquired under the virile preaching of Mark Trafton who drew large audiences which outgrew the chapel. An account in Zion's Herald by Mr. Trafton, who had gone to Massachusetts, one of who's districts he represented in Congress, tells of the first musical instrument or organ. This was no doubt the handiwork of the late Rufus Johnson who built organs for several Saccarappa churches. George Browne was the organist, a native of the village and afterward rector of a large Episcopal church in Keene, New Hampshire.

In 1841 Nathaniel Haskell conveyed the Church Street lot to Henry C. Babb, George Hayes, Moses Quinby, 2nd, Benj.Partridge, Samuel Lamb, Lewis Hardy, (then of Windham), Charles Evans, and (Colonel) Simon Cutter. The Society prospered under the ministry of well-known clergymen. During the ministry of Rev. Asabil Moore March 27, 1865 the church, including a fine vestry in the lower story, was burned to the ground. In 1867 the present church edifice was erected under the care of the Rev. A. W. Pottle and dedicated. In 1869 the State Conference was entertained in June. Bishop Clark presided. It was also attended by such able preachers as Dr. Torrey of Kents Hill, the Brothers Alen, C. C. Mason, Chaplain McCabe, and others. The young pastor was retained for another year.

The members of the infant society who helped build the old Iron Works church and later the small vestry, are long since gone, but their names are cherished as Hopey Pike, George Pike, Mark Pike, Charles Pike, all children of Timothy Pike whose house was where the Haskell Silk Mill office stands, and although he was not a Methodist he had generously opened his home for a meeting place for the people. Others whose names are on the list of that first society are Charles Small and wife, Capt. Nathaniel Hatch and wife, Sarah Newcomb, Margaret Babb, Elizabeth Lary, Mehitabel Henshaw (Aunt Hitty) who served the early families as housemaid and in her declining years lived in a one room house on the land of Daniel Pierce on Christian Hill. She was deeply religious, content to break bread of honest charity until her final resting place in one of the old cemeteries in Saccarappa, but which one tradition says not. Besides these names there were Sally Proctor and Rebecca Babb, nee Proctor, wife of Charles Babb.

Tradition has it that Methodism was early preached in Saccarappa by one Robert Fellowbee, a circuit rider, in 1790. He was the first of a long line of circuit riders to traverse this district and preach whenever and wherever he found opportunity. Houses and schoolhouses were the usual places, and one old record ells of a meeting being held in Quinby's saw mill. As a rule these early Puritans to whom a smile was suspicious. Still there were exceptions.

While they met with opposition the newcomers were not to be driven away; the doctrine that they preached had come to stay.

In 1841, as has been said, the Methodists erected a place of worship on Church Street in the vicinity of the house now occupied by Mr. John Keefe. This was occupied until March 29, 1865 when on Monday of that day it was destroyed by fire. In this same year the Rev. A. W. Pottle, destined to become one of Westbrook's most popular and well-liked clergymen, came to the town and found his parishioners much discouraged at the loss of their place of worship. Full of enthusiasm he raised their courage and labored with them in the erection of a structure still standing on Main Street, at the corner of Foster Street. This church was dedicated October 17, 1867.

Four years later the first Methodist conference ever held in Westbrook was held here. Bishop Clerk presided. Since that time the conference has twice visited the city, the second time in April 1893. Bishop Minde presided and the third time in April 1917 with Bishop Hamilton in charge.

In 1889 the present parsonage was purchased at 33 Pleasant Street, the Ladies' Aid assuming and paying a debt of $1600 that this might be possible. In that same year $3,300 was spent in improvements on the church and December 5, 1889 the church was rededicated with Rev. Israel Luce as pastor.

A rededication followed January 26, 1910 under the pastorate of Rev. A. T. Craig, and again on May 4, 1923, Rev. E. H. Post, pastor.

In 1892 a bell was added to the tower, this being made possible by a gift of $300 from the late Mrs. Maria Plummer. In the same year the late John J. Knowlton, founder of the Knowlton Machine Company, prevailed upon the congregation to subscribe $2,000 for the purchase and installation of an organ taken from the State Street Methodist Church in Portland. He personally subscribed $500, Mrs. Plummer contributing a like amount.

In 1916 during the pastorate of Everett L. Farnsworth the church boasted the largest Bible Class in the state up to that time, having 258 enrolled, the original members being Mr. Farnsworth, Harry L. Pride, Leroy T. Gorrie, Earl K. McFarland, E. Leroy Hawkes, and Ralph Cousins.

Numbered in the Methodist Ministry are several who as boys received their first religious training in the Westbrook parish. Leading them is Bishop Edgar Blake, Rev. John Blake, a brother, Rev. Charles Spear, Rev. Robert Clark, and others.

Clergymen who have regularly occupied the Methodist pulpit since 1850:

Rev. Parker Jacques	Rev. Howard B. Abbott
Rev. M. F. Farrington	Rev. P. C. Richmond
Rev. E. Robinson	Rev. William Rideout
Rev. John C. Perry	Rev. J. Benjamin Foster
Rev. A. F. Bernard	Rev. Ashel Moore
Rev. A. W. Pottle	Rev. W. B. Bartlett
Rev. H. B. Mitchell	Rev. S. F. Strout
Rev. W. W. Baldwin	Rev. D. B. Randall
Rev. Israel Luce	Rev. Charles W. Bradley
Rev. Everett Stackpole	Rev. Ezekiel Martin
Rev. M. C. Pendexter	Rev. A. W. Pottle
Rev. C. C. Phelan	Rev. C. E. Parsons
Rev. A. T. Craig	Rev. W. F. Holmes

Rev. E. L. Farnsworth Rev. J. S. Crossland
Rev. H. E. Leach Rev. E. Hilton Post
Rev. Charles H. Draper Rev. Albert E. Luce

Universalism in Westbrook

Universalism made its appearance in Portland in 1821 under the ministry of Rev. Russell Streeter. It grew and prospered so that in 1831 a school of learning was established on Stevens Avenue, then Westbrook, under the name of Westbrook Seminary, which has survived through good years and years not so good, and is known today as Westbrook Junior College, although no longer located in Westbrook as that part of old Westbrook in 1839 was set off as the town of Deering, later City of Deering, and has for years been a part of the City of Portland.

It may not be amiss to briefly mention Westbrook Seminary as it is so intimately connected with the history and growth of Universalism in Westbrook.

The first principal of this new institution of learning was Rev. Samuel Brimblecomb, a native of Lynn, Massachusetts, where he was born in 1799 and graduated at Harvard College in 1817 and the divinity School of Harvard in 1820. After serving pastorates as a Unitarian in Sharon, Massachusetts and Norridgewock, Maine, he allied himself with the Universalists and by virtue of his superior scholarship he was selected for the leadership of this new denominational school.

It was in 1833 that the Universalists of Saccarappa withdrew from a society organized a few years earlier by the people living in Stroudwater, Stevens Plains and Allen's Corner, and became a corporate body, worshipping meanwhile in the old meeting house, or perhaps in a hall owned by Capt. Abial Cutter who, throughout his long life, continued to be an ardent Universalist, until 1840 when they were able to point to a church edifice of their own, attractive in everything except situation, still standing and in the midst of usefulness, but now of an industrial type as a machine shop.

It was under in impassioned preaching of the Rev. Zenas Thompson that the church was built. Mr. Thompson might have prided himself upon being the founder of the Universalist societies in several of the villages of the vicinity and not to have left them to their own exertions until they had buildings of their own, most of which had one architectural peculiarity which could still be seen for many years in many of the churches erected in 1840, to wit: the pulpit faced the audience from between two doors inside the front entry, while the singing seats faced the doors from in front of the read wall on a platform a little elevated above the main floor. In this way people who had entered the church at random, when their desk was in possession of some unacceptable preacher, could not retire until they had first been seen by the audience.

Mr. Thompson, who is still affectionately, one might say reverently, remembered by a still surviving remnant of the older people of Westbrook and Portland, especially the Deering district of the later, was a convincing speaker like Rev. John Greenleaf Adams who, it will be remembered, was mentioned in the story of the "Old Ironworks" as delivering his first sermon there while he was spending a year under the tutelage of Rev. Samuel Brindlecomb, preceptor of Westbrook Seminary.

Mr. Thompson was born in Auburn, this state, December 4, 1804, and came of a sturdy Scotch ancestry, remarkable for mechanical ability, a grandfather of Mr. Thompson, a few degrees removed, having made the first spinning wheel ever constructed in New England; and it is said of Mr. Thompson himself that he inherited the mechanical genius of his ancestors, and that he could not only make an elegant fly rod or rifle, but was skillful in the use of both.

After the close of his activities in these parts he became the first of his denomination in Bethel. He was never happier than when demolishing the argument of an opponent. His wife who outlived him was Leonora Leavitt of Turner, and always proved herself a wonder-ful helpmate. They had several children, one of whom was the first wife of Prof. Vose of Bowdoin College; also two well-remembered sons, Zenas and Frederick Thomp-son, for years among the well-known business men of Portland.

From the first those who espoused the Universalist faith in Saccarappa appear to have included many of the substantial and influential families, such as the Valentines, Quinbys, the Walkers, several of the Babb families, the Roberts families, and others.

Interest in religious matters seems to have been active in other denominations and several of the rightist young men prepared for and entered the ministry of Universalists. Mention might be made of George W. and Edward W. Quinby, sons of Esq. Benjamin Quinby. The former, although self-educated, early became master of fine English and was well known for many years for his conduct of a denominational paper, the Gospel Banner. Another young man whose interest was awakened under the preaching of Mr. Thompson, who was afterwards known throughout the state, a political writer and founder of the old Portland Press, was John T. Gilman who left a pulpit in Bath to become editor and proprietor of the Times of that city.

Of the leading laymen of the society of Father Thompson's time should be mentioned Leander Valentine, who was Westbrook's first mayor, Aaron Quinby, Asa P. Leavitt, Lewis Q. Pierce, Dana Brigham, and John Cloudman; also Isaac F. Quinby. Mr. Valentine served the society for many years and through many vicissitudes as the clerk, and both he and Mrs. Cloudman, being childless, left the society generous bequests at their decease. One half the land on which the present fine church stands was a gift from Mr. Cloudman. Mrs. Cloudman was no less interested in the welfare of the church than her husband, and was an earnest worker.

As was said, the first structure was erected in 1840 and dedicated in December of the same year, with bare floors and uncushioned pews and $500 in debt. The vestry was not finished until wanted for a grammar school some eight or nine years later; money was raised by the sale of the pews, many paying for the same in labor on the church building. The ladies furnished the pulpit; Mrs. Martha Waterhouse, a zealous worker and strong Universalist, gave the Bible.

Mrs. Paul Cloudman, grandmother of the late Frank H. Cloudman and great grandmother of F. Harold Cloudman of the Westbrook Hardware Company, another ardent Universalist, helped her husband set the glass in the windows, and still other ladies helped cook the dinner on the day of the raising. This church prospered for many years, then came a change, lack of interest in the cause, and with small means to support preaching it was at last decided to wait for better days. Then followed years of inactivity when only an occasional sermon was given until in 1883. That year the church was opened every other Sunday, and the next year every Sunday. In May 1885, Rev. Q. H. Shinn came to Deering and Saccarappa and he at once began to agitate the matter of building a new church. The leaders worked long and hard with the result that the present commodious edifice was erected during Mr. Shinn's pastorate. He was a native of West Virginia. He had imbibed liberal views from reading a discourse by Rev. James P. Weston, who is still affectionately and widely remembered for his services at two different times at Westbrook Seminary, which, finding at a low financial ebb, he raised to financial prosperity.

Much credit is due Mr. Shinn for his untiring zeal and personal work, without which it is doubtful if an effort would have been made to build, so many were the obstacles to be overcome, while the steady and persistent work of the women of the society made possible the attractive church of today.

Rev. Harry E. Townsend, or I should say, D. Harry Townsend for he received that well merited title some years ago, has been with the church for thirty years, and has so become a part of the community that he is not only the well-loved pastor of the church of his faith but the friend of everyone, for a case of need or sickness has only to be known when Mr. and Mrs. Townsend are there, whether of his flock or not.

The year 1904 saw an old landmark that rightfully belonged to the past history of Westbrook, as the Deering district until seventy years ago was an integral part of the town of Westbrook. This landmark to which I refer was the old Universalist meeting house which stood at the corner of Stevens and Brighton Avenues. Following closely on the destruction of the old Parson Bradley church to make way for the Eunice Frye Home, and of Parson Bradley's house to supply a lot the erection of a modern home, the changes in this locality have been significant of the spirit of the times.

The old meeting house had a checkered career, a life of varied usefulness. It served for a house of worship less than a score of years from 1830 until the decline of the parish for various reasons; then it was used by the town of Westbrook for a townhouse until the town of Deering was set off in 1871. Deering town meetings were held there until the adoption of a city charter in 1891. Eight years later Deering was annexed to the larger city of Portland, and gradually the old church has fallen on evil times, both inside and out. In summer the city of Portland has stored sleds there, and in winter wagons. In the rear the stone crusher ate away the lodge which was the old meeting house's foundation, each day a little more, and finally the land was wanted for a school building so the old building was taken down. None of the charter members of the old First Universalist Church are living. It was in 1829 that the parish and church came into being and the founders met in the school-house on Capisic Street. The schoolhouse stood where the present chapel of the Eunice Frye Home is situated. This old schoolhouse was built at Stroudwater in 1787. It was moved to Capisic Street in 1812 and remained there until 1850, when it was moved to Nason's Corner and was there remodeled into a tenement house. The chapel of today is the converted school-house which was built that same year, 1850, on the same site.

In those days the support of the churches of a town was by a tax levied on the parishioners. The State of Maine was then a Province of Massachusetts. Upon the separation from the Commonwealth in 1820 a new order of things began. Very shortly the Maine legislature annulled the law, or rather failed to enact one such as had been in force formerly. Parson Bradley completed a pastorate of thirty years in the old Congregational church in 1829, and the last few years of his life he was supported by the voluntary contributions of parishioners, as is the custom now.

Westbrook included what was formerly Deering. The town, large in area, had several growing villages; Saccarappa was over at one side near the Presumpscot River, while the Stroudwater settlement and that at Woodfords were growing in population and importance on the sites they still occupy. In winter it was too far from the churches for the Saccarappa worshippers to journey, hence the brief existence of the old Universalist Society.

It was decided in a meeting held in the old schoolhouse in 1829 to form a Universalist society and to have a "proprietors" church as was the custom in those days when currency was scarcer that it is now; accordingly the old meeting house was built. No records in existence as to who were the proprietors. They built the church, sold the pews, and a pastor was secured; no records can be found. Capt. John Jones gave the lot. He was a well-to-do sea captain. It is not known how many pews were sold, nor the outcome finally. The Universalists were considered altogether too liberal in those far off days; Orthodox, as Congregationalists were often called, church members did not consider Universalists as Christians or conscientious worshippers. Parson Bradley says of Capt. Jones as follows: "He was a good man when he went to my church."

Religion and politics were mixed up very materially in the history of Westbrook at that time. The Universalists flourished under the storm of abuse and calumny that was heaped upon them at that time. They numbered among them at that such men as Jonathan Smith, Stroudwater, who played the bass viola, and lived to a ripe old age, being employed in the Customs House in Portland; Levi Morrill, the leading spirit in Morrill's Corner for a third of a century, the builder of the Morrill mansion; Samuel Jordan, postmaster of Portland; the King and Stevens families--they were Democrats and worked together in church and town affairs.

In one election the entire town was lined up against the Universalists; the latter won out electing three selectmen of the town committee. Those were lively times in Westbrook. All this time the Congregationalists were prospering also. The old structure which had been used since the close of the Revolution was torn down and the church erected on the same site, which remained until 1902 when it was removed to make room for the Eunice Fyre Home. It was built in 1835 and Parson Bradley's diary contains much of interest in regard to the old days.

One of the hymn books used in the old church was styled "The New Hymn Book" and was published without music, and the words were sung to the few tunes which did duty for a diversified repertoire according to the rhyme rather than the sentiment. The old Bible is cherished in Scarboro, a ponderous book.

Box pews were set up, plain, square pens, long and dignified, with doors along the sides and small crickets for short-legged persons to rest their feet on while the long sermon continued. The frame of the building was of pine, immense timbers for the sills and sides, with the roof frame to withstand the winds that came down from the "White Hills," as they were called in those far off days.

Such logs as were sawed into those timbers are not seen floating down the Maine rivers these days. There was a gallery in the rear. The windows were immense, tall and wide. A great platform was raised for the pulpit. Mr. Thompson remained as pastor of the church several years. Finally differences arose and smote the church; the Westbrook members began to rebel against the long distance they had to travel to attend the services. At length the Saccarappa members withdrew and built a church in their own village. Other trouble followed. Mr. Thompson went to Bethel. The old church was unable to support a minister. Finally the church was sold for a townhouse. There had been turbulent scenes; along with its devotional exercises, now cam political battles which had much to do with the history of the town.

Westbrook was large and growing but the old-time centers had changed. Morrill's Corner, Woodfords and Saccarappa continued to grow rapidly, while Stroudwater seemed to stand still. Then came a time when Deering people leaned toward Portland, whereas Saccarappa had little in common with the seaport city. This went on for several years and it was in and around the old church that the orators and fighters had their settow. It is difficult to give an accurate picture in words of the scenes that occurred. A fighting spirit was in the land; the Civil War was not long over.

"They say" that about a thousand voters were crowded into the room about 75 years ago during the agitation which accompanied the making of two towns out of old Westbrook. The stand-pat people howled down the divisioners when they attempted to speak. It was the greatest session ever held in the old church. They couldn't take a vote by show of hands so great was the confusion, and the voters were lined up out in the street. The motion to divide was lost and the Deering people finally resorted to sending a petition to the Legislature and an new town was granted February 16, 1871. This action was ratified by 876 voters. Deering, the new town, became a city October 12, 1891.

For many years the old church had served as a townhouse. The pews had been taken out and the pulpit removed, and Henry J. Fowler of Scarboro secured the Bible. His maternal grandfather had given it to the society. The building was kept in good repair and signs on the door indicated that the town offices were here. Three churches had grown from this old church, the Saccarappa church, All Soul's church at Deering, and the Woodfords society.

The Westbrook Seminary, now Westbrook Junior College, represents the educational side of the old church. Underneath the upper window in the front of the church was a tablet of stone 6 1/2 feet long, 1 1/2 feet wide, 4 inches thick, weighing 600 pounds. It bears the inscriptions "First Univeralists Society, Westbrook, 1830."

The Episcopalians

European settlers were at Richmond's Island as early as 1630, but it was not until 1658 that this great expanse of forest, lake and river, which took in the island and neighboring mainland, extended inland so as to include "Sacrabigg" and "Ammoncongan," and was organized into a municipal corporation with its selectmen and other necessary officers.

It is observed by William Willis, Portland's historian, that the first settlers along the coast of what is now Maine did not leave their own country for freedom of worship but for hope of gain. To quote: "the first and only clergymen that we have any account of before the jurisdiction of Massachusetts was extended over this territory were Richard Gilson and Robert Jordan." Both of these men were priests of the church of England and were in succession chaplains of the Trelawney plantation, which included all the territory embraced within the limits of Cape Elizabeth and South Portland, besides Richmond's Island.

John Winter was Trelawney's agent. Robert Jordan seems to have won the affection of Winter's daughter, Sarah Winter, through whom are descended the many Jordans of this vicinity.

Winter died in 1645 and Jordan, as his administrator, secured of the Trelawney heirs a large landed estate which he left to his posterity. Of him M. Willis says: "Although he came as a religious teacher, the affairs of the world and the gratification of ambitious views appear soon to have absorbed the most of his attention and to have alienated him from his profession."

By his will dated January 28, 1678 he gave to his wife, Sarah Winter Jordan, who was still living "the old plantation at Spurwink containing 1,000 acres more or less," and to each of his sons land enough "to constitute a respectable English Barony." So extreme were their possessions and so great a family that in 1762, more than 80 years after Robert Jordan's death, we find them petitioning the General Court sitting at Boston to incorporate them into a proprietary that they might the better protect their inherited estate.

Mr. Willis seems to have underrated Mr. Jordan's devotion to the church of which he was a member, for in the execution of his rites he more than once came in conflict with the

Puritan magistrates and found himself in prison for administering the ordinance of baptism in families where only priests of apostolic succession were deemed worthy of officiating.

While they did imprison Mr. Jordan for baptizing children, whether he ever came out to old Saccarappa bringing the quaint bass font that is still treasured among the invaluable relics of the Maine Historical Society, we shall never know. Worship according to the ritual of the church of England has never taken definite form here, except between the years 1820 and 1836 Saccarappa was the abode of a few very intelligent, and no doubt fashionable, people who maintained Episcopal worship in Small's Hall which was in the second story of the building which was removed from the corner of Main and Bridge Streets to make place for the brick block now used by the Warren Furniture Company.

Daniel T. Pierce, who built the beautiful old house now the home of ex-mayor Walter F. Haskell on Bridge Street, was the leading layman among the church people and was reinforced by Colonel George Small the owner of the hall, and Dr. William Marrett, who had recently come from his native place, Standish, and settled in Saccarappa in the practice of medicine.

The rector was the Rev. Petrus Stuyvesant Ten Broeck, who had just reigned from the St. Pauls' in Portland, and seems to have resided in Portland during the period of his ministry in Saccarappa. There must have been others of this little handful of communicants and among them doubtless was Mrs. Codman who had been Miss Smith of Windham, and was the mother of the late George C. Codman, one-time superintendent of the Westbrook Manufacturing Company who, with his estimable wife, always remained very zealous adherents of the Church of England, notwithstanding a Puritan ancestry.

Both Mr. Pierce and the Rev. Mr. Ten Broeck, and Dr. Marrett, as well, if they saw fit, were entitled to boast of their lingeages.

Mr. Pierce was one of the sons of Josiah Pierce, Esq. of Baldwin, a half-brother of the famous Sir Benjamin Thompson, afterward Count Rumford. Dr. Marrett was a direct descendant of Rev. Henry Dunster, first president of Harvard College; while Mr. Ten Broeck was a great grandson of Governor Peter Stuyvesant of New Netherlands and rector of Saint Paul's, Portland,

1818-1831. During these years he did missionary work at Saccarappa.

Both before and since those days missionaries have come here and it seems rather strange that no better success has rewarded their efforts, for laymen of the Episcopalians have lived, if not in this town, near including Colonel Tyng, second sheriff of the County, and Judge Solomon Lombard of Gorham, who resigned his pastorate as minister of the First Parish of that town to become layman in the Episcopal Church.

Advent Christian Church

Previous to 1885 there were no regular Advent meeting held in Westbrook. There were some families of this faith, and while there was no lack of interest or zeal on their part, yet it was only possible to meet the expenses of occasional public services. There were held in various places which could be secured from the time to time as need arose.

Many became interested, the company of Advent Christians began to grow, and with added numbers their faith became stronger to carry on the work they felt divinely called upon to do.

In July 1886 the Advent Christian Parish, which holds in trust the church property, was organized and incorporated with the object of securing a suitable lot and resetting thereon a house of worship.

This was accomplished by liberal subscriptions from the people, together with aid from many friends an sympathizers, and on Sunday, December 26, 1886, the present church home was dedicated to the worship of God. The dedicatory sermon was preached by the Rev. William H. Mitchell of Kennebunk, Maine. From that time on regular services have been held in the church on each Sunday and during the week. For one year the pulpit was supplied by various itinerant ministers of the Advent Christian denomination.

In September 1887 Rev. Orvin H. Wallace, pastor of the Kennebunkport Advent Church, was invited by the parish committee to supply the pulpit regularly and bring about a better organization of the work. The invitation was accepted and Mr. Wallace began his work as pastor January 1, 1888, and on the 20th of January of that same year the Advent Christian Church was organized with 20 members with Stephen Andrews and John Stevens as deacons. Mr. Wallace served the church four years, during which period the church membership increased and much interest was manifested in the work. Mr. Wallace resigned to go tot the Advent Christian Church in Lowell, Massachusetts, and with much regret his resignation was accepted.

On September 27, 1891 the church called Rev. Orrin S. French, president of the Maine State Advent Christian Conference, to become pastor. Rev. Mr. French accepted the call and became the second pastor. During his pastorate there were many additions to the membership, and on January 1, 1894 he resigned, having completed a very successful pastorate. The church then called Rev. John H. - - ? who served faithfully two and a half years and then resigned. Rev. Warren N. Teft (?) was the next pastor who resigned after six months of labor. Rev. A. H. Kearney, pastor at Dover, Maine, was elected pastor. He served the church two and a half years and resigned to go into the mission field. He was elected Field Secretary by the State of Maine.

The church was without a settled pastor for a year, during which time Rev. E. P. Woodard supplied the pulpit.

A call was then extended to Rev. John A. Cargile, a man who had labored for years as a missionary in the southern states and been most successful. Mr. Cargile accepted the call and began his work as pastor February 15, 1903. Many improvements were made and the church remodeled and redecorated, also rededicated, the sermon being preached by a former pastor, Rev. O. S. French. After two years Mr. Cargile resigned to return to his former missionary work in the Southland. Rev. Mr. Cargile's resignation was regretted by many outside the church membership as he had won the respect of the citizens of the city.

In 1905 Myron M. Adams, a student at the Boston School of Theology, came as pastor and was ordained in the church October 15, 1905. He served the church three years.

On April 12, 1908 the Rev. David Jack, a graduate of the Divinity School connected with Bates College, came as pastor and served two years and a half.

In November 1910 Rev. Thomas W. Kennington, from England, accepted the pastorate and served until 1912 and resigned to go as a missionary to Wuhu, China.

Rev. James Albert Nichols was elected pastor and served the church three years. During his pastorate the tower and stained glass windows were added and a new organ was installed. He resigned to become the editor of the denominational publication "the World's Crisis."

Rev. William P. Brown of Newburyport, Massachusetts was elected the next pastor and served two years and resigned to attend Bangor Theological Seminary at Bangor, Maine.

Rev. A. B. Blanchard was elected the next pastor and served eight years. During his pastorate the parish house was built at a cost of $6,500. Mr. Blanchard resigned and the Rev. Charles Linn Smith of South Elliott, Maine served as pastor three years.

Rev. Howard A. Mitchell of Old Orchard, Maine was engaged as supply pastor and he continued until March 31, 1932.

At the close of Mr. Mitchell's pastorate the church extended a unanimous call to Rev. Curtis L. Stanley, a young man of marked ability, to become the pastor, and on May 1, 1932 Mr. Stanley began his work. Under his faithful labors the church has prospered spiritually, numerically and financially. It was with the deepest regret that the church accepted his resignation, which came as a great surprise May 7, 1939.

Mr. Stanley has proved himself to be an excellent preacher, a faithful pastor, and a sympathetic friend to all who have enjoyed the privilege of knowing him, either in the church or outside it.

Miss Bertha E. Cassidy, a member of the church, is a well-known missionary teacher in Wuhu, China.

The Church officers are as follows:

Pastor	Rev. Maurice S. Amnott
First Deacon	Melville C. Perry
Second Deacon	Charles H. Leighton
First Deaconess	Mrs. Lucy V. Leighton
Second Deaconess	Mrs. Nettie J. Wentworth
Clerk & Treasurer	Mrs. E. W. Rome
Auditor	Harry J. Robinson
Organist	Dwight L. Leighton
Pianist	Zane Loring
Chair of Music Committee	Mrs. Mildred S. Perry

St. Hyacinthe

It is almost 100 years since the first mass was celebrated in the city of Westbrook. Early history has it, perhaps I had better say tradition has it, that in 1850 the first Catholic mass was said in a brick house on Cumberland Street which is still standing. There were very few Catholics here in that early day and priests came out from Portland to officiate. There were very few French speaking people here then.

But in the seventies it was different. So that regular masses might be said each Sunday a hall in Warren block on Bridge Street was secured. This was used for a brief period only, a more fitting place being found in the Walker-Brigham block, now the home of The Remnant Store. A chapel was fitted up in the upper floor where mass was said and the various functions of the Catholic church carried out.

There was no settled pastor, priests coming out from Portland to officiate. The first mass in this little mission chapel was said by Father Bogardtz in 1873. In this first place of worship were baptized several of the young people who afterward were prominent in St. Hyacinth parish for many years. This now mission and the neighboring one at Gorham, which had been held in Ridlon's hall, as has been said, were ministered unto by Portland priests.

In 1877, so rapidly had the congregation increased, that Right Rev. James A. Healy of Portland purchased a building lot on Brown Street. In 1878 ground was broken for the church. The work of completion was directed by Father Linehan who celebrated the first mass Easter Sunday, 1879. In July of the same year Rev. A. D. Decelles, a professor in St. Hyacinth Seminary in Canada was appointed as first resident pastor of the parish. That was really the beginning as heretofore it had been a mission of the Cathedral of the Immaculate Conception of Portland. The church was a structure unadorned, walls were plain white, beams and pillars bare, settees in place of pews, no tower or bell.

The residence of Father Decelles was a small old-fashioned house, perched high on the hillside. This property had been purchased by a committee of laymen.

It is an interesting fact that hardly was the church completed when it had to be enlarged to accommodate the congregation. This of course delayed the dedication which did not take place until August 22, 1880. Two years after the present commodious rectory was built and the grounds graded terraced. In 1882 land on Stroudwater Street was purchased for a cemetery. In 1887 the tower was added and the parishioners added a bell. A vestry was built and the interior thoroughly renovated. In 1890 a pipe organ was purchased and in 1901 a granite school building was erected on Walker Street. The school had been started in the early 80's. This structure represented an outlay of $25,000, contained well appointed classrooms. The nuns of the Presentation of Mary from St. Hyacinth P. Q. were installed as teachers. The parish suffered a great loss in the death of Father Decelles in 1901 of pneumonia, he having accomplished stupendous tasks in organizing and carrying on the new parish in his work of 22 years.

The next pastor was Father Alexandre Dugre who served from 1901 to 1911. He was succeeded by Father A. A. Hamel, 1911-1916. In 1916 came Father Desjardins, the present incumbent, who is much beloved and respected, not only by his own people, but by the citizens of Westbrook at large.

In his various fields of activity he has achieved more than ordinary success, and not content with things accomplished, his program is a forward-looking one always looking to expansion and improvement. He has seen erected a new convent and Sisters' Home. The land on Brown Street, almost the church, has been acquired, and in more prosperous times a new church will be seen rising, so the people of St. Hyacinth say.

Father Decelles and Father Desjardins have held the longest pastorates, Father Decelles 22 years and the present pastor 24 years. Much might be written of these years. Several memorable occasions have occurred; that in 1897 to celebrate the 25th ordination of Father Decelles to the priesthood, and his 18 years in Westbrook, is especially noteworthy. It was a splendid tribute to a popular man and beloved pastor. There was a very large attendance, the church and many residences being beautifully decorated with both the tri-colors of France and our own Star and Stripes. The principal and most interesting part of the program was in the evening.

Ernest LeBel, in behalf of the French parishioners, delivered an address of congratulation to Father Decelles which plainly showed the love and esteem in which he was held. Edward Doyle, in behalf of the English speaking people of the parish, delivered an eloquent speech of love and appreciation in a most congratulatory manner to Father Decelles. It is worthy of notice how for many years the two nationalities have worship-ped side by side in a most brotherly way, until the constantly increasing attendance made it seem best for the Irish membership to have a church and pastor of their own, of which mention will be made later.

Copies of both addresses were really works of art and were presented to Father Decelles. These were printed in script by the Sisters of Mercy of Portland.

Father Decelles replied most feelingly to these addresses expressing his deep appreciation of the attendance of the Mayor of Westbrook and the aldermen, as well as the large number of town people. He spoke particularly of the amity in which they dwelt together.

Of course music figured largely in the day's happenings. It was an occasion long to be remembered by those privileged to attend.

Another rather unusual tribute to Father Decelles was the solemn occasion of his funeral obsequies. The people of this city outside the faith of the dead priest showed their respect and esteem of the life just closed, not only by their attendance, but the closing of all places of business during the funeral. The influence of such a man, pastor of a third at least of the city's population, was not confined within the boundary of his fold, and one and all felt to honor his memory.

There is one peculiar and particularly pleasing fact about the French-American and Irish-American parishioners of St. Hyacinth church, and that is the amity between these two diametrically different nationalities. However, they have always been united in parochial matters. This reflects great erudite on those in charge.

However, in 1917, the English speaking part of St. Hyacinth had so increased that it seemed wise to form a new parish. So this was done, the congregation worshipping for a year or so in Speirs Hall. In 1917 the present church was built;

this is called St. Mary's. The building also contains classrooms the large and flourishing school.

    Rev. William J. Culbert was the first pastor. The two Watson Houses on Main Street were purchased, one being moved away and the other remodeled into a parochial residence. The structure used for both church services and school activities is in the rear of the large lot which extends back some little distance. The convent, which is the residence of the Sisters of St. Francis who have charge of the school, is on the corner of Main and Speirs Streets and was built in 1927. Classes are graduated each year. In 1933 Father Culbert was obliged to give up his charge on account of a throat trouble. His place was taken by Rev. John J. Finn on January 1, 1933. Father Finn takes great interest, as but natural, in everything pertaining to church and parish, but his work does not stop there for his is a wide outlook over community affairs. The parish is in a most flourishing condition.

Saw and Grist Mills
Mast Industry

When pioneers came to make their homes in a new country there are two indispensable requirements - food and shelter. As wild animals abounded in the virgin forests of Old Falmouth this prime necessity was obtained with little difficulty; but what about bread?

There must be grist mills to grind the corn which the fertile land easily furnished. So hand in hand with the saw mills came the grist mills, perhaps a little before for their rude huts were first made of logs which required only the felling. Joseph Conant, whom tradition tells was the first settler, early saw the need, as well as the profit, in mills, and to him has been ascribed the first grist mill in this region.

Lumbering operations here afforded many fortunes for those engages therein. Before telling of the lumber kings it may be of interest to mention rather briefly the first great industry of Maine, and incidentally of Cumberland County, particularly Old Falmouth, namely, the mast industry, in which Thomas Westbrook, for whom our city was named, figured largely as mast agent for King George III of England's Royal Navy.

Maine has well been called the Pine Tree State and Cumberland County has its full share of these towering pines, sought and procured for ships' masts, yards and bow-sprits, the lesser in size being used for mill logs in the many saw mills which quickly sprung up.

Mast procuring in those days was an industry of no little proportions, compared with the means at the disposal of those engaged in the business. The market was England and the business was under the ban of statutory law. The province of New Hampshire seems to have been where the industry had its starting point.

Brigadier General Samuel Waldo appeared before the legislature of that province for the purpose of explaining it. It is believed he transferred his interest in the business to Colonel Westbrook in 1718. Colonel Westbrook established himself, temporarily at least, at a place now know as Dunstan Landing in Scarboro, living, it is conjectured, in a lumber camp. Rev. Thomas Smith, the first minister of Falmouth Neck, frequently alludes in his diary to the act of loading and the sailing of mast ships. There is, and most carefully cherished, an account book which was the property of Nathaniel Knight. Who is he? He was the son of Nathan Knight whose wife was a sister of Colonel Westbrook. In 1720 Nathan Knight came to Dunstan and purchased land at the landing and built a dwelling house, which was sold to Richard King, gentleman, of Scarborough in November 1748 for 45 pounds.

In 1735 he bought 100 acres of land at Stroudwater Falls, a mile southerly of old Saccarappa Village, where he built a good two-story building, the cellar of which was plainly visible at the end of the last century.

Nathaniel Knight retained the homestead and farm; the house was destroyed by fire in 1829 while owned by John Knight, a descendant. In course of time most of the farm came into the possession of Edward Chapman, now deceased, and at the present time is the property of the City of Westbrook. Edward Chapman was a sort of hermit, to put it mildly; the writer recalls him vividly in the early 80's (1880's). The house in which he lived was destroyed by fire and he had built a fine barn, a much better building than the usual farm barn. He had a hallucination that someone was pursuing him so he had finished off a room in the top of the barn where he slept. He had fixed a ladder arrangement which he could draw up after him and thus make himself safe. He became much worse mentally and finally became a ward of the city, which took his farm in payment of his care.

In the ancient book above referred to there is nothing recorded as to when it was first used, but under date of February 9, 1828 is the following:

Colonel Westbrook Esq.
Then began ye Oak contract

To dyating ye men when hewing at Dunston	77-4-0
To making Walter Hinds Trowsers	0-5-6
To one day carrying things to Stroudwater	0-8-0
To sundry times my horse and boy to Stroudwater	3-0-0
To 32 days hewing masts at Dunstan @ 7 pr day	14-8-0
To a house	44-0-0

This evidently was the house that stood at what is known as the southerly corner of Westbrook and Bond Street, Stroudwater, which was given the name of "Harrow House" but is better known in history as the "Garrison House," which was removed to make room for the so-called Fickett house, built more than a hundred years ago by Samuel Fickett.

The account then goes on: July 24, 1732

To whole years work which was our agreement for	40-0-0
To finding myself in victuals in foul whether and from Saturday night to Monday morning the whole year	10-0-0
November 26, 1732	
To myself 127 1/2 days	63-15-0
To 28 loads of hay	84-0-0

The last entry is as follows:

To hunting masts, fitting them, and clearing of roads.

The time covered was forty-seven weeks and he charged a pound per day for his services, but there is not a date entered after the first.

The highways as now used in this vicinity were laid out for the purpose of transplanting mast logs in connection with the rivers, and were cleared and opened by Col. Westbrook and others engaged in the mast business.

Among some of the items are charges for going up the Stroudwater river "twitching masts into the river, clearing river, bringing down he river." Another item is for hauling masts at "Horse Beef (Little Falls) and at Saccarappa - self and 4 oxen four days @ 5-10-0."

Thomas Westbrook died in 1744, a sketch of whom will be given later. Westbrook's industrial importance is due largely to one fact--the superb water power furnished by our river, the Presumpscot. Sir Christopher Levett in 1623 first realized the possibilities of the Presumpscot. Saw mills were built by John Larrabee and later by John Phillips. Their activities were confined to the Lower Falls almost entirely. The banks of the Presumpscot held many saw mills and grist mills, too, of course, were a necessity for providing food for the growing communities. Hand in hand with these lucrative industries was the mast business.

Of course this was a boon to the early settlers, for by cutting and shipping masts to a central point they were able to secure real money, which in these days was a scarce article.

Most of the settlers were obliged to resort to barter to gain their livelihood.

Colonel Westbrook had constructed a paper mill at Stroudwater which was I active operation for several years, and it can be counted on as a pioneer in the industry. A dam built at the Lower Falls of the Presumpscot River and a paper mill erected there, but owing to the raids of the Indians and other causes the mill was never in full operation and was later destroyed by the Savages. Col. Westbrook began building a dam at the upper Saccarappa Falls, and tradition has it that a block house was erected on Pork Hill (now Park Hill) for protection. This dam was never completed.

The felling of a mast tree and hauling it to the nearest navigable water was an event of no little local importance, and when it was known that such a happening was to take place many gathered to witness the spectacle.

Colonel Westbrook, as was said, was mast agent and it was his duty to select such trees as would furnish suitable masts and bow-sprits for the ships of the Royal Navy of King George III. These were usually of white pine and the rule governing their fitness was that after they were hewed to the proper dimensions, the mast must measure as many yards in length as it did inches in diameter at the butt. Upon the tree thus selected was put the broad arrow, or "King's Mark" so-called, which was out with an axe. For the felling or destroying of a tree so marked without the Royal license a penalty of a hundred pounds sterling was imposed. To cut a mast tree was quite a process. First the small undergrowth in the vicinity of the tree to be felled was cut down to make a bed for the mast on which to fall. If a tree was allowed to fall where it would, it might break. After the forest monarch was laid low, oxen, yoke after yoke, were employed to haul away the sled with a fallen tree. The long line of oxen made quite an imposing sights, and sometimes a tragedy occurred when a yoke of oxen became choked. Those in attendance waited in breathless interest as the tall pine began to totter and bow its lofty head with a mighty sweep fell prone upon the prepared bed. Chains and ropes were now brought and fastened securely about the tree and it was fastened upon the sled. Then the oxen were hitched in place and amid many "gee haws" the log team started. Now came the dangerous moment as the first yoke would go up a hill. the last ones would be in a hollow and standing on lower ground then their leaders they were hung up by their yokes; sometimes this resulted in a tragedy.

The tree was then hauled on its sled to the nearest water and in the spring floated to the nearest landing where the mast house was.

The war of the Revolution of course put an end to the mast business.

The Presumpscot River flows through Westbrook for a distance of 2 1/2 miles, and is a boundary for about 3 miles. The Stroudwater river is a stream of many sources and flows through the northern part of Westbrook for a distance of 4 miles. Many saw mills were operated on this river. With the cutting off of the forest the flow gradually become less,and correspondingly its mills fell into disuse and finally into decay.

It would be a hard task to enumerate the saw mills on the Presumpscot. At one time, in the early history of Saccarappa, there were nineteen saw mills in operation day and night in Saccarappa alone, one at least which spanned the river. Many were the drives of logs each spring. It is easy to imagine that the river men were not the most polished of gentlemen, especially since that which cheers but does not tend toward sober sense was an easily obtained article. Almost every house contained it for daily consumption, not for medical purposes only. Every tavern, as they were called, every store, offered it for sale. No wonder Saccarappa acquired anything but a savory reputation which it took years to live down; in fact, it has never acquired the spotless name of some of its neighbors.

Until the early 80's saw mills were fairly flourishing here, then came the decline until today the sawing of timber is done almost wholly by portable mills not dependent on water power.

Daniel Godfrey swamped out the first road for the passage of log and lumber teams. It was without doubt a part of our present Main Street. Considering the "Saccarappa blacking" of more recent years, what must the road of more than one hundred and fifty years ago have been when traversed by heavy ox-teams in the early spring. Tradition has it that log teams of 26 yokes of oxen often conveyed the heavy lumber loads to the ships in waiting at Stroudwater. Saccarappa was doubtless a busy and noisy place in those far-off days. As was said lumbering was carried on well into the 19th century, and some of the lumber kings of that day were John and Nathaniel Warren, Daniel T. Pierce, Archelaus Lewis, Joseph Walker, Dana Brigham, George and Lewis Warren, and Samuel Clements and others.

Not only were there saw mills but grist mills as well. Long after the settlement in Gorham in 1736 the only grist mill available to the inhabitants of that town was at Presumpscot Lower Falls, to and from which they transported their girst by boat, carrying boat and cargo around the falls at Saccarappa and Ammoncongin. The Conants early took advantage at Saccarappa by the middle of the 18th century is shown by the following entry in Parson Smith's journal: "February 27, 1748. Went to Saccarappa. Mr. Conant tells me he has ground 1,000 bushels of corn this winter, there being no other mill than his between York and Saco."

Besides the many mills in Saccarappa and Ammoncongin there were saw mills erected in the 18th century at Stroudwater Falls so-called, on the present Spring Street; and also at the outlet of Duck Pond, now called Highland Lake, and upon Mill Brook near the residence of the late Nathan W. Boody

Saccarappa, which was the name of the largest village in the town of Westbrook, has been immortalized by Richard Henry Dana in his book "Two Years Before the Mast," and earlier has been heard of in history by the following doggerel:

"Old horse, old horse, what brought you here?
From Saccarap to Portland Pier
I've carted boards this many a year,
Till killed by blows and sore abus
They salted me down for sailors's use.
The sailors they do me despise,
They throw me over and damn my eyes,
Cut off my meat and scrape my bones,
And throw me over to Davy Jones."

The years went by and in 1814, when Westbrook became a town of which an account will be given later, the chief industries were its many fertile farms, saw mills, tanneries, and lumbering and farming industries.

According to the tax assessors' list then, Saccarappa had nine saw mills, two grist mills, two carding and fulling mills; Congin three saw mills, one grist mill; Duck Pond and Duck Pond Brook five saw mills and one grist mill.

The year 1815 was a memorable one in local history. Every month in the year frost was reported throughout this section. Frost was reported on the window panes in July. Crops were a total failure; meat, game and fish were the principal articles of food. Cereal foods could only be purchased at luxury prices.

When Saccarappa saw mills were at their peak of production, times must have been strenuous. The working force were happy-go-lucky fellows who often made play of work. They were noted for strength, and wrestling was their chief pastime. Their fame even went beyond the confines of the State and often strangers came here to do combat. Often the sturdy river drivers wre the victors, and the word went abroad that a wide berth had better be given to "Old Saccarap. A man now gone to his reward was my informant for the following anecdote which was told him by his father:

Stephen Babb, who weighed less than 130 poundes, was one of the best wrestlers in the bunch. One night a stranger came to town and put up at Barker's Tavern, as the Old Presumpscot House was then known, and after supper walked round among the men, evidently looking them over. Finally he said, "I'm somewhat of a wrestler and hearing that you have several good wrestlers here, I came out to try my strength wiht the best of you. Now who want to take hold of me first?" The men gathered in a corner to talk the matter over, beign very careful to speak loud enough for the stranger to hear, The conversation ran something like this: "We'll let Babb try him first; if he throws Babb, then So-and-so will take him. If So-and-so goes down, then So-and-so can have a try at him." Babb came from the conference and told the stranger that he was ready to try conclusions with him, and at the first send-off stood the latter fairly on his head. "I would like to see you do that again" said the stranger, and Babb immediately accommodated him.

"Guess I've had enough" he said. "What would happen to me if some of you bigger fellows should tackle me I don't care to find out. Let's take something." and I haven't a doubt they took.

Now, the fact was that Babb, I spite of his weight, was the strongest, most active man in the bunch, in fact he was abnormally strong, and they had merely been stringing the stranger with their talk about the other wrestlers.

While the "river drivers" as they were called, were well aware of their strength; they were seldom quarrelsome. For many weeks in Spring they were away from home and had little time to cultivate good manners, yet they took life as it came, cheerfully. Drink? Well, yes. In fact, liquids was a large part of their daily menu. Each Spring as the men started for the drives, his father, so my informant said, swung a couple of kegs of New England rum over a horse, mounted him and followed the men in their work, dealing out the "grog" as it was called for. When the supply gave out he replenished it and again took up his rounds.

The Westbrook Manufacturing Company

As was said, the first great industry of Westbrook, then Old Falmouth, was lumbering and kindred occupations, which flourished well into the 80's of the 19th century. In the meantime there were various small industries which will be mentioned later. But in 1829 another most flourishing business had its beginning in Westbrook, not Old Falmouth for 1814 had seen a part of Falmouth set off and called Westbrook: this was the Westbrook Manufacturing Company which in the aforementioned year became incorporated body. It was sponsored and financed largely by Portland business men who saw an opportunity for establish a flourishing and paying business.

The first mill was built in the early 30's and was known as the Duck Mill. The foundation can still be seen just beyond the bridge on Bridge Street. It was a large brick building and did duty for many years until it was declared unsafe.

The product manufactured in this first building was sail duck, overall duck, and blue drilling. This sail duck found a ready market for this was in the days of sailing vessels out of Portland Harbor. During the Civil War was a large amount of money was made by the company. Not long after the first mill was built, another of four stories was erected in the mill yard. It was topped by a belfry. The bell which for many years called the operatives to their daily work is now doing duty on the Baptist Church, and calls weekly worshippers with its mellow notes. It was given to the church several years ago by the Dana Warp Mill proprietors whose property it had became.

In speaking of summoning the workers to their daily toil brings to mind the tales of those days as related by Mr. John Brown, for many years station agent for the old Portland & Rochester Railroad. He was for some years a worker in the Mills. The hours of work were much longer than those of today. The day was begun at 5:30, he stated, and ended at 7:00 or 7:30 with time out for meals. The pay was much less, but the cost of living was much less also. The operatives were recruited largely from the surrounding farms, as the weavers were largely farmers' daughters.

The blue drilling was made from indigo blue cotton yarn which was had dyed and fast colors. The two dyers who were longest in the employ of the company were George and Nathaniel Murch. George was the father of the late G. Fred Murch, a well-known businessman of this city whose daughter, Mrs. Caroline Murch Diran, resides on Spring Street.

Nathaniel Murch was the father of the late Harlan P. Murch, for more than half a century deacon of the Westbrook Congregational Church. Others of the overseers of the mills, I should say among others for doubtless some who read these words will call to mind others not named, were David Webster Babb who had charge of the weaving; his son Fred W. Babb resides on Chestnut Street; William Valentine Harmon, father of Adalbert R. Harmon of Portland; Charles W. Lane who lived where Dr. E. S. Hall now lives. This Mr. Lane should not be confused with Mr. Lemuel Lane who purchased the property of the first mentioned and later his heirs sold to Dr. Hall. There was no connection between the families. Another well-known overseer was Alfred F. Sweetser who had charge of the finishing of the overall duck. The second mill built in the mill yard was given over to the making of coarse sheeting.

In 1881 the new mill on the opposite of the street was built for the manufacture of gingham; it is now the loom section of the Dana Warp Mills. At this time also was built the dye house in the mill yard, and also many tenement houses on Scotch Hill, so-called. The company also owned several houses on Brown Street and Mill Lane. These last named houses were in what old deeds were designated as "Widow Freeman's garden."

Shortly after the beginning of the making of gingham in the early 80's skilled help was needed so 40 girls were brought over from Scotland. I remember very vividly their coming in March 1882. They were not used to our climate, and certainly not to Saccarappa mud. The first thing the girls did was to purchase much needed articles, rubbers, which they thought a great lark. They looked as strange to us with their little shawls over their heads as no doubt we did to them. They were a fine lot of girls, good weavers, and good citizens; in fact, they and their children are numbered among out substantial citizens. Later many of their friends and relatives came over from Scotland to make their homes in their adopted country. This mill operated from 1882 to 1896. Finally the business became unprofitable and had one or two periods of shutting down for a short time.

In March 1896 there came a terrible freshet when the Presumpscot went on a rampage. There were more than 1300 cases of gingham stored in the basement of the old mill, and these were damaged beyond repair. The Westbrook Manufacturing Company was a heavy loser. This gingham was almost a total loss and was afterwards sold for 2 cents a yard. This closed down the mill and the machinery was sold to junk dealers.

The first agent of the mills was Henry Smith. He resided in the house on the corner of Bridge and Brown Streets in what was known for many years as the agent's house. In fact the house was built for the first agent, Mr. Smith. Mrs. Smith had the oversight and planning of it. She was a woman who interested herself in all the affairs of the town. She was active in the Congregational Church, then in its infancy. Mr. Smith was followed by Mr. George Codman who lived for many years afterward on Ocean Street, Portland. In 1858 James Haskell of Rockport, Massachusetts was sent for to come to Westbrook. He came and was hired directly. He succeeded in the late 70's by his son, Frank Haskell, who served until his death. He was the last agent.

The superintendents of the Gingham Mill were John Henderson. Next came Charles W. Dennett who built the house now owned by Mrs. Alexander Speirs on Stroudwater Street. Mr. Dennett went to North Adams from Westbrook and he took several of the old operatives with him. John W. Kimball was next on the list. Charles Rollins was the last; he served until the company suspended business.

Unfortunately the first records have been destroyed, at any rate lost. In the early 80's the president was Edward H. Davies, William R. Wood, treasurer; in the early 90's Mr. Frank Haskell replaced him, but Mr. Wood continued as a director. The directors were Joseph Walker. As has been said, the begin-ning of his fortune was made when a lumber merchant in Westbrook. He built the house now owned by Dr. Wheet, which he occupied until he removed to Portland. In his will he left a sufficient sum to finance the Westbrook Library, or the Walker Memorial Library, to call it by its right name. The circumstances of the bequest will be told in the story of the library. To resume the directors: Jacob S. Winslow, Fred Dow, Henry St. John Smith, Edward H. Davies. The now dye house was built in 1881.

Previous to this time the company had been sending overall duck to outside commercial dyers, principally to the Lewiston Bleachery and Dye Works. The new dye house was designed to take over this work that had been going outside, and at the same time equipped to take over some outside commercial work here, and for several years this was successful business. In addition to this, machinery was installed for dying yarn in colors used in making ginghams in the new mill just erected. The third floor of this building was the finishing department where the goods were packed and shipped. Among the dyers of 40 or more years ago were William Kerr, a fine Scotchman of much experience. He was followed by Robert Bryson, also a Scotchman. There are many others whom doubtless the readers will recall.

In the repair shop were Henry Blatchford, Walter V. Knight, Albion P. Stiles, Hiram B. Sproul, James Sproul, and George H. Winslow. The latter is now in South Hadley Falls and another old-time employee was Nathaniel Winslow. Nearly every one of these mentioned lived on Brown Street, in fact the houses they owned are still standing.

These employees and their families were not here today and gone tomorrow as is the case with many of today. This was their home. They attended our churches and their children made up our school population.

A rather unusual sight was the five horse team that drew the productions of the mills to Portland for shipping. There were two pair of horses and a leader. The men who carried on this work for years, in good weather and bad, were Stephen M. Dresser and Joseph H. Hazelton. The incline leading into the mill yard was very steep and at the end an archway rather low and narrow. One day Mr. Dresser, miscalculating the distance, came into violent contact with the archway; in consequence he suffered a broken shoulder.

Another everyday sight was George Goodell and his three horse team. In quite recent years the three upper stories of the mill in the yard have been removed and the lower story is still retained for storage.

After the closing out of the business the property finally came into the hands of the Dana Warp Company. The original gingham mill has been added to greatly and is now a large plant extending from the bridge to the Old Haskell Silk Mill office.

Haskell Silk Mill

It was a matter of extreme regret to every citizen of Westbrook when the Haskell Silk Mill, owing to market conditions, silk no longer having the vogue it had enjoyed for many years, suspended operations and the business was closed out. It was essentially home company, a family concern, employing largely people who lived in Westbrook and had homes here.

In 1874 James Haskell, who as has been said, came to Westbrook in 1859 to act as agent for the Westbrook Manufacturing Company, from which organization he resigned in 1874, that same year, with his sons Frank and Edwin J. Haskell, formed a company for the manufacture of silk. This company was known as the Haskell Silk Company and the make-up was: James Haskell, president; Frank Haskell, treasurer; while eventually Edwin J. Haskell acted as general manager.

Work was started on a wooden building on Bridge Street, south of the bridge, in July 1874. In size the structure was 50x50 feet, a long walk leading to it as it was on the rear of the lot. This building had formerly been used by a Mr. Vogel who attempted to carry on the silk business but with indifferent success. It is told how one night his place was broken into and many of his tools stolen. When Mr. Vogel discovered his loss he packed up the remained and departed.

This building was later used by Lawrence & Horne for a saw manufactory. Later still it was run as a laundry by Marr Brothers; and again Stephen Sibley of Charlestown, Massachusetts, also carried on a laundry here.

When the property was purchased by the Haskells there also stood on the lot several other buildings, among them a large two-storied house known in local parlance on account of the many occupants it domiciled as the "beehive." Mr. Abiel Foster also had a small building on the lot which he used as a dye house. This later was moved to Preble Street, Portland, and was the beginning of the well-known Foster's Dye House.

The Haskell Silk Company began in a small way at the start. Only spool silk and twist was manufactured, the first being made in September 1874. Only six operatives were employed.

As the years went by, as they have a way of doing, additions were made to the original building until finally it became necessary to choose a new site for expanding business. The King farm on the north side of the river beyond the Dana Warp Mills, comprising some 65 acres, was purchased and a large mill two stories in height, 55 x 300 feet in dimensions, also a stone and brick dye house 100 x 60 feet, and a large office were erected.

In 1881 the manufacture was started of dress silks. At first only black silk was made. Later beautiful colored silks were made or several years, but his was abandoned and black only was produced which was justly known all over the United States.

Of course as the enterprise grew the number of those employed grew until several hundred found work here. It was to be noticed that there was no age limit; as long as work was satisfactory no one was ever discharged.

All the silk used in manufacturing came from Japan in the form of skeins. These as soon as received were rewound; then came the doubling, so-called. It is then ready for the spinners. It is then reeled, dyed, and wound again, then warped and quilted from which it is woven into yard goods. The inspection or "picking" followed, and finally the finishing. Much care has been exercised in running the looms, which is the reason why an operative can run only two looms.

The picking of the silk was for many years sent out to the various homes and was quite an industry.

In 1891 Mr. James Haskell died which was a great loss, not only to the Haskell Silk Company and his immediate family, but to the community as well. The Haskell family suffered another severe loss in the sudden death of Mr. Frank Haskell who died suddenly at this cottage at Sebago Lake. This, too, was a severe loss to the business life of Westbrook. Mr. Edwin J. Haskell who had virtually acted as manager still looked after affairs.

In the meantime Mr. Lemuel Lane and William W. Poole, family connections, had become associated in the business and remained so until the closing out of the organization.

Such is the history of the Haskell Silk Company. The fine mill, with its many windows, seems to look with reproachful eyes at the passerby.

Several attempts have been made to start manufacturing here but as yet without success, and Maine has no silk mill for this was the only one within its borders.

Within the past year the office has been sold to St. Hyacinth parish for a club home for the unmarried young Frenchmen of Westbrook.

S. D. Warren Company

In point of time the next great industry of Westbrook is that of the S. D. Warren Company, which has grown from a small beginning to its present size. This is said to be, it not the largest, among the largest and best equipped paper plants in the world.

We have mentioned that there had been two or three small attempts to manufacture paper in Westbrook but which, owing to the unsettled state of the country with Indian troubles, were not successful.

But the paper industry had really its beginning in Westbrook when in 1847 Grant and Lyon the erected the first paper mill on the northerly side of the Presumpscot River at Cumberland Mills, or as it was called at that day, Ammon-congin, but which shortened to Congin. It was a little low wooden structure totally different from the fine building which now not only occupy the sides of the first mill, but also stand out and cover many acres.

From a hamlet in 1854 which consisted of a dozen houses and a country store, this part of the city has kept pace with the mills in rapidity of growth, the whole section being covered thickly with commodious and comfortable homes making a residential section of much beauty and charm. These homes have in some cased been built for the operatives by the company. In the more recent residential sections, in streets leading off from Main Street and also on Main Street itself, are many attractive homes built by those connected with the huge mills in their various capacities.

In the year 1854 Mr. Samuel Dennis Warren of the paper firm of Grant, Daniel & Co. of Boston, purchased the paper mill of Grant and Lyon. With the advent of Mr. Warren a change came over the place. He began building, renovating, and remodeling; also continued improvements that have made Cumberland Mills a model place in which to live and rear a family. When purchased by Mr. Warren the paper made consisted of first quality newspaper, manila and brown paper or wrapping paper. The principal market was in Boston for a finer grades, while Portland and surrounding town consumed the coarser grades. All the rags, coal, and other supplies, as well as the manufactured product, were hauled from Portland by team.

In 1860 Mr. Warren purchased the water power and land on the south side of the river from the Winslow heirs. He also kept on increasing the plant and brought the daily product from 3000 pounds to 7 tons. Mr. Charles Fairchild in 1871 was admitted as a partner and the firm name was S. D. Warren and Company. Mr. Fairchild withdrew in 1880. In 1883 Mr. M. B. Mason was admitted, the firm name being the same.

Mr. Warren died in 1888. His death was a great loss and was most keenly felt. He was more than the proprietor of an immense business. He was friend of the community; to the church which bears his name which without his benefaction and continued interest could not have reached its present status and prosperous life and growth. He was interested in the welfare of his employees and a personal friend of each. Many of the advantages enjoyed by the community are largely due to the generosity of Mr. Warren and his family. In the early seventies Westbrook became alive to the needs of the town in the matter of health and civic improvements and in this the S. D. Warren Company lent an able hand. In 1873 much work was done in regard to laying of sewers and cesspools. S. D. Warren Co., furnished a large amount of the material and labor in their construction, free of cost to the town.

Some ideas of the immensity of the S. D. Warren Co.'s paper mills can be gained when it is learned that there are nearly ten acres of roofing and about 27 acres of flooring. The paper plant with its 92 machines produces on a average of 75 tons of paper daily. There is used from 50 to 60 cords of poplar wood every 24 hours.

Mr. Warren was the pioneer in using foreign rags, the supply came largely from Japan. Of late years rags have been largely superseded by pulp wood. The number of persons employed is more than 1700, and the payroll is correspondingly large. In 1855 the tax paid by the company was $300. It is now more than one third of the entire city tax. The firm supplies book and magazine paper for many periodicals. It is a busy hive of industry.

A distinguishing feature of the industrial life of Westbrook is the absence of labor troubles. A higher encomium upon the men who managed the great industry could not be pronounced than no cause for discontent has ever been given their employees. A peculiar and interesting incident occurred in 1858. There was at that time a great depression in the paper trade and it seemed necessary to reduce the labor scale 10 per cent. This condition in business being well known to the workmen, no objection was made by them. But in a year or so business had revived somewhat so the men sent a request to Boston for the restoration of the 10 per cent which had been taken from their pay.

The Company answered by a letter which was forwarded to the men assembled and the agent at that time, Marshall ?---ales, read the communication to them. It said in substance that the wage scale would be restored if the output of the mill could be increased to 6500 pounds daily as an average. The men accepted the situation and the output averaged a little better than 6700 pounds daily for the following year.

Of course this happening was no strike as we understand the word at the present time. There has never been a union tolerated in the almost century of the business life of the company. However, 24 years ago, September 18, 1916, the dwellers along Main Street were surprised to see a labor parade with all its accompanying of shouts, banners, noise, and general near lawlessness.

What is it? The question ran from lip to lip. A strike at Cumberland Mills was the answer, hardly to be believed. But it was true. It was an attempted strike.

It seems that some five or six men from Portland, and others farther away, typical labor agitators, had visited the mills for a week or so and found five men who were ripe for trouble to to make trouble, which was not surprising in a company of nearly 2000 human beings. These visiting agitators not only attempted to inflame the operatives by single contact, but speeches were made in the park nightly, which, of course, drew large crowds of curious hearers, and a sort of union was formed which, as was said, on September 18, 1916 resulted in a strike parade. Not all the operatives joined; some reluctantly, as my informant told me, were over-persuaded to do so, but as soon as they consented, heartily repents. Why? They really had no grievance. They had always been treated fairly and as justly as circumstances of business permitted. After a few days those who had gone out came back and generally resumed their old places. The company was not vindictive and the movement died a natural death. All were received back save rive of the most violent leaders whom the company refused to reinstate. So died the really only strike the S. D. Warren Co. has had in its 100 years of existence, and that disturbance was so slight as to be hardly worthy of the name of strike.

Another great benefit to Westbrook which the city owes to the Warren family is the gymnasium, the real beginning of which dates from the winter of 1903-4 when Miss Helen Coe of Portland came here and conducted classes for girls in the old Cumberland Hall. The expanse of the venture was paid by Miss Cornelia Warren, a daughter of the late S. D. Warren, founder of the firm bearing his name. The benefit derived from these classes caused Miss Warren to consult with Mr. Maurice Ross, then an instructor in the Young Men's Christian association in Portland, in regard to fitting up a regular gymnasium here. Together with Mr. Herbert Mason they looked over the ground and in the winter of 1904 began preparations for fitting up a gymnasium for girls. This was finished about the first of March 1904, and for the balance of the season Mr. Ross came twice a week and gave instruction. Miss Warren also arranged or the completion of a department for boys which was accomplished in March 1905, and Mr. Ross was engaged as the regular instructor. The gymnasium is in Cumberland Hall and is fitted up with all modern devices. A small fee is charged.

In the summer of 1905 a large bath house on the south shore of the Presumpscot was erected and is conducted in connection with the gymnasium. This bath is for the use of the public and no fee is charged unless instruction is required. The only restrictions in conducting either are that the paper mill employees shall be given first opportunity, then town people, whoever, and then if there is room the general public will be admitted.

This sketch of the Warren Paper Mill would be sadly incomplete were there not on extended notice of the man who for years made it the principal industry and power for good in the municipality of Westbrook. Did space permit there are doubtless many others who merit praise for their business integrity and good citizenship who should be mentioned.

The man entrusted with the management of a business owned by non-residents, following an English custom, was styled agent. Among the agents of the S. D. Warren Company John L. Warren stands out most prominently. Mr. Warren was born in Grafton, Massachusetts, the early home of his kinsman, the founder of this business. In early childhood his father's family moved to Wisconsin and settled in the town of Wanwatosa where John grew up on a farm, not leaving the town until he went with the first regiment of soldiers furnished by the state of Wisconsin in May 1861. He served in the ranks of the Union Army during the whole duration of the struggle and was cap-tured in June 1864 in Mississippi, and spent several months in Andersonville Stockade. In the early part of 1867 he came to Cumberland Mills and went to work for the S. D. Warren Co.

In 1884 he became Agent and the gratifying results of his business acumen is shown in the phenomenal growth of the plant. When one realizes the large number of persons employed in the mills, the many different processes from raw material to finished product, and the enormous financial interests involved, some comprehension of the great responsibility resting on the Agent is seen. During the long term of years Mr. Warren was a citizen of Westbrook he was never found wanting in a private or public capacity. He had also reprinted the District in the Legislature, and when a city charter was granted Westbrook, he was a member of the first Council. It is but fair to say he has been just in the discharge of his duties both to employer and employees.

Westbrook will long hold in grateful affection the memory of John E. Warren.

Dana Warp Mills

When one's eyes fall upon the words Dana Warp Mills the name Woodbury K. Dana instantly is spoken for <u>he</u> is the Dana Warp Mills.

In the winter of 1866 - 67 Mr. Dana came from his home in Portland and started in business in Westbrook. John S. Dana, Woodbury's older brother, first suggested that Mr. Dana, then nineteen years old, should become a manufacturer. One of the staple articles sold in large quantities in his father's store on Commercial Street, Portland, was cod lines, and it occurred to John that his brother Woodbury, who had just completed his academic course at Lewiston Falls Academy, might well institute the manufacture of that commodity. Woodbury fell in with the idea and a small building at Gray was leased, and John acting as financial backer, and Mr. Dana began his long business career by the making of cod line, bags, and bunch yarn. A dozen people were employed. The mill in which the enterprise was started is still standing.

It was hard work at Gray and the founder of the Dana Warp Mills soon realized that his capital was insufficient, as also was his experience. He was discouraged when he found he had lost the few hundred dollars invested; but grit, determination, and dogged perseverance won the day. He began now plans at once. He would learn the business at someone's expense.

He came to Westbrook and got work at card grinding in the old brick mill of the Westbrook Manufacturing Company where duck and denim were made. He remained here a few months. He did not find the opportunity of learning the business so he left for Lewiston where he found employment in the Lincoln Cotton Mill, where he worked twelve hours a day. Later, until he enlisted in the Union Army, he worked at different positions in the Bates, Continental, and Lewiston Mills. He was there for a purpose. His pay was only $1.25 a day; it was but a small part of what he was earning for himself. In this way Mr. Dana spent the important years from 1859-1863.

In June 1863 he was mustered into the United States service as Private Dana. He was mustered out August 22, 1865. Who can say what kind of a man he would have become were it not for those plastic years when he participated in that awful struggle.

It was not long after his return from the war in 1866 that with Thomas McEwen he formed a copartnership under the firm name of Dana and McEwan for the manufacture of cotton warps at Saccarappa Falls in Westbrook. In the winter of 1866 the machinery was hauled from Portland on sleds an installed in a small two-storied frame building painted red, located on a site near the present extensive plant. At the start machinery was installed for 600 spindles, but before the first year was over 300 more were added. Mr. McEwan took no active part in the business and in a few years he sold out his interest to Mr. Dana.

By 1873 the business had outgrown its quarters and it was moved to a larger mill located on Main Street, just west of the Foster and Brown Machine Shop. In 1879 a still larger mill was needed and a move was made to the Island of Saccarappa Falls. Here, too, a dozen additions were made to the mill before it, too, had to be abandoned.

In 1892 a corporation was formed known as the Dana Warp Mills Co., with a capital stock of $130,000 of which $90,000 was paid in. On Labor Day 1893 a very disastrous fire occurred. The wooden building with its oil soaked floors burned fiercely, while the loose cotton and yarn was all that was needed to spread the flames. But that very next morning Mr. Dana had builders on the ground and a larger and better plant planned.

In 1896 a freshest occurred, sweeping away the bridge. A rope ferry was devised and things went on, although under difficulties, while the bridge was rebuilt.

In 1900 the large brick gingham mill was bought which furnished a large and well-planned building, well adapted to the growing business. In 1906 the size of the mill was doubled and a picker room, dye house, and boiler room added. Since then three additions have been made to the dye house and now it can dye the entire product of the mill which amounts to over 80,000 pounds each week. A new dye plant has been installed for dyeing warp on the beam. It is the first mill in the country so equipped.

The corporation or organization had as its first president Mr. Lyman M. Cousens of Portland, and Mr. W. K. Dana treasurer and general manager.

After graduation from Bowdoin College in 1896 Mr. Philip Dana, older son of Mr. & Mrs. W. K. Dana, took a course in the Philadelphia Textile School and then came into the mill to assist his father in the management of the business.

In 1902 Luther Dana, the younger son of the family, finished his course at Bowdoin College and immediately took up his share of the work in the rapidly growing plant.

This brief capitulation of the history of the Dana Warp Mills shows inadequately the remarkable success of the enterprise as the Dana warps have been favorably known to the trade for forty years

The process of making warp is most interesting. The bales of cotton are taken to the picker room where it is put into machinery from which it emerges in a wide white alt. It is now taken to the carding room and made into rolls, and from here to the doubling frames. Then the yearn goes through four pro-cesses, making it each time a little finer. The next step is spinning, then comes the spooling and warping; the warps are dressed into beams and are ready for shipment.

Besides the manufacture of warps there are made about 2,000 bags daily. These grain bags go all over the United States. The Dana Warp Mills have about 19,000 spindles and is one of the largest warp plants in the country. On the payroll there are several hundred people and the yearly payroll is about $82,000. The cotton used is from different parts of the United States, and some come from Egypt.

A personal write-up of the founder of this enterprising business will be found later telling of his various activities for they were many.

Just a few words of the original building on the Island. In 1876 Mr. George Warren started building a woolen mill for his two sons, William and Charles. He died before its com-pletion. It was finished, however, and the manufacture of fine blankets carried on for several years. Mr. Robert P. Tibbetts of Limerick was the superintendent. In size, when purchased by Mr. Dana, the mill was 44 x 80 feet with three stories and an attic.

In the summer of 1940 The Press Herald and Evening Express issued a State of Maine edition which contained the following advertisement, which shows the present status of the Dana Warp Mills:

Dana Warp Mills
Westbrook, Maine
Cotton Yarns and Warps
Fast Colors
Capacity 100,000 pounds per week

Specialists In
Cottons - Woolens - Worsted
and Rayon Novelty Yarns
A Maine Institution

Pewter Manufacture

Pewter manufacture was largely a seasonal occupation as the snow blocked roads of Maine at that time in winter and isolated many markets. Rufus Dunham was the first to provide work for a force of men all the year round.

Rufus Dunham was a Maine boy, born at Saco May 10, 1815. He was the ninth in descent from John Dunham who came over to Plymouth in 1630. Young Rufus was obliged to make his own way from the age of nine years. At first he worked as chore boy for a farmer who, when drunk, beat him so badly that he ran away to Portland and found a place as errand boy in the old United States Hotel. Working and attending night school he obtained the foundation of an education.

One Sunday when about sixteen he, with a companion, walked out to Steven Plains, then the headquarters for 100 or more tin peddlers who traveled not only through Maine but New Hampshire, Nova Scotia, and eastern Canada. Much interested in the display of pewter, decorated Japanned are, and high backed horn combs in the shop windows at the Plains, he asked for time the next week to see the factories in operation.

As a result of this visit he bound himself as an apprentice to Freeman Porter for his board and $50 cash and two suits of clothes a year. In 1833 he broke the contract alleging he had not been paid for overtime due him, and went by sailing packet to Boston.

He found work with Roswell Gleason, a pewterer, of Dorchester, remaining there and in Poughkeepsie, New York until 1837. At 22 years of age, with $800 which he had been able to save, he decided to open a shop of his own at Steven Plains. With his brother John as helper he made the venture successful. The following year he received a silver medal for the best specimen of pewter shown at the Mechanics Fair in Portland. In the Portland Transcript was the following comment: "R. Dunham of Westbrook presented some elegant Britannia ware," and elsewhere his exhibit was described as block tin. Britannia seems to have been applied to articles of rolled metal, white pewter was moulded. As time went on the Britannia ware seems to have displaced pewter, but the terms seem to have been used rather indiscriminately by the public of that time.

According to Dunham's family tradition he bought his first metals in Boston and did his own melting and casting, subsequently turning the parts of each article on a hand lathe and soldering them together. Later on he is said to have been the second man in Maine to use a steam engine as a source of power.

At first Mr. Dunham sold his products to Eben Steel, a Portland dealer in crockery, but he soon extended this field of sales. In those early days the only Maine thoroughfare open all the winter was the road to Montreal by way of Crawford Notch, Lyndonville, Derby Line, and Coaticook, Quebec, traversed by the four and six horse wagons transporting freight from Canada to Portland to be shipped by water to Boston.

Rufus Dunham filled a wagon with his goods, took to the road, and sold by barter, returning to the city at the end of a trip with hides and sheep pelts for the tanners and wool pullers; bristles and oxtails which he sold to the brush makers; cattle horns for the comb makers; and a supply of furs, yarn, mittens, and stockings which he sold in Boston. By degrees his itinerant sales people numbered 23 and at length he was constantly employing between 23 and 30 men in his factory. Some of his helpers worked for him all their lives, and his custom of paying good wages brought him the best workmen of his craft. His advertisement in the Portland directory of 1844 lists his articles as communion ware (many old churches are today treasuring these articles), teapots, waterpots, coffee urns, and lamps, and this footnote is added, "All kinds of Britannia ware mended so as to baffle detection." almost every piece of this ware is marked, especially the pewter, on the bottom with R. Dunham, Westbrook, in a round circle. I said almost every piece. I should add, except the plates of which there were small, large, and very large ones. These large platters were generally used for boiled dinners and made a fine colorful showing, all on one platter not unlikethe plate dinners of today.

He continued business at Stevens Plains until his building burned in 1861 and he removed to Portland. He did little pewter manufacturing after 1850, but he increased his output of Britannia ware. An advertisement of 1866, when he was established at Fore and Union Streets, mentions in addition to the wares previously made, caster frames, ale pitchers and mugs, kerosene lamps, teaspoons and tablespoons. In 1876 he took two of his sons, Joseph S. and Frederick, into partnership and the firm of Rufus Dunham and Sons was dissolved in 1882.

Rufus Dunham had eleven children and his hospitality was proverbial. It is aid that on one occasion, probably a family gathering, there were 32 who were entertained over night.

When he died on September 21, 1893, at the age of 78, he was spoken of in his obituary as a wholesale manufacturer. His business ability was praised but nothing was aid of his early making of pewter.

Today the three pewterers A. Porter, F. Porter, Westbrook, and Rufus Dunham, are receiving the belated praise which is their just due, and if you are so fortunate as to possess a piece bearing their trade mark, cherish it.

Lesser Industries

While the larger industries of Westbrook as being of major importance have been treated at length, nevertheless it will be of interest, doubtless, to give a brief history of the comings and goings of lesser ventures that were apart of Westbrook's business life for a brief period, especially during the 19th century and a little later.

As was mentioned, lumbering was the first great industry from which many large fortunes were realized; and with lumbering came the blacksmith who could hammer out things needed provided you gave him time. It must be remembered that time wasn't such an important part of life in those earlier days as it is today. And so the smithy was left to his work with an assurance on the part of the customer that the article needed would in time be forthcoming; this was something akin to blind faith.

Everything was done by hand; even nails were the product of the blacksmith. Can you image a man sitting and patiently waiting for a bunch of nails to be hammered out for the purpose of mending a fence prone on the ground?

One of the pioneer nail makers of Westbrook was Major William Valentine, father of Hon. Leander Valentine, Westbrook's first mayor. He turned out a choice brand and they were much sought after. He built the house now known as the old Haskell house, just west of the residence of Herbert R. Chute on Main Street; in fact, Mr. Valentine sold the house to Mr. Haskell.

It has been erroneously stated that Leander Valentine was born in this house. Such s not the case, and the authority is no less a person than Mr. Valentine himself, who stated he was born in a house which stood for many years where the Springer block now stands. It was known in its later years as the Dr. Martin house where Dr. Noah Martin lived and practiced medicine for years. This house was later moved back on the river bank and occupied as a tenement house. Quite recently it has been taken down. While speaking of the Martin house it may be well to mention the Office which was a small building near the street on the west side of the house, used by the Doctor as an office for years. Later R. C. Boothby rented it for a grocery store, which was a paying venture. Later, after several moves, always for the better, he came to anchor in the store where Maurice Parker is now. Mr. Boothby remained here until failing health caused him to sell out his business, having acquired a competence.

Speaking of blacksmiths, there was Mr. Dillingham who devoted much of his time to the making of locks to order, and hasps, especially padlocks and staples. He was a cheerful as the "village blacksmith" of Longfellow fame. The boys never lost an opportunity to watch him work as he was a prime favorite.

Among the older blacksmiths was Edmund Woodbury who had a stop on Main Street in the vicinity of where the children's summer playgrounds are now. Just how long Mr. Woodbury had a shop there cannot be learned. But during the early years of the Civil War Mr. Charles London of Bridgewater came to this region and settled. His wife, who was Miss Cordelia Hanson of that section, had gone down, as the phrase is, with her people where she taught school. Her parents, Mr. & Mrs. -- Hanson wished to return to their former home in Buxton, York County. Mrs. London and her infant son, then nine months old, came with them and went to Buxton. Their conveyance from Bridgewater was a prairie schooner, and it was a journey in those days from Bridgewater, which is 22 miles north of Houlton, to Buxton. Mr. London did not arrive until a little after. He used to tell how when he arrived in Portland he had $1.05 and he walked to Buxton where his family was rather than spend that dollar plus. He worked in Biddeford for a short time, then came to Westbrook where he went to work for Mr. Woodbury for $1.50 a day, which was fair wages for those days. Mr. London worked in that same building for a little over 40 years. After working for Mr. Woodbury some little time he bought him out. Mr. London ran the business alone for most of those 40 years, although for a short time his brother-in-law,
William Hanson, was in company with him. The old smithy tree which shaded the building still stands after all these years. In 1910 Mr. London, owing to ill health, retired, selling the business to Jeff Phaneuf. The land passed into other hands and the building was removed. Here might be seen slings for the shoeing of oxen, now an unusual sight and one to be remembered by one fortunate to witness it. Here by honest and hard work a competence was acquired.

Almost opposite across the street was another old landmark, the blacksmith shop of Samuel E. McLellan which was in active operation by Mr. McLellan and his sons for many years.

Mr. McLellan's progenitors were among the Gorham McLellans and were among the makers of history of that historic old town. As a young man he early came to Westbrook and for many years carried on a successful business with his sons, Henry and William R.,the latter known to everybody in Saccarappa as "Ed." After his death his sons still continued the industry. The death of Henry left the junior partner alone. He carried on successfully for some years, but the coming of the automobile made the shoeing of horses take second place, and gradually work fell off, and finally the shop was closed. Later he went to Gorham where he died a few years ago. His shop was a most interesting place to visit. He did a great deal of carriage work and his oxen slings were quite a novelty to the younger generation.

There have been, and still are, blacksmith shops in town but so near to our own time as not to need mention.

Another industry of the olden time that flourished here was a knife factory carried on by one George Ropes. His factory stood by the river where the old Duck Mill formerly stood, and the stones of the underpinning can now be seen. This was quite an establishment at one time. It even ran nights sometimes and a lady, long since dead, used to tell how the temping machine used to keep her awake, as she lived quite near. This must have been in the late thirties or early forties of the last century. Mr. Ropes made steel knives and forks which were universally used. They were not handsome, however useful. They were made of good steel and stood well the constant scouring necessary to keep them as bright and shining as the particular housewives of that bygone day deemed necessary. The advent of silver knives and forks, manufactured to suit the pockets of everybody, doubtless had much to do with the waning of this industry.

Then there was the cooper shop where Jones Pennell made headings much in demand in those days. This, too, was a center of attraction for the youngsters of the place.

Paper bags were also made in Saccarappa. Mark Adams, grandfather of Ernest Adams of the east end, was the man who ran the industry. He had a shop under the old Universalist

Church. He cut the bags out of paper and farmed them out among the boys and girls of the town to paste. They really did not get very much for their labor, only a matter of three or five cents a hundred, and they had to go after their work and return the completed bags. The late Leonard Valentine and George A. Jordan were two of the boys who pasted bags for Mr. Adams. The former told me that ten cents was a big afternoon's work. But that was 75 or more years ago before short hours and long hours were thought.

In talking with Mr. Valentine it was disclosed that he also remembers as a boy how sparsely settled the town was on Main Street between Saccarappa and Cumberland Mills. He said that after one left what is now Spring Street the first house on the north side was a little structure where the Universalist Church now stands. Then came what we know as the Roberts house, just east of the present park; and lastly was the Haskell house just west of the present Chute residence. There was no road by what is now the Warren Church. There was a road branching off over the Rochester track to the Eastman store. On the south side toward "Congin" was the Debeck house. Next to that was the Montgomery Anderson house on the "flat."

It may be of more than passing interest to designate who and what was on Main Street about 60 years ago, as remembered by a man in the late sixties who used to pass hand bills as a boy, and recalls the picture vividly.

He says, "Main Street of Westbrook as I remember it nearly 60 years ago: Beginning at the Portland and Rochester Railroad on the northerly side were living Wesley Hawkes whose son, E. Leroy Hawkes, still occupies the house. Mr. Hawkes lived downstairs and the family of Mr. Joseph Babb, the father of Mrs. Irene Harding late of Gorham, who now resides in Portland. In the next house lived Mrs. Charles Brackett with her son Leo, so well known as a painter, and her daughter, Ida. In the other side of the house lived her sisters, maiden ladies by the name of Anderson.

"But between their house and the Hawkes house was a double house occupied by the families of Washburn Elwell and Herbert Cutter. In a small house lived David Dyer and sister; this house was afterwards moved up on Central Street. Next to this was a tenement house where lived a family by the name of

Dumphy. Then came the John W. Warren cotton warp mill, which was taken down years ago. Then came the Hanson shoe repairing shop. This was kept by Benjamin Hanson, the father of Mrs. Charles London. Next was the London blacksmith shop. A little back from the street stood the house of Mrs. Dolly Simonton and son, John Stimson. The Old Universalist Church was next. The next in order came the Foster & Brown machine shop with the woodworking shop of George E. Raymond upstairs.

"The Keeler and Bailey underwear mill came next. This business was flourishing for a time. Mr. Keeler built the large house on Central Street at the top of the hill, just this side of the old Highland House, which was used as a hotel for some years. Now both houses are tenement houses. Following the underwear mill was the leatherboard mill which was a prosperous concern for several years under the management of George R. Davis. George H. Raymond had a feed and grain mill. Next in order of place in the rear was the Crocker and Dunn cotton renovating mill. Now came the second-hand store of Jerry R. Andrews where all kinds of furniture could be found. The grocery store of Rufus and Cyrus King was a well known landmark; it is now occupied by Leland W. Knight as a hardware establishment. The small store of William Best where cigars and candy might be found was next on the list. Following was the store of Jenness Cash who also sold cigars, candy, etc. Close to was the grocery store of Wesley M. Hawkes. The large wooden building of Lewis W. Edwards stood on the corner; here Mr. Edwards did a flourishing business for many years. Later the wooden building was replaced by a fine brick block which is now occupied by the Warren Furniture Company. "On the opposite corner was Harlan P. Murch, groceries. The Men's Furnishing Store of Charles R. Andrews has been omitted; it stood between the Edwards store and the store of Wesley M. Hawkes. Then came the millinery stores; the proprietors were first Miss Eliza Barker, Miss Harriet Gower, and lastly Mrs. Mary A. Bean, Dry Good and Millinery. A large two-story house stood next which was occupied by Mrs. Bean and the family of Robert P. Tibbetts downstairs, and the families of Harlan P. Murch and Hebron Mayhew upstairs. Beyond this house was the candy shop of Mrs. William Best with tenement above. Then came the shoe repairing shop of Nathaniel Swett. Moccasins were made in Westbrook in that far off day.

The firm doing this was Lord, Haskell and Neal, and they carried on quite a business in this shop.

"Now came the residences. First was the large house of Dr. Noah R. Martin whose office stood in the west end of the yard, for there were no lawns then, we called them dooryards. The Springer block now occupies the space. The house was moved back on the river bank and has quite recently been taken down.

Next came the house occupied by the families of William W. Cutter and George T. Springer which is now the plumbing establishment of Knight Brothers, with tenement above. East of this house was the small cottage house of Mrs. Deacon Walker, or as she was affectionately called, Auntie Walker. Mrs. Walker was a very patriotic woman. She loved her country's flag. Every Memorial Day she saw to it that there were no soldiers' graves undecorated. Her love for her country and its defenders was deep and abiding. The Henry Sands house came next, followed by the Crague house which stood quite near the Marion, or now the residence of Mrs. Lauiston W. Sawyer. This Crague house was moved away and Ruel W. Woodman, who had a furniture factory on a street running in nearly opposite the old electric car barn, built the house as his residence. The brick house, now the home of John W. Hay, was then the residence of Samuel Clements, a prominent business man of that day. This house had been built by Hanson Clay who had moved to Portland some years previous to the time we are telling of. The next house was the home of Mr. Jerry R. Andrews which, I am told, had been built by a Mr. McGuire. The house directly opposite Spring Street had been built by John M. Allen in 1870; an item in an old paper gives this information. The next house was the home of Bryce M. Edwards,Jr. who was of the well-known firm of Edwards & Walker who, about this time, removed to Portland; then for a short time it was occupied by Rev. H. B. Meade, pastor of the Westbrook Congregational Church, to be succeeded by Edmund Woodbury who occupied it for years. Then came the William Trickey house which was built by Joseph Walker who gave to Westbrook its public library. Mr. Walker was like many of our former residents who moved to Portland; although not of us, yet still retain a warm place in their hearts for Westbrook. The old wooden high school building, which is now on Valentine Street and still doing duty as a school building, stood between Mr.

Trickey's house and the Methodist Church. Foster Street came next, which was then called Methodist Lane. The Dana W. Brigham house, now the residence of Clarence A. Hughes, came next. On the land where now stands the Baptist Church was a house occupied by a family by the name of Cobb. The John Cloudman house came next. The Universalist Church had not been built; in that vicinity stood a house shifting tenants and a small house occupied by James Beasley. In the corner of what is now Dunn Street was a two-storied house occupied by G. Fred Murch and Eugene Graffam. The Johnson Quinby house came next. This house is now the property of the city and is occupied by Willis C. Mitchell. The next house was the B. F. Roberts house which is just east of the Park, which was not then in existence. Then came the two Watson houses, being the property of two brothers, Henry and John Watson; one has been removed, the other is now the dwelling place of the pastor of the parish of St. Mary's. The old Haskell house, as it is called, was occupied by a Hallock family. The next house was occupied by a Mr. Stevens who, at that time, was building it by piece-meal; he had the ell completed and was living in it. The Stephen Emery house came next which, as today, is followed by the Brown house, Mrs. Emery and Mrs. Brown occupying them respectively. Next was the B.G.Pride house, now the home of the family of his son, Merritt Pride. The last house before the Maine Central, mountain division, was the house of Ansel Stevens and his store. This house has been added to and remodeled and is now the Westbrook Hospital.

"On the southerly side of Main Street, for the same distance extending from the Maine Central to the Portland-Rochester at Longfellow Street, the buildings are: first, the house of Benjamin Elwell, John W. Wheeler whose windmill in his wood yard was long a landmark; then came the house of William A. Babb, now the property of Joseph ----. the home of Dr. A. F. Murch came next, to be followed by the house of Solomon Haskell. The Warren Schoolhouse had recently been built. In succession came the residences of Isaac Cross, Frank Moses, Edward Fogg, Irving Rowe, a tenement house; next an old yellow house formerly on the site of the Odd Fellows' block at the west end. Now came the John Debeck house which is still standing. Next the John Dunn house, now the home of Mrs. W. B. Boothby.

The next was two-family house where Alvin L. Parker and a Hopkins family lived. Where now stand the large house, to us of the olden time known as the Dr. Horr house, stood the home of Charles Ritchie. The late Dr. Thomas P. Smith lived in the house on the corner of Stroudwater Street, now the home of Mrs. A. H. Burroughs. The home of Charles Lane came next, now the Dr. Hall residence. What is now the residence of Dr. Miller was then the home of John C. Schwartz. Mrs. Westcott came next and Lemuel lived on the corner of Pleasant Street. The Ricker house had not been built then, but was shortly after. In a house where now stands the residence of Dr. D'Arche stood the home of Emma and Eugenia Haskell. Then came Spring Street. George H. Raymond lived in the corner in a house which is now down on Main Street opposite the Universalist Church, owned and occupied by Mrs. Alice Varnum. Shortly after this period Mr. Raymond moved the house and erected the structure which now stands there, and is owned and occupied by Stephen F. Hopkinson. The Lewis W. Edwards house came next, now the home of Henry S. Cobb. Where now stands the Walker Memorial Library stood a white cottage house, the property of Capt. William Barker, which was moved away to make room for the library. At this time the family of Edward Phinney lived here. Then came the Bryce M. Edwards house, now the property of his grandson, Frank H. McCann. The Rev. Israel Luce, pastor of the Methodist church, lived there. The Alonzo Libby house was next. Bond Street is between the Libby house and what was then the residence of Mrs. George Warren, now the home of Dr. Louis L. Hills. The residence of Dr. George M. Woodman was then the home of F. M. Ray, which is on the corner of Church Street. The house on the opposite corner was the home of Leonard Chase. There were then no more buildings until just this side of the Westbrook Congregational where stood the small building just east of the church occupied by Otis Wyer and Asa P. Whitney, carpenters. The church was on the corner of Brackett Street, as at present located. On the other corner of Brackett Street was the store of the late James Pennell, which at that time dealt principally in stoves, and after was a plumbing establishment. The grocery store of John N. Allen came next in order. The Post Office was next; this was followed by the store of C.B. Woodman, druggist. One of the oldest houses of the town was next, the old

Presumpscot house, then in a most prosperous condition. It was later moved down on to Fitch, or as it is often called, Depot Street, and is now a boarding house, and the Scates block stands on its site. F. X. Girard and Leander Clements occupied the next building. The grocery store of J. K. Dunn came next, also that of W. F. Bettes. A coal office of A. T. Skillings and the saloon of Leonard Valentine followed. A building which served as a sort of city hall stood next; it also served as a band house. Later it was moved to several places on Main Street and on near lots. In the corner of Central Street stood a stable run by Charles Schwartz. The Star Theatre and Odd Fellows block now cover the space. The next building was what was known as the Jerry Clements house; it is still standing. John Adams' carriage shop came next, then the blacksmith shop of Samuel E. McLellan, which has already been mentioned. The house west of the blacksmith shop was occupied by the Allen and Hale families. Mr. Joseph Babb had a tin shop next. The house now standing next was the Phinney house occupied by the families of Fred Phinney, his mother, Mrs. James Phinney, and her brother, George Mayberry. A lumber yard was in the Saco Street corner; John W. Warren had a storehouse, and the Simon Cutter house was next to the Portland and Rochester railroad.

The Underground Railroad

During the Civil War, which most of us now living know of only as we read of it or by tradition since it occurred eighty years ago, an enterprise of much secrecy, as well as much assistance to unfortunates of another race and color, known as the underground railroad, flourished in Saccarappa.

It was under the direction and active help of four well-known citizens of this village hamlet, Mr. Sewall Brackett, Captain Isaac F. Quinby, Rev. Horace J. Bradbury and Mr. John Brown. Mr. Brackett will be remembered by many in Westbrook as carrying on a stove and tinware business; Captain Quinby was an active business man about town, dealing largely in real estate; Rev. H.J. Bradbury was a Universalist minister, and of course interested in all helpful activities; while Mr. Brown was the station agent at the Portland and Rochester Railroad depot at this end of town.

The large block on the corner of Main and Brackett Streets, at that time owned and occupied by Mr. Brackett as his place of business, (earlier in the century it had been built by Mr. Bracket's father for his son's occupancy), had in its fourth story a large dark room. To this refuge slaves were taken by one of the men above mentioned, and kept there until a particularly dark night or a good opportunity made it feasible to take the hunted black people to some place from which Canada could easily be reached. An old-fashioned "carryall," rightly named for it was surprising how many could be crowded into it capacious interior, was used for this purpose, with closed curtains and as swift a horse as was obtainable. Would that these humane people had had our swift locomotion of today!

So careful were these men to keep their doings secret that even the members of their families were in total ignorance of this rescue work being carried on. Mrs. Brackett was greatly mystified as to where her food was disappearing. She accused the apprentices, of which Mr. Brackett had two or three, of pilfering her pantry; which of course they indignantly denied.

After the war Mr. Brackett confessed that he was the culprit. These four men all lived at that time on Brackett Street, and thus kept in touch with each other easily. Mr. Brown, being station agent, of course knew what and who came in and went out of the town. Now and then there would be a child among the fugitives, and then of course great care had to be taken to prevent noise. That dark room sheltered many a quaking heart and despairing souls who was helped to light and life by these kindly men.

This block is now put to a much different use. It is now the property of the LaFond Estate and the whole lower story is the LaFond Department Store; yes, and the second story as well, where dresses and hats are on sale. The third and fourth floors are remodeled into attractive flats, and the "underground railroad," with its fears and escapes, has become a forgotten story.

The Cumberland and Oxford Canal

Just a little over 150 years ago, to be exact, in 1741, the matter of a canal from Sebago Lake to the Presumpscot River, Saccarappa, was agitated and a committee to consider the practicability was chosen. The report of this committee is told by Philip L. Milliken in his most excellent pamphlet, "The Cumberland and Oxford Canal and The Canal Bank." This committee reported "that the products of the country could be brought to the Falls at Saccarappa from a distance of some sixty miles."

As a result of this favorable report, in 1795 Woodbury Storer and other of Portland obtained from the General Court of Massachusetts, for it must be remembered that we were still dominated by Massachusetts, an act incorporating under that name of "Cumberland Canal Company" to open a canal from the Lake to Presumpscot River at Saccarappa. Another corporation was incorporated at the same time called the "Proprietors of the Falmouth Canal," for the purpose of uniting the waters of the Presumpscot and Fore Rivers.

The first charter allowed a capital of $20,000 which in 1804 was increased to $120,000. But after ten years' efforts the amount could not be raised. The charter was extended five years with no better results, and the charter was allowed to lapse.

Then came the fateful year of 1812 with its attendant business depression. In 1820 Maine became a state by itself and business improved. In 1821 a charter was obtained from the new legislature authorizing Arthur McLellan, Albion K. Parris, Charles Whitman, Asa Clapp, Samuel Anderson, Leander Gage, Daniel Brown, Nathaniel Howe, Enoch Perley, Josiah Whitman, and Ira Crocker to construct a canal from Waterford in Oxford County, to the navigable waters of Fore Rivers, under the name of "The Cumberland and Oxford Canal Corporation." This corporation was empowered for the management of the canal, also to lay out, make and maintain a canal with a suitable number of locks, to begin at the waters of Thomas Pond in Waterford in Oxford County, thence to proceed to Sebago lake, and thence to Fore River at a place they may designate.

The corporation was authorized to take the private land of persons along the course of the canal, not exceeding 20 rods, and paying a just compensation. They were authorized to use the water from any pond, river, or other water course as was necessary, and to make such locks, floodgates, embankments, docks, piers, wharves, as was found convenient and necessary. It was also provided that the property of the corporation would be divided into 2,000 shares, subject to assessment not to exceed $50 a share.

If this amount were not sufficient the corporation was to create and sell the necessary number of shares. A toll was to be established for the benefit of the corporation on all commodities passing through the canal, at specified rates.

If the canal was not complete in five years this act should be void. In 1823 the new legislature passed an act on February 1, 1823, granting the forming of a lottery to the Cumberland and Oxford Corporation to raise $50,000 for the benefit of the corporation.

In 1825, as a further means to help out the enterprise, the canal bank was incorporated at a capital of $200,000 with the condition that one-fourth of the capital should be invested in the stock of the canal.

The work was begun in the spring of 1828 and completed in a little less than three years. The first boat towed through Sebago Lake bore the illustrious name of George Wash-ington and was called a "pleasure boat." It was built by William A. Rich who lived at Great Falls on the Presumpscot River.

Mr. Solomon Cloudman had a vivid remembrance of the events of those far off days, and told me much concerning the old canal. He said the boat was painted in stripes, red, white and blue. On its stern were the heads of George and Martha Wash-ington, finely carved, with the name George Washington in a half circle above them. The favored passengers on this first trip were the stockholders and business men of Portland, Westbrook, Gorham, Sebago, and Standish.

The outfit of the boat was in full sympathy with the times which was far from temperate, having a bar and all things that go with its equipment.

The boat was not a success financially, and it was soon remodeled into a freight boat, and finally sunk in a small cove near Kents Lock. The common freight boat was 65 feet long and 10 feet wide, with a cabin 9x9 feet in which were a cook stove, 3 bunk beds, a table, three chairs, all the cooking apparatus and clothing for three men.

The boatmen used a long tin horn to notify the lock tender that a boat was approaching; also this horn was used in giving the signals where the cut was too narrow for two boats to pass. a long shrill blast announced the down boat which had right of way. The down freight was mostly sawed lumber, boards, shocks, staves, and cord wood. The price of the last was from $2.50 to $3.00 a cord. Ten to fifteen cords was the average load for one horse, and the speed four miles an hour. The 7 miles without a lock was between Horse-beef, as Little Falls was called, and Stroudwater, known as the Long Level. Then there were 7 locks near together; the last one was located near the foot of Clark Street, Portland, called the Lower Guard Lock, and opened into salt water. The canal proper from Portland to Sebago Lake was about 20 miles.

Boats ran to all points on Sebago Lake, often taking freight from Bridgton and Harrison. The Canal Company owned but one boat called the "The Corporation Boat" managed by Lothrop Libby, Timothy Skillings, and Joseph Libby. These men had the oversight of all needed repairs on the whole line. This was found to be too expensive and was dropped. The Company had nothing to do with furnishing boats for transporation. Each individual furnished his own boat and paid a certain per cent a mile for transporting goods and merchandise.

The old records show the toll on molasses was 10 cents a mile for each hogshead, rum 2 cents, staves and shock 3 cents per thousand, all other goods in about the same proportion. The following yellowed receipt found among Mr. Ray's papers in very legible writing and hardly faded ink tells its own story:

October 12, 1840
Caleb Rhea to James Crockett Dr.
to use of Canal Boat from
the 12int. to the 17th two
trips four dollars. James Crockett
one trip at one dollar
Oct.21st rec'd
Payment by cash.
James Crockett

The whole matter of collecting revenue was regulated by a board of directors, paid to the treasurer by the superintendent, Charles E. Barrett of Portland, who was treasurer for many years.

Joseph E. Lary of South Windham was on old time blacksmith; he was employed for over 30 years. His shop was near the locks. The names of some of those oldtime boats were: The Waterwitch, Sebago, Jack Downing, Honest Quaker, Speedwell, and many others.

The by-laws of the company required all boats to have the name printed on the stern in letters not less that four inches in height.

Among those who owned boats and ran them on the lake and canal were Luther Fitch, John Lindsay, William Chadbourne, Elliot Libby, Jesse Plummer, Henry Chadbourne, and Nathan Winslow.

The process of locking a boat through was simple and very practical. If the boat was on the way up the lake, the towline was cast off at the foot of the lock and it sailed into the empty lock. Then the two huge wooden gated behind the boat were shut and the up stream pads opened with a big iron wrench, admitting near the bottom of the boat two streams of water, each two feet square, under a pressure of ten feet head. In about three minutes the boat came up to the level water above, gliding easily about, and was again on the way to the Lake. With the down stream the process was reversed; it sailed into the filled lock and the upper gates were closed, the lower pads opened and the boat gently settled to the level below. Five minutes were sufficient to lock through.

As was said, the State Legislature gave permission for a lottery scheme to the Cumberland and Oxford Corporation sufficient to raise $50,000. One good old freewill Baptist deacon (Deacon Shaw) was the lucky man and drew the largest prize $5,000. Perhaps as a sop to his conscience he appropriated a large share of the prize to the building of a church for his denomination. The share owners never received a dividend as there was nothing to divide form the venture; the Canal received $27,000.

In the thirties the Canal Bank furnished the Canal large sums of money, and for security took a mortgage on the property which they held until 1857, when they sold to F. O. J. Smith, Thomas S. Abbott, and Isaac Dyer for $10,000.

After this, misfortunes seemed to multiply. It finally got into the courts and as late as 1876 some cases were pending. Finally, after many struggles for existence, the few boats left on the line ran their last voyage in the fall of 1876, and the Canal became a thing of the past.

In the summer of 1830 the whole line was alive with Irishmen, newly imported with picks, shovels and wheel-barrows. The banks were dotted all along with shanties, crudely built, which overflowed with small pats (?). In some dwellings were two, three, and sometimes four families.

In the most prosperous days of the Canal there were nearly 100 boats actively employed. For a short time the whole venture was popular. No carriage riding was permitted on the tow path; no horse was allowed to go faster than a walk. If cattle were found on the Canal owner was liable to a fine. The shore line of Sebago Lake and its near vicinity were stripped of its valuable pine and hard timber. Thousands of cords of wood were cut and sold for just enough to cover the cost of cutting. The deep cuts through many fine farms reduced their productive value 25 per cent. Few are now left who recall the unfortunate events associated with the beginning and ending of the Cumberland and Oxford Canal.

While the business of the old canal had been growing less and less, it received its death blow with the building of the Portland and Ogdensburg Railroad. This railroad furnished a much quicker and cheaper means of transporation not only for all kinds of merchandise besides human traffic and opened a large territory on which to draw.

Colonel Westbrook's Dam

While other factors were involved, still it was primarily the sea salmon which came up the Presumpscot River to Sebago Lake that caused a bloody war of six long years. These fish were a great food of the Indians who speared them, not alone for fresh food, but also they were cured by a smoking process.

The early settlers along our river eked out their food through a hard and long winter by this custom learned from the Red Man; they also salted them down.

The trouble began in 1739 when Colonel Thomas Westbrook, for whom our city was named, and who had large lumbering interest in this and adjoining sections, built the first dam on the Presumpscot River. This dam was on the upper Saccarappa Falls and was never wholly completed. About his time a block-house for defense was erected on Pork Hill, as our present Park Hill was called for many years. Tradition has it that the origin was as follows: the garrison in the town who sent their meat supplies very quickly disposed of the pork, but the beef lasted longer, therefore, they were admonished to go lightly on the pork; hence to pork eaters, be that as it may, it was Pork Hill, and still is to the older inhabitants.

This dam was on obstruction to the salmon ascending the stream to Sebago Lake, their spawning ground.

Chief Polin soon discovered this. He was the leader of the Rockameecooks, a band of the Sokokis, who frequented the Saco River. The same year that the dam was built Polin walked to Boston, where he had an interview with Governor Shirley and demanded that Westbrook's dam be removed. When Governor Shirley told him that a fish way would be built, which was promptly doe, he was pacified for a time. But as the white settlers increased, the supply of salmon for the Indian lessened.

Again Chief Polin went to Boston and interviewed the Governor. He was at all modest in his demands as he claimed all the land on both sides of the Presumpscot River from Sebago Lake to tide water, Portland, where the river empties into the Atlantic ocean.

Receiving no satisfaction, he swore vengeance on the white settlers along the stream. The first attack fell on Gorham April 19, 1746. In the meantime two forts for defense had been erected, one on Fort Hill at Gorham, the other at Windham on what is known as the River Road in the Anderson neighborhood; in fact, it was situated in what is now the garden of the house owned and occupied as a summer home by the Goodells of Cumberland Mills, descendants of the Anderson family. These forts were occupied from necessity during this six years' war provoked by Col. Westbrook's dam.

May 14, 1756 an attack was made by Polin and his band of warriors on the Windham settlers, who had ventured forth from the fort to plant some corn.

The Indians had assembled at White's Bridge, Sebago Lake, and came down the Presumpscot at a point near the blockhouse. Hearing the report of the guns of the savages, members of the fort occupants hastened to the relief of those attacked. Among this party were Abraham Anderson and Stephen Manchester. Polin in ambush fired at Anderson and missed. While eagerly reloading, in his haste he came out of hiding. Manchester, quick to take advantage, raised his gun and fired, with the result that this dreaded chieftain fell, to rise no more.

The woods resounded with the yells of the red skins. The Indians, as was their custom when suffering a defeat, became panic stricken, and quickly carrying the dead leader, they made their escape in their canoes up the river to Sebago Lake, where they proceeded to uproot a beech tree and place the body of Polin in the cavity thus made. Released, the tree quickly sprang back into place, deftly covering all trace of the burial.

This death put an end to future trouble with the red foe in this region. While Westbrook had never suffered, as had the two adjoining towns, nevertheless many depredations had been suffered, and the passing of Polin was far from being regretted. It seems as though this historic event took place in our own town, it is so near and so many of the descendants of those taking part reside here.

Lowell H. Woodbury is the grandson of Joshua Lowell Hawkes, on whose farm the battle took place, which is adjacent to Westbrook, and Mrs. Carrie Manchester Foss is a lineal descendant of that same Stephen Manchester. There are others, too, residing in Westbrook, in whose veins runs the blood of the heroes of that bloody day.

Old North School

The church and school are twin educators and we find they usually come together in very pioneer town or hamlet; and so it was in old Saccarappa, as this hamlet of old Falmouth is called, for it must be remembered Westbrook as a town came into existence in 1814.

The erection of the first schoolhouse in this territory was no doubt the "Old North Schoolhouse," as it was called, which was built in 1811. Doubtless there had been small "dame schools," as they were called previously. These were held usually in some room of a house, and taught generally by some maiden lady of uncertain, or perhaps certain, age. Small children were the pupils generally, for in those days when everyone began work as early as possible, when physical ability admitted, young people as a rule could not be spared for extensive learning.

But in 1811 the need for a school for older young people became apparent, and so the building was erected. It sat at what was called, and still is, the Four Corners on Bridge Street, where it crossed Cumberland Street. Here the farmers' sons and daughters received their education's. The school teachers of that period, while thoroughly conversant with the studies taught, and so great was his faculty in imparting knowledge that he left a lasting impression, particularly is he remembered for the dexterity with which he handled the ruler and switch, for there was no law then against whipping an unruly pupil as at present. Perhaps the need was no greater in those far off days, but certainly the art was practiced much more. Who can tell if it was for the betterment of the learner? Certain it is that a sturdy, honest, upright race was the result.

These pupils of the "Old North School" who entered upon their various vocations in life were in earnest; some went far and won both fortune and fame, while not a few remained in their place and have been among our most honored citizens, occupying positions of trust in social and political life.

This district included all the territory on the north side of the Presumpscot River to the Windham line, Rocky Hill to nearly Prides Corner, and what is now Cumberland Mills on both sides of the river.

Many of the scholars were obliged to study, in those days, evenings, by the light only of burning pitch knots in open fireplaces; and they used birch bark on which to "cipher" or perform their problems in arithmetic.

Many were obliged to walk two or three miles, but those who had the farthest to come were generally the first there. Tradition has it that the old schoolhouse was haunted, from the fact that a workman was said to have been killed and his body buried beneath the teacher's desk. As the story goes, lights had been seen in the window at night, and one day, to all appearances, a veritable ghost with winding sheet was seen gliding in and out among the alder bushes, for the adjacent ground was then a swamp. The story goes on to say that the teacher dismissed the school and the pupils hastened away in great fright.

In the early 90's of the 19th century a reunion of as many as possible of the old pupils and teachers who were living was held in Captain Chase's then new barn at the Four Corners, near the spot where the old schoolhouse used to stand. This was the first reunion in many years and it was a glorious one. Gray-haired men and women, many bent with the infirmities of years, grew suddenly young at heart as they met friends and schoolmates of by-gone years on that spot which was hallowed ground. Here they lived over again the by-gone years of more than a half a century when their laughter and shouts rang out on the clear air.

The barn was decorated with flags and bunting for the gala occasion. An old pung was completely covered with evergreen and flowers, and over the seat was a placard reading "Lovers' retreat for this day only." A most bountiful dinner was served at noon, and then came not the least enjoyable part of the day, namely the speeches. Among those present on this happy occasion, who have since entered that greater school beyond this earth, were Benjamin Blair of Boothby Harbor; Honorable Leander Valentine, Westbrook's first mayor; Rev. Benjamin Freeman of Scarboro; Frank Cobb; Mrs. Elizabeth Cobb; Mrs. B. J. Woodman, the grandmother of Dr. George M. Woodman of this city, herself a native of Westbrook; Stephen Grant; Mrs. George Millions; Mrs. Henry Jewett; all of Westbrook; Mrs. Preston Day of Warren, R. I.; Mrs. Thomas Akers. Lowell, Mass.; B. F.

Roberts, Mrs. Jane Jones, Stephen Winslow, Zachriah Small, Harlan P. Murch, Oliver A. Cobb, Mrs. Apphia Davis, Mrs. Isaiah Hacker, Mrs. P. C. Dole, Mrs. H. K. Griggs.

Now, on that spot where in the long ago only a bird song might have been heard as the school was dismissed, now, as was said, can be heard the roar of big water falls, the whir of the machinery of the largest paper mills under one roof in the world; also the sounds of other manufactories of the city, as Westbrook has for more that forty years been a city; until quite recently the buzz of the electric cars, now superseded by buses; the noise of a passing automobile, and perhaps from a nearby house, for the region has now many homes, the voice of one talking over the ever-present telephone to one nearby or perhaps many miles away; and last, that modern wonder, the radio; and all this has come to pass in less than a hundred years.

An old elm tree still stands near the spot where once the children of long ago gathered, and perhaps beneath this very elm, ate their noonday lunch.

Some of the teachers of the first fifteen years of the school were Master Garvin, Nathan Harris - he had a country store at Congin, as Cumberland Mills was called, and his last resting place is in old Saccarappa cemetery. Mr. Ray told me that he was spoken of as "old Nathan Harris," and from a passing curiosity he took occasion to look at the date of his death on his gravestone and found it read 42 years. Evidently age was considered somewhat differently then than now. But to continue with our list: Francis Purington, Levi Fulsome, John C. Bake, Myril Sawyer, Rachel Hall, Lydia Austin, Ann Hawkes, Louise Hawkes, Lucy Colby. The winter terms were usually taught by men as the old boys were harder to discipline and were needed on the farms in the spring and summer.

The teachers from 1827 to 1841 were Olive Dole, George Quinby (late editor of the Gospel Banner at Augusta), Benjamin Freeman, Nathaniel French, W. Hall, Sarah Blair, Rebecca Harris, Abbie Webb Mary Freeman, Sophronia Quinby, Abbie Cutter, Caroline King, Betsey Quinby, and Sarah W. Winslow.

The first school in this part of the town was taught by Master Blair, the great grandfather of Mrs. Ida Griggs Quinby, herself a well- known teacher in the early eighties of the past century. It may be of interest to recall the fact that until 1814 this part of Westbrook was a past of old Falmouth. Mr. H. K. Griggs, Master Blair's granddaughter, was on of the pupils of the Old North School and lived and died in the home where she was born, the Pines at Rocky Hill. This first school was taught by Master Blair in a room in the old Boody house near Riverton.

Mr. Blair was of Scotch lineage, though emigrating from Ireland to the United States. It was said of him that he could "make an almanac or navigate a ship." He was also a Quaker preacher and began to teach ten days after landing in this country.

One of the teachers mentioned was very unsuccessful in his government of the boys who were full of pranks of mischief. One day, seeing the teacher enter an outbuilding, they rushed upon it and tipped it over and the poor man was extracted with much difficulty. Master Fuller (or Fulsome) was engaged particularly to tame the boys as he had a reputation as a disciplinarian. One day a boy by the name of Moses Babb was severely punished. The boy remained at home the next day nursing his wrath. Finally, taking the fastest horse obtainable, he rode up to the open window of the schoolhouse and yelled the following doggerel:

> "Levi Fulsome (or Fuller) did come down
> To teach a school in Westbrook town
> Called Jim Davis out in the floor
> Told him "Here's the rule and there's the door."

He also shouted out other lines reflecting on the Master's partiality for Lydia Austin.

Miss Sarah Blair stand out prominently among the early teachers. She was a daughter of Master Blair. She died at Rocky Hill in 1850.

Miss Rebecca Harris adopted the monitor system. All around the outside of the building were tents made of shawls where pupils could go for study or recitation, in charge of a monitor.

Among the best loved of the teachers of those days was Miss Jane Bixby, a sister of the late Mrs. Rufus King, and Miss Caroline Jordan, mother of ex-mayor Rufus K. Jordan. She was born in Saccarappa and was highly educated for the times. She had much artistic ability and painted with her own hands the "Rewards of Merit" given the children. She died while teaching, leaving the cards unfinished in some cases. The following is one she had finished:

> "Oh, make religion thy magnetic guide
> Which tho' it trembles as it lowly lies,
> Points to the light which changes not,
> To Heaven." Remember Jane.

Miss Betsey Quinby was the next teacher who had such will power that it needed only a nod. Miss Sarah B. Winslow was a gifted teacher who married Dr. Milton Seavey of Portland, for whom Seavey Street at Cumberland Mills is named.

Calvin Stowe, afterwards the husband of Harriet Beecher Stowe, also was a successful teacher here.

John C. Baker also taught here. He was proprietor of the Mousam House, Kennebunk, at the time of his death.

Rev. George Quinby taught several terms; he was much beloved and his farewell leave-taking made a lasting impression.

Leander Valentine was a much esteemed teacher; no teacher was honored or loved.

W.W.Hall was long remembered for his plain methods of teaching.

Dr. Albus Ray was distinguished for his scholarship. He was a stern disciplinarian. He was an uncle of Fabius M. Ray. He practiced many years in Portland, where he died.

Another teacher was Rev. Benjamin Freeman who was a successful Methodist preacher for many years.

Quite a stir was made by the report that Miss King was teaching dancing in her school. An investigation showed that the so-called dancing was calisthenics.

Miss Blair, spoken of above, taught 3 years for $2.50 a week. She was nearly 15 years getting her pay and was finally obliged to take 1,000 fence boards in part payment.

The children were taught "manners" in those days. When a class was called into the floor, "toes to the right" was the order. When the teacher said "attention" the girls courtesied and the boys bowed.

When visitors entered the room the scholars rose and stood until the visitor was seated. The same was done when the visitor left. The old schoolhouse is gone, also the early pupils and teachers, but all live in the influence they exerted.

As time went on there were various school districts established throughout the town, and in 1873, following a custom throughout the state, the school committee recommended to the people the need of a high school. The school committee at that time was made up of Charles E. Boody and John E. Bean. This recommendation was adopted and in 1873 there were five terms of high school in the town, three at Main Street, Saccarappa, and two at Pride's Corner. The school on Main Street was held in the building which was later moved to Valentine Street to make room for the present high school building, which much enlarged and expanded, stand as our present high school.

Frederick E.C. Robbins was the principal with Miss Sarah R. Bradley as assistant. The high school at Pride's Corner was in charge of F.O. Mower. Later the two schools were united.

In 1882 Bridge Street schoolhouse was built, and that too has been enlarged by several additions as time passes.

In 1888 music was introduced in the schools, Mrs. Walton N. Files (Miss Etta Babb) being the first teacher.

Tradition has it that there were small schoolhouses in several sites throughout the town. One stood on Main Street, west of the Methodist church; another, it is said on Main Street also, not far from Dunn Street. There was also one at Cumberland Mills, or Congin as it was called, on Main Street. In the seventies a two-storied wooden building containing two rooms stood not far from the present Forest Street schoolhouse.

In the seventies an attempt was made to grade the schools, as the school population was growing so rapidly. Now there are not far from 2,000 pupils in our city, 623 being in the high school alone. Sixty-seven teachers are employed, 20 in the high school alone. This is a far cry from the first terms when two were all that were needed.

The first graduation as held in 1883 with three graduates, Hattie Hacker, now the wife of Charles E. Cobb of Denmark and Florida, Mr. Cobb being the proprietor and among the first originators of the boys' and girls' camps now scattered so thickly all through our eastern states; Charlotte Woodman, now dead, the wife of Bishop Edgar Blake; Eleanor Murch, now Mrs. Albert N. Carter of Portland. Her twin sister, Helen Murch, now Mrs. Walker, recently of North Adams, Mass., was a member of the class but did not graduate. In 1884 there was no class to graduate and in place of a graduation an exhibition was held in Odd Fellows Halls, with members of the different classes taking part. A program of the exhibition is in existence. It was printed by Marcus Watson, that veteran newspaper man, who came to Westbrook from Saco and established the Westbrook Chronicle which flourished for several years. The following program will doubtless be of interest to those connected with the Westbrook High School:

Part 1
1. Oh, Calm and Lovely the Evening Bells Polymnia Quartette
2. Uncle Sam's Farm Fence, as essay   Willie Farley
3. Reading, King Robert of Sicily   Edith Lane
4. Source of a Nation's Wealth   Josie Libby
5. Clarinet Solo, C. E. Bettes, with
                                Miss Nellie Bettes, accompanist
6. Rome was not built in a day   Lillian Mayhew
7. Declamation, Battle of Lookout Mountain
                                Fred Marriner
8. Essay, Imagination   Lizzie Hallowell
9. Quarrel Scene from Julius Caesar, Edgar Blake &
                                Lewis Haszelton

Part 2
10. Songs of Seven   Jean Ingersoll, Missses Lillian Haskell, Lillian Pennell, Lizzie Hallowell, Lillian Mayhew, Bertha Pennell, Lizzie Adams, and Josie Libby.
11. Essay, An Allegory   Minnie Hodsdon
12. Clarinet Solo   C. E. Bettes, with Miss Nellie
                                Bettes, accompanist
13. Essay, Poetry of Nature   Marcia Dunn
14. Declamation, Toussaint 18 Overture   Edwin Brown
15. Essay, Nathaniel Hawthorne   Eva Roberts
16. Reading, Money Musk   E. Maude Sampson
17. Essay Peter Cooper   Mitta Jones
18. Friends, Good Night   Polymnia Quartette

In 1885 William C. Farley was graduated as salutatorian, with a class of seven young ladies. Miss Elizabeth Hollowell, now deceased who later married Leroy Chase, now dead, was valedictorian. Other members were Marcia Dunn, later wife of Ernest Brewer; Lillian Mayhew, who married Albert Adams; Minnie Hodsdon, a teacher in Westbrook for many years;

and Miss Bertha Pennell, the wife of Harry D. Brooks. All these girls are dead excepting Mrs. Brooks.

In 1886 the graduating class had only two members, Joseph A. Warren and Edwin L. Brown, both now living on Cumberland Street, Cumberland Mills.

Since then yearly graduations have been held, and each year sees more than a hundred graduates.

In 1885 manual training was introduced. In 1906 Home Economics became a part of the regular course, and in 1909 Industrial training was established.

In 1882 Bridge Street schoolhouse was built, and that too has needed a sizable addition since.

In 1884 Warren school building was erected, and for some years also housed the manual training school; in fact, until the industrial building in the rear of the high school was available.

In 1886 the Main Street High School building was moved to Valentine Street and fitted up for school purposes. The present High School building was erected; since that time, as need arose, two large additions have been made.

The present Saco Street school building was built about 1868. Persons still living in Westbrook recall vividly attending school there, and also their attendance in the school building which preceded this present one. This first building stood on the same site. It was a large structure, a long weather beaten building with the end to the road. It had two rooms, and doubtless took the place of the "old Ironworks" so-called, which stood on the same site.

There are adequate buildings for pupils at Rocky Hill, Pride's Corner, and Highland Lake, this last being known to many as Duck Pond. The school at Spruce Swamp on the County Road off Spring Street has been discontinued for several years for lack of pupils.

Such in brief is the history of the schools of Westbrook, which from a small beginning, have grown to their present large and most efficient status. They compare most favorably with any municipality of its size in the state, and we may well be proud of the Westbrook schools.

Archelaus Lewis

It is probably true that our townsmen bore their part in that struggle which gave to the world it greatest republic; but the name of only one has been found who went into the Revolutionary Army from what is now Westbrook, and that one was Archelaus Lewis.

He was born in North Berwick, the son, it is said, of a Welsh sea captain, and a nephew of Francis Lewis, one of the signers of the Declaration of Independence. At the age of twenty-one he came to Saccarappa and set up business as a tailor, having his shop and "garden spot" on land which he bought of Daniel and Sarah (Pearson) Dole, the shop being near where the brick block of the late Lewis W. Edwards, now the Warren Furniture Store, now stands. The deed is dated August 8, 1780. This land, it is stated in the deed, came to Sarah Pearson Dole from her late father Moses Pearson.

It is probable that Mr. Lewis had occupied the land some years before purchasing it, for he came here in 1744, so his descendants say.

In 1776 he entered the army and was in the service five years. At Valley Forge he held a lieutenant's commission. After his return he lived for a short time at Stroudwater. It is probable that he was employed by the Smalls and other living on the Munjoy lands to negotiate a settlement with the Waldo heirs who were disturbing their possessions.

Mr. Lewis purchased from Waldo large tracts of land at Rocky Hill and Ammoncongin. Choosing for his residence an elevated site on the northerly side of the river at Ammoncongin, he erected the large mansion house now for some years occupied by Hon. Joseph A. Warren, which has been added to and greatly improved by Mr. Warren. Tradition has it that Mr. Lewis caused the County Road from Portland to Windham to be laid out in such a manner as to pass the westerly end of his dwelling.

He was a leading citizen and was known as "Square Lewis." He was several times married and had a numerous family. His descendants still live in Westbrook and adjoining towns, and one in particular still calls Westbrook his home, a great grandson who bears his precise name.

Mr. Lewis died January 21, 1834 at the age of eighty-one years, and is buried in the old cemetery at Stroudwater. At the time of his death he wad deacon of the church at Capisic, then called the First Congregational Church of Westbrook. This church stood on the lot where the Eunice Frye Home now is. It was organized April 8, 1765 in connection with the Fourth Parish of Falmouth, and the original members were: John Bailey, Thomas Haskell, Nathaniel Knight, Henry Knight, James Johnson, Jeremiah Riggs, Joseph Riggs, James Morrill, Clement Pennell, Anthony Morse, Solomon Haskell, and Benjamin Haskell. Bailey and these last were of Saccarappa.

Martha Washington Charitable Society of Saccarappa, Maine

Finding of an old Bible brings to light valuable information Original members are all dead.
Among them are many familiar names of women who were active in good work several years ago. Constitution not much unlike those in use by present day societies.
* * *

An old, leather-covered Bible, yellowed with age, but without a defaced or torn leaf. On the flyleaf is written, The Martha Washington Charitable Society of Saccarappa. On the title page is the date 1845. What was the Martha Washington Society? Who were its members? A long search disclosed little until one day the right person was asked. "do you know anything or have your ever heard anything of the Martha Washington Society?" "Why, no, I don't know much about it; but stop, I'm secretary of the Ladies' Sociable of the Westbrook Congregational Church and a numbers of books were given me when I was elected, and there's an old one I haven't looked at."

The secretary did look, and, sure enough, the old book was none other than the record book of the old society. The book is perhaps 6x8 inches with marbled blue and green covers. Some of the leaves are falling out, some are torn, all are colored by the artist, Time.

There must have been an earlier society, for on the first page one reads, "Constitution of The Saccarappa Martha Washington Society, as amended from the Constitution of the Female Charitable Society adopted Sept.6, 1842." Of this earlier society there is no record.

"For ye have the poor always with you, and whenever ye may, ye may do them good," is a truth as applicable now as when first uttered by the Savior of the world. Believing as we do that to alleviate the miseries of the poor and extend the hand of charity to the suffering and the destitute is a duty incumbent on all, we whose names are here affixed for the purpose of affecting this object, do agree to form ourselves into a society to be governed by the following constitution:

Art. 1. This society shall be called the Martha Washington Charitable Society.

Art. 2. The object of the society shall be to aid the poor without regard to religious sect by giving or lending such articles of clothing or other means of promoting comfort or happiness as the society shall possess. Another object of the society shall be to promote total abstinence from all intoxicating liquors as a beverage.

Art. 3. The officers of this society shall consist of a first and second directress, secretary and treasurer, which two latter shall be included in one person; also a board of managers consisting of nine, of which the first and second directress and secretary shall be members. All of which officers shall be chosen by ballot

Art. 4. The first directress shall preside at all meetings of the society; in her absence the second directress; if both be absent the senior manager shall preside.

Art. 5. It shall be the duty of the secretary to keep a record of all the meeting of the society, also an account of all money received in and paid out, and collect the subscriptions and all other dues and present a quarterly report to the society.

Art. 6. The board of managers shall have charge of all business of the society and shall see to the distribution of the funds. In drawing money form the treasury they shall give an order for the same to the treasurer.

Art. 7. The annual meeting of the society shall be holden on the first Tuesday of September for the choice of officers and the transaction of such business as may come before the society. The subscription shall become due at each annual meeting.

Art. 8. This society shall meet once in two weeks on Tuesday p.m. at 2 o'clock, in such place as may from time to time be designated.

Art. 9. Any member may become a member of this society by signing the constitution and contributing to its funds not less than 25 cents.

Art. 10. This constitution may be altered or amended by a vote of two-thirds of the members of the society present at any regular meeting provided notice of such alteration be given at a previous meeting.

This constitution is surely not unlike that of many a club today. Then came the bylaws as follows:

Bylaw adopted by the M.W.C. Society, Nov.26, 1846.

1st. The hour for assembling at the regular meeting of the society shall be at 2 o'clock p.m. The society shall be called to order and the meeting be opened by prayer or by reading from the Scriptures. If the weather should be unfavorable and no members present at the appointed for the regular meeting, it shall be considered as adjourned for the next two weeks unless there shall be special notice given for a previous meeting.

2nd. In order that our association may promote our social virtues, we deem it important carefully to abstain from all approach to scandal, to allow no conversation which may produce or foster a spirit of detraction, to avoid the repetition of all slanderous reports, and in neither word or deed to offend against the law of love.

3rd. Being strictly a charitable society we deem it inconsistent with our object to provide expensive entertainment and to prevent this we limit ourselves to but one kind of cake in addition to bread, butter and tea.

4th. Every member shall take care of her own work, folding and putting it up before leaving the meeting.

5th. None but members of the society shall attend the meetings of the society. If members have friends visiting them they are at liberty to take them if desirable.

A set of bylaws modern associations might do well than copy, especially number 2.

A list of members came next in the book. among them are many familiar names but, alas, all of the first members have gone to their last long homes. The name of Mrs. Henry Smith heads the list. She was the wife of Henry Smith who was at that time agent for the Westbrook Manufacturing Company. Her maiden name was Sally Maynard. She was born in Jamaica, W.I. She was a sister of Mrs. Neal Dow and a woman of keen intellect and much force of character. It was stated in the constitution that the society should be non-sectarian, and evidently it lived up to the letter of its creed, for the next name is that of Mrs. Benjamin Roberts, a woman as pronounced a Universalist in her way as Mrs. Smith was a Congregationalist. Mrs. Roberts was the mother of the late B. F. Roberts. Mrs. Levi Pierce follows, (she, too, an ardent Universalist), whose death occurred a few months since at her home on Stevens Ave., Deering District, in the house in which she was born, where she had lived since leaving Westbrook, which she did after the death of the husband who was in business under the firm name of North and Pierce on the corner now occupied by the Edwards Block, and whose successor, Lewis W. Edwards lives. Mrs. Benjamin Woodman, the mother of the late Charles B. Woodman, a pronounced Methodist, comes next in order. Then we read Mrs. Joseph Walker. Mr. and Mrs. Walker occupied the house just west of the high school building, which house Mr. Walker built. He afterwards removed to Portland and lived for many years on High Street next to the Congress Street Church. Westbrook has cause to reverse his memory for he gave to her the Walker Memorial Library. And if Westbrook has cause for gratitude, no less has Portland, for his generosity made possible the Manual Training school and the large addition to the Public Library, as large, in fact, as the first edifice. Mrs. Bryce Edwards, mother of Lewis W. Edwards, who died many years ago. After Mrs. Edwards comes the name of Mrs. Dan Carpenter (and the name is Dan, not Daniel as many typesetters insist) who removed to Portland many years ago but always hold a warm place in her heart for Westbrook friends as her frequent visits up to the very year of her death attested. Mr. Carpenter was also connected with the Westbrook Manufacturing Company. Mrs. Quinby was the mother of Mrs. H. H. B. Hawes and Mrs. Charles E. Quinby. Mrs. John Merrill, a most faithful attendant, Mrs. Rufus King and also Mrs. Cyrus King, well remembered figures whose deaths occurred only a few years ago.

Then follows Mrs. Deacon Akers. Mrs. Akers was the mother of Paul Akers, the sculptor, whose Pearl Diver is in the Portland Public Library. They lived in a house on Pork Hill, now the property of the S.D.Warren Company.

Mrs. Sewall Brackett, another well-remembered name as prominent in her day in the Congregational Church as are today her daughters, Mrs. Abbie B. Stackpole and Mrs. George H. Raymond. Mrs. Hayes, the wife of Deacon Hayes who lived out a long life in the house on the corner of Bridge and Brown Streets. The next name is Mrs. Marrett, the wife of Dr. Marrett, who lived and died in the Marrett house, corner of Main and Church Streets. Mrs. Marrett lived to the advanced age of 91, dying in 1901, February 14.

Mrs. James Walker is next on the list. She was the wife of Deacon Walker of the Congregational Church and was known as Auntie Walker to everyone in town. She was an intensely patriotic woman and did much in our Civil War. Long before Memorial Day she set apart to day to decorate the graves of those who had fallen in their Country's aid who were buried in Saccarappa cemetery. And now that she herself has become one of "the great majority," Cloudman Post every Memorial Day pays loving tribute to her by decorating her grave, not only with a bouquet but the place is also marked with a soldiers' flag. There are many other names added from time to time, but as far as I can learn, Mrs. Catherine B. Warren is the only person living. She it is who has the Bible in her keeping. It was given her by Mrs. Leonard Bond, the last secretary. It is Mrs. Warren's intention to cut this little account from the Sunday Telegram, paste it in the Bible, and give the book to the Walker Memorial Library for safe keeping.

It is most interesting to read of the meetings. The society never meets at the home of Mrs. So and So, but always of Mr. So and So. The first officers recorded are First directress, Mrs. Henry Smith; second directress, Mrs. B. Roberts; secretary and treasurer, Ellen Mosher; managers, Mrs. Pierce, Mrs. Woodman, Mrs.Akers, Mrs.J. Roberts; examining committee, Mrs. Deacon Walker, Mrs. John Brown.

There must have been months, perhaps even years, when they did not meet, for there seems to have been no records from 1846 to 1850. There are full records of 1850, '51 and '52. The annual report is interesting. It is very full, showing every cent received and also paid out. They evidently had a way of meeting and sewing on garments to be given away. If, however, a member wished to devote the afternoon to her own work, or not to sew, she paid three cents into the treasury and sometimes six cents. The list of articles to be given away is long and sounds rather strange. The list for 1851 includes quite a quantity of linsey woolsey, factory cloth, shoes, cradle quilts, undergarments, sheets and pillow cases, hose, shawls, calico, medicine, and last but not least, money.

The last record is September, 1853. Evidently the society was declining whereas in 1846 it numbered 58. It now has but 37. Mrs. Bond, the secretary, reports 22 meetings, the whole amount of money received $40.23, with a balance in the treasury of $17.82. The articles given the last year are mostly money and barrels of flour. Flour was cheaper than it is today as $4.75 is the price recorded. The society probably did not meet regularly again, the last record ending "meet in two weeks at the house of Mr. Walker to choose officers for the ensuing year."

If these officers were ever chosen there is no record made in this book at least. And in 1859 there is a record of a well organized and evidently not new, church circle in the Congregational Church and probably the other churches also, for early in the Civil War all societies here had circles or mission bands which did much for the good of the cause.

Pioneers in a worthy cause, it seems but fitting that some record should be left of the Martha Washington Charitable Society of Saccarappa.

(Copied from the newspaper clipping
pasted into the front of the Bible)

—A—

Abbott
 Thomas S., 199
Adams
 Albert, 208
 Eleanor Newton, 95
 John, 95, 192
 John Greenleaf, 112, 140
 John, President, 68
 Mark, 186
 Myron A., 151
 Sally, 117
 Silas N., Rev., 127
Adams' carriage shop, 192
Akers
 Paul, 101
 Sally, 118
 Thomas, 203
 William, 117, 118, 120
Albany, Maine, 31
Alden
 Charles, 40
 Nancy Quimby, 40
Alen
 Brothers, 135
Allen
 Hope, 81
 John M., 189
 John N., 191
Allen family, 192
Allen's Corner, 139
Ames, Charles T., 27
Amesbury, Mass., 39
Ammoncongin, 6, 8, 10, 38, 47, 210
 Falls, 88
 Old farm, 8
 Planting ground, 9
Anderson
 Abraham, 201
 Edward, Col., 105
 Family, 201
 Montgomery, 102, 187
 Sally Babb, 102
 Samuel, 195
 Sisters, 187
Andersonville Stockade, 176
Andres, Nancy M., 124
Andrews
 Charles R., 188
 Jerry R., 188, 189
 Nancy M., 132
 Stephen, 150
Androscoggin, 10
Armstrong, Edward, 47
Ash Street, 118
Ashbury, Francis, 133
Ashby, John L., 123
Austin, Lydia, 204, 205
Ayer, Albion P., 135
Ayres, Wilson, 114

—B—

Babb
 Abigail Freeman, 100
 Adaline P., 101
 Alexander, 99
 Almira Jordan, 100
 Anna Conant, 102
 Anna Haskell, 102
 Apphia, 101
 Bailey, 101
 Betsey, 99
 Betsey Hawkes, 101
 Betsy, 117
 Caroline, 99
 Charles, 101
 Charlotte, 101
 Cyrus K., 101
 Daniel, 99, 100
 David Webster, 166, 100
 Edward, Mayor, 100
 Elias, 101
 Eliza Jones, 101
 Elizabeth, 37, 99, 100, 117

Elizabeth Conant, 55, 99, 100
Elizabeth Webb, 54, 100
Elizabeth Wescott May, 100
Ellen, 99
Emily, 99
Emily Small, 100
Esther Wescott, 99
Etta, 207
Fred W., 100, 166
George, 99, 100
Hannah Thurlow, 101
Harlan P., 100
Harriet, 101
Harriet Farmer, 101
Henry, 98, 100
Henry C., 101, 135
Henry S., 101
Henry, Capt., 54
Howard S., 100
Isaac G., 37
Isaac W., 101
James, 37, 60, 98, 100, 102
Jane, 101
Jesse B., 101
Joanna, 99, 117
Joanna Libby, 102
John, 98, 100, 101, 102
Joseph, 101, 102, 187, 192
Josiah, 102
Judith, 98
Lemuel, 101
Lewis, 99
Lois Walker, 60
Louise T., 99
Lucy, 100
Lucy Bailey, 100, 102
Margaret, 101, 136
Maria, 99
Mark, 102
Marshall L., 101
Mary, 100, 102
Mary Ann, 99
Mary L., 101

Mary W., 99
Melissa Libby, 99
Miriam, 102
Moses, 205
Nathaniel, 98, 102
Nelson, 100
Oren, 99
Peter, 98, 100, 102
Peter, Jr., 101
Philene, 102
Philip, 98, 102
Rebecca Proctor, 101, 136
Rebecca Skillings, 102
Rhoda, 101, 102
Sally, 102
Samuel C., 99
Samuel S., 102
Sarah, 99, 100, 101
Smith, 90, 99
Solomon, 99, 100
Stephen, 99, 163
Susan, 102
Tabitha Darling, 102
Thomas, 98
W. Scott, 99
Warren P., 102
William, 37, 98, 99
William A., 101, 190
William, Jr., 99, 100
Zebulon, 102
Back Cove, 8, 12, 47, 68, 81
Bacon
   Edward E., Rev., 125
   Gardner, 100
   Jane Plummer, 100
Bagaduce, 50
Bagnall, Walter, 5
Bailey
   Daniel, 31
   David, 100
   Jane, 54
   John, 38, 110
   Lucy, 100, 102
   Mill, 56

Baker
  John C., 204, 206
  Susannah Brackett, 82
Bakerstown, 60
Ballad, Rev. Dr., 10
Bancroft, Keziah Brackett, 84
Bangor Theological Seminary, 151
Barbour
  Adam, 77
  Herbert D., 12
  John, 12
  Margaret, 96
Barker
  Eliza, 188
  William, Capt., 191
Barker's Tavern, 118
Barrett, Charles E., 198
Bates College, 151
Bayley
  John, 13
  Joseph, 64
  Lydia, 64
Bean
  John E., 207
  Mary A., Dry Good and Millinery, 188
Bears, 5
Beasley, John, 190
Beaver Dam Brook, 5
Beaver Pond, 5
Beaver Road, 5
Beberly, Mass., 36
Beckwith, George C., Pastor, 119
Berry, George, Capt., 45, 47
Best
  John L., 102
  Martin W., 102
  Miriam Babb, 102
  Tritten, 102
  William, 188
Bethel, 140

Bettes
  F. A., 102
  W. F., 192
  William R., Mrs., 40
Beverly
  Daniel, 107
  Elizabeth, 107
  Mary Webb, 107
Bickford
  Abner G., 124, 131
  Lydia, 59
  Salome, 124, 131
Birch Hill, 90, 104
Birney
  Elizabeth Pearson, 70
  Joseph, 70
Bishop
  E., 57
  Harvey, Jr., 114
  Nancy Hamblen, 57
Bixby, Jane, 205
Black William, 4
Blackley, Thomas, 98
Blacksmith, 42
Blacksmiths, 184, 192
Blackstrap, 75
Blair
  Benjamin, 203
  Sarah, 204, 205
Blake
  Edgar, 137
  Edgar, Mrs., 207
  Edward, 60
  John, 137
Blanchard, Addison B., Rev., 125, 132, 152
Bodge
  John, 104
  Rebecca Chute, 104
Bolster
  Freelan, Rev., 128
Bond Street, 158, 191
Boody
  Benjamin, 120

Charles E., 207
Nathan W., 38, 45, 68, 162
Boody house, 205
Boothby
  R. C., 184
  W. B., 191
Boston, 10
Boston & Maine, 3
Boston School of Theology, 151
Bowdoin College, 140, 179
Bowler, S. L., Rev., 124, 125
Boxford, 14
Boyd
  Agnes, 113
  James, 113
Boynton, Theophilus, 134
Brackett
  Abigail Chapman, 81, 82
  Abigail Reed, 85
  Abraham, 81, 82
  Alton C., 82
  Ann Mitton, 81
  Anthony, 44, 49, 81-83
  Barnabas, 85
  Charles, 40, 187
  Charlotte, 40
  Dower, 83
  Elizabeth, 84
  Esther Cox, 82
  Genealogy, 49
  Happy, 84
  Herbert L., 49
  James, Dr., 82, 84
  Jane, 81
  Jane Cobbey, 65
  Jane Warren, 83
  Joanna Springer, 81
  John, 48, 49, 83, 84
  John Snow, 82
  Joseph, 85
  Joshua, 65, 81, 82, 83, 84
  Judith Sawyer, 82
  Keziah, 84
  Lucy, 84
  Mary, 44, 46, 48, 82, 84
  Mary Fabyan, 83
  Mary Mitton, 81, 83
  Mary Snow, 82
  Nathaniel, 84
  Richard, 49
  Sally, 84
  Samuel, 82, 84
  Sarah, 40, 44, 65, 81, 83, 84
  Sarah Bangs, 85
  Sarah Knight, 83
  Sarah Lamb, 65
  Sewall, 85, 193
  Susannah, 82
  Tabitha, 82
  Thomas, 45, 46, 47, 81, 82, 83, 84
  Widow Kerenhappuck Hicks, 83
  William, 77, 83
  Zachariah Bangs, 81, 82, 84, 85
Brackett Street, 84, 191, 193
Brackett's Company, 75
Brackett, Thomas, 77
Bradbury, Horace J., Rev., 193
Bradley
  Caleb, Rev., 26, 55, 66, 109, 117, 119
  Sarah R., 207
Braintree, 10
Bramhall farm, 81
Brewer, Ernest, 208
Brewster, William, Elder, 33
Bridge Street, 32, 38, 100, 119, 148, 153, 165, 167, 169, 202
Bridges
  Great, 19
  Saccarappa, 19, 20
Bridgewater, 185
Bridgton, 197

Brigham, Dana, 141, 162, 190
Brimblecomb, Samuel, 139, 140
Bristol, 107
Britannia ware, 181
Brooks, Harry D., 209
Brown
  Daniel, 195
  Dorcas, 118
  Edwin L., 209
  George D., 132
  John, 165, 193
  Maggie, 113
  Melissa, 132
  Thomas, Rev., 59
  William P., 151
Brown house, 190
Brown Street, 32, 153, 154, 166, 167, 168
Browne
  George, 135
  Thomas, Rev., 26, 38, 61
Brunswick, 10
Bryant, J. B., 114
Bryson
  Elizabeth, Mrs., 113
  Robert, 168
  Robert, Mrs., 113
Buckfield, 50
Bucknam, William, 27
Bunker, Harriet L., 107
Burbank
  Eleazer, 84
  Mary Brackett, 84
Burnham, Aaron, 41
Burroughs, A. H., 191
Button, Nanaadonit, Waraad, 18
Butts, Samuel, 104
Buxton, 185, Lt., 77
Buxton Road, 37, 98, 102

—C—

Calais, Maine, 31
Canada, 193
  Bolton, 87
Canal Bank, 198
Canal Company, 197
Canned corn factory, 97
Cape Elizabeth, 4, 60, 63
Capisic, 6, 8, 26, 42, 55, 65, 87, 100, 117, 119, 127
Capisic River, 3
Capisic Street, 143
Cargile, John A., 151
Carlton
  P. J., Hon., 101
  Sarah Smith Babb, 101
Carter
  Albert N., Mrs., 207
  Edwin R., Rev., 129
Casco Bay, 4, 6, 8
Casco Fort, 62
Casco House, 67
Cash, Jenness, 188
Cassidy, Bertha E., 152
Cemeteries
  Conant, 29, 53, 66
  Haskell, 25
  Saccarappa, 21, 40, 54, 55, 118, 204
  Scotch Hill, 22, 30
  St. Hyacinthe, 90, 154
  Stroudwater, 39, 211
  Woodlawn, 22, 24, 30
Center Street, 91
Central Street, 187, 188, 192
Central Wharf, 71
Chadborne, William, 198
Chadbourne, Henry, 198
Chapman
  Abigail, 81
  Edward, 158
  Ruth, 38

Chase
- Captain, 203
- George, 91
- Leonard, 191
- Leroy, 208
- Lydia Shove, 91

Chatham, Harriet, 113

Chesley
- Fanny Hamblen, 57
- Isaac, 57

Chestnut Street, 166

Chicago, 10

Christian Endeavor Society, 115

Christian Hill, 136

Church of England, 98

Church Street, 5, 191, 134-136

Churches
- Advent Christians, 150, 152
- Baptist Church of Dighton, Mass., 113
- Baptist, 113-115, 165, 190
- Bishops, 136
- Capisic, 31
- Central Church of Portland, 130
- Christian Endeavor, 116
- Church of England, 148
- Clegymen/Methodist, 137
- Congregational Church of Cumberland Mills, 115
- Congregational, 26, 66, 109, 110, 127, 130, 167
- Cumberland Baptist Association, 115
- Farther Lights Circle, 115
- First Baptist Church of Westbook, 116
- First Baptist of Portland, 113
- First Catholic mass, 153
- First Church of Westbrook, 119
- First Congregational Church of Westbrook, 117, 211
- First minister at Capisic, 38
- First Parish, 12, 26
- First Universalists Society, 140, 143, 146
- Fourth Congregational, 26
- Fourth Parish of Falmouth, 211
- Freewill Baptists, 135
- French-American, 155
- Immaculate Conception of Portland, 153
- Irish-American, 155
- Methodist Episcopal, 133
- Methodist, 191, 207
- Mt. Vernon of Boston, 130
- Nuns of Presentation of Mary, 154
- Old Iron Works, 135
- Old South Church of Boston, 130
- Old Universalist, 188
- Parson Bradley's, 142
- Philathea Class, 116
- Sebago Lake Chapel, 131
- Second Congregational Church of Westbrook, 118, 121
- Sister's Home, 154
- Sisters of Mercy of Portland, 155
- Sisters of St. Francis, 156
- Sociable of the Westbrook Congregational Church, 212
- St. Mary's, 156, 190
- St. Paul's, 148
- St. Hyacinthe, 153, 155
- State Street Methodist, 137
- Third Congregational Church of Portland, 119

Trinity Church of Boston, 131
Unitarian, 139
Univeralism, 123, 139
Universalist Church, 112, 186, 190, 191, 193
Warren Church, 187
Warren Congregational, 132
Warren Parish, 130
Warren, 124
Wesley Chapel, 134
Westbrook Congregational, 130, 166, 189, 191
Young Peoples Society, 116, 131
Chute
  Herbert R., 184
  Rebecca, 104
  Thomas, 104
  Thomas, Capt., 19
City of Westbrook, 158
Civil War, 193
Clapp, Asa, 195
Clark, Robert, 137
Clark Street, 197
Clay, Hanso, 189
Clements
  Betsey, 118
  Jerry, 192
  Leander, 192
  Samuel, 162, 189
Cleve, George, 81
Cloice
  Heirs, 31
  Thomas, 21
Cloudman
  Ella, 126
  Esther, 40
  Frank H., 141
  John, 141, 190
  Josiah, 102
  Paul, 141
  Reliance, 40
  Solomon, 196
  Susan Babb, 102
Cloudman Street, 113
Cloudman, Frank H., 131
Coal Kiln Corner, 59
Cobb
  Charles E., 207
  Ebenezer, 46, 67, 68
  Elizabeth, 203
  Enoch B., 99
  Frank, 203
  Henry S., 191
  Hope, 96
  Isaac, 39
  Marrett, 120
  Mr., 113
  Oliver A., 204
  Sarah F. Babb, 99
  William, 25, 39
Cobbey, Jane, 65
Codman
  George, 167
  George C., 148
Coe, Helen, 175
Coffin, Nathaniel, Dr., 16, 24
Coke, Thomas, Bishop, 133
Colby, Lucy, 204
Colley
  Deering, 74
  Molly Frink, 74
  Mr., 77
Collins, Mary, 35
Commercial Street, 71, 177
Conant
  Anna, 102
  Anna Frink, 15
  Anna Haskell, 25
  Barthelomew, 15, 16, 69, 75
  Brothers, 38
  Daniel, 37, 110
  Elizabeth, 14, 37, 55, 99, 100
  Eunice, 75
  Hannah, 14

Hannah Worcester, 36
John, 27
Joseph, 13-16, 19, 21, 36, 46, 62, 67-69
Lot, 14, 15
Mary Peabody, 36, 37
Roger, 14
Samuel, 15, 27, 36, 37, 53, 107
Sarah, 14
Susan S., 26, 49, 83, 84
Thomas, 14, 15
William, 37, 38
Conant Street, 38
Conant,
  Mary, 38
  Samuel, 38
Congin, 6, 204
Connecticut, Killingly, 123
Connely, Mary, 100
Cooper
  Claim, 9, 15, 18, 27, 28
  Thomas, 18
Cordwell
  Stephen A., 124, 131
  Stephen E., 132
Cornish, 7
Corporation Boat, 197
County Commissioner, 62
County Road, 63, 68, 209
Cousens, Lyman M., 178
Cousins
  Edgar M., Rev., 131, 132
  Ralph, 137
Coverly, Mary, 54, 55
Cox
  Esther, 82
  John, 46, 47, 82
  Sarah Proctor, 46
  William, 100
Craig, A. T., 137
Cressey, William, 77
Crocker, Ira, 195

Crockett
  James, Dr., 197
  Sally, 57
Cross
  Abigail Webb, 63
  Isaac, 190
  Mary Munjoy Lawrence, 9
  Stephen, 9
  William W., Hon., 63, 64
Culbert, William J., 156
Cumberland and Oxford Canal, 195
Cumberland and Oxford Corporation, 198
Cumberland Block, 135
Cumberland County, 157
  Sherif, 69, 70
Cumberland County Registry of Deeds, 13, 21, 57
Cumberland Hall, 175
Cumberland Mills, 2, 6, 65, 172
  White House, 65
Cumberland Street, 111, 202
Cummings, Mary, 113
Cushing
  Ezekiel, Col., 20
  Mehitable, 100
Customs House, 144
Cutter
  Abbie, 204
  Herbert, 187
  Simon, 192
  Simon, Col., 135
  William W., 125, 189
Cutter, Abial, Capt., 139

—D—

D'Arche, Dr., 191
Dana
  John S., 177
  Luther, 116, 179
  Philip, 179

Richard, 19
Richard Henry, 162
Woodbury K., 41, 54, 125, 128, 177, 178
Dana Warp Mill, 13, 30, 32, 41, 56, 165, 168, 170, 177
Dye-House, 32
Gingham Mill, 32
Danielson, Joseph, Rev., 123, 125, 127
Darling, Tabitha, 102
Dary
Albert N., 113
Carrie E., 113
Davies, Edward H., 167
Davis
Apphia, 204
George R., 188
Jim, 205
Day
Mrs., 39
Preston, 203
Dean, Lee Maltbie, Rev., 127
Deane
Eunice Pearson, 70
Journals, 16
Rev. Dr., 54, 70
Debeck, John, 190
Debeck house, 187
Decelles, A. D., Father, 153,
Declaration of Independence, 210
Deer Hill, 19, 26, 47, 65, 86, 87
Deer Isle, 50, 58
Deering, 4, 47, 142, 145
Nathaniel, 73
Deering, 139
Democrats, 144
Dennett, Charles W., 167
Depot Street, 192
Desjardins, Father, 154
Dillingham, Mr., 185
Diran, Caroline Murch, 166

Dodgeon, Thaddeau L., 102
Dole
Daniel, 38, 70, 71, 210
Olive, 204
P. C., 204
Sarah, 38
Sarah Pearson, 71, 210
Dorchester, 181
Dow, Fred, 167
Doyle, Edward, 155
Drake, Francis S., 75
Dresser, Stephen M., 168
Duck Mill, 165
Duck Pond, 15, 38, 63, 69, 75, 162, 163
Duck Pond Brook, 163
Duck Pond Stream, 44
Duclos Block, 119
Dugree, Alexandre, Father, 154
Duke of Wellington, 133
Dunham
Frederick, 183
John, 181
Joseph, 183
Robert, 181, 182
Rufus, 181
Dunn
A. T., Rev., 113, 114
J. K., 192
John, 190
Marcia, 208
Dunn Street, 190, 207
Dunstan, 98, 158
Dunstan Landing, 157
Dunster, Henry, Rev., 148
Durham, 14, 29
Dwight, M. T., Rev., 119
Dyer
David, 102, 187
Isaac, 199
Mary Babb, 102
Michael, 25
Rachel, 25

—E—

Early settlements, 4
Early settlers:
　Proctor, Barbour, Thomas, Wass, Doughty, Rounds, Mills, Hall, Scales, Coller, 12
East
　John, 89, 90
　Mary, 89
East Bridge Street, 2, 45
East Limington, 31
Eastman Store, 187
Eaton, Joseph, 114
Edwards
　Brice M., 117, 118, 121, 122, 124
　Bryce M., 191
　Bryce M., Jr., 189
　Lewis W., 118, 119, 191, 121, 210
Electric power house, 38
Elm Street, Portland, 39
Elwell
　Benjamin, 190
　Washburn, 187
Emery, Stephen, 190
England, 157
　Abbottaham in Devonshire, 9
　London, 50
　Redrift, 50
Episcopalians, 83, 127
Essex County, Mass., 35
Evans, Charles, 135

—F—

Fabyan
　Joshua, 84
　Mary, 83
　Sarah Brackett, 84

Factory Village, 84
Fairchild, Charles, 173
Falmouth, 4, 6, 8-10, 12, 13-16, 18-32, 35-37, 39, 41, 42, 44-47, 49-51, 53, 59, 60, 62-64, 66-71, 73-77, 82, 83, 87-91, 93, 96, 102, 104, 107, 109, 111, 117, 133, 157, 165, 195, 202, 205
　Neck, 12, 16, 42, 44, 62, 67, 69, 87
　Old, 59, 81, 83, 93, 157
　Proprietors', 13, 18, 45, 47, 97
　Selectmen, 13
Falmouth Social Library, 32, 42
Farley, William C., 208
Farmer, Harriet, 101
Farmsworth, Everett L., 137
Farrar
　Bethiah, 52
　Hannah Worcester, 107
　Isaac, 106
　John, 52, 105, 106, 107
　Persis Holbrook, 107
Farrow
　John, 52
　John Pendleton, 106
Father Bogardtz, 153
Fellowbee, Robert, 136
Fellows, Abigail, 35
Felt
　George, 18
　Neale, 18
Female Charitable Society, 212
Fenderson
　Fred, 83
　M. Fred, 53
Ferris, Agnes, 113
Fick, Oscar, 99
Fickett, Samuel, 159

Files
  Adeline, 99
  Alton N., 99
  Caroline Babb, 99
  Peter L., 124
  Peter W., 131
  Sargent S., 99
  Walton N., Mrs., 207
Finn, John J., 156
First National Bank, 71
First Parish Church, 63, 71
First Schoolhouse, 202
Fitch
  Almira, 71
  Judge, 72
  Luther, 71, 198
Fitch Street, 54, 119
Flucker
  Hannah Waldo, 92
  Lucy, 94
  Thomas, 92, 94, 95
Fluent Block, 101
Fogg, Edward, 190
Fore River, 14, 195
Fore Street, 44
Forest Avenue, 117
Forrest, Isabella, 113
Fort Hill, 134, 201
Fort Loyal, 6, 8
Foss
  Carrie Manchester, 201
  V. R., 114
Foster
  Abiel, 169
  Asahel, 84
  Lucy Brackett, 84
  Mr., 66
  Rebecca, 117, 118
Foster and Brown Machine
  Shop, 178, 188
Foster Street, 136, 190
Foster's Dye House, 169
Four Corners, 202
Fowler, Henry J., 145

Foye, Annie, 124, 132
Freeman
  Abigail, 100
  Benjamin, 33, 59, 203, 204, 206
  Betsey Webb, 59
  Enoch, 15, 69, 89
  Enoch, Jr., 29, 30, 100
  Enoch, Major, 28, 67
  Eunice Seavey, 59
  Hannah Atwood, 30
  Joshua, 70
  Josiah, 59
  Lois Pearson, 70
  Lydia, 24, 30
  Lydia Sparrow, 34
  Mary, 118, 204
  Mehitable, 117
  Mehitable Cushing, 100
  Nathaniel, Capt., 33
  Widow, 32
  William, 30, 34
Freeman's, Widow, 166
Freese, Hannah, 34
French
  Embassador, 76
  Nathaniel, 204
  Orrin S., 150, 151
French King, 69
Frink
  Anna, 15
  John, 74
  Molly, 74
  Samuel, 74
Frost
  Apphia Babb, 101
  James, 101
Frye
  Anna March, 49
  Dean, 49
  Eunice, 109, 117, 144
  Eunice, Home, 211
  John M., Col., 49
  William P., 49

Frye's Island, 56
Frye, Eunice, 142
Fitch Street, 192
Fuller, Levi, Master, 205
Fullerton, Jeremiah E., 132
Fulsome, Levi, 204, 205
Fur-bearing animals, 5

—G—

Gage, Leander, 195
Galdhill, Isabella, 132
Garrison House, 159
Garvin, Master, 204
Georges River, 94
Gerrish, Charles, 27, 28
Gerry
   Dorothy March, 49
   Jacob, 49
   Peletiah, 49
Gettysburg, 107
Gibbons, Rey, Rev., 129
Gibbs, Lois, 60
Gibson, Richard, 133
Gilman
   Ebenezer, 86
   Edward, 86, 88
   John, 86
   John T., 141
Gilson, Richard, 147
Girard, F. X., 192
Gladhill, Isabel, 124
Gleason, Roswell, 181
Gloucester, 21, 24, 34, 85
Godfrey
   Benjamin, 27, 104
   Daniel, 26, 27, 28, 29, 52, 105, 161
   Joseph, 27
   Lydia, 34
   Richard, 34
   Sarah, 27
Goodell
   George, 168
   John, 59
   Louise, 109
   Mary, 109
   Polly Webb, 59
   Reginald, 109
Goodell family, 201
Gooding, Mary, 49
Goodwin, Mary, 49
Goold
   Benjamin, 100
   Moses, 86
   Sarah, 100
Gorham, 84, 186, 200
   David, 53
   First Settlement, 36
   Grist Mill, 36
Gorham Road, 83, 84
Gorhamtown, 53
Gorrie, Leroy T., 137
Gowen Family, 69
Gower, Harriet, 188
Graf's Meat Market, 125
Graffam
   Caleb, 107
   Eugene, 190
Graham
   Elizabeth, 131
   James, 124, 131
   Lizzie J., 124
Grand Trunk Station, 6
Grant
   James, 110
   Stephen, 203
Grant and Lyon, 172
Grant, Daniel & Co., 172
Graves, William, Rev., 119
Gray, 30, 45, 74, 177
   First school teacher, 33
Great Falls, 102, 196
Great Walt, 4
Greenwood, M. G., 119
Griggs, H. K., 204
Gustin, George E., 12

—H—

Hacker
  Hattie, 207
  Isaiah, 204
Haggett, Captain, 16
Hale, J. L., 119
Hale family, 192
Halidon, 2
Hall
  Charity, 96
  Dr., 191
  E. S., Dr., 166
  Hate-evil, 96
  Rachel, 204
  Susannah, 44
  W., 204, 206
Hamblen
  Bethiah Webb, 57
  David, 57
  Dennis, 57
  Dorothy, 57
  Fanny, 57
  Joseph, 57
  Katy, 57
  Nancy, 57
  Prince, 54, 57, 58
  Sally Crockett, 57
  Samuel, 57
  Solomon, 57
Hamel, A. A., Father, 154
Hammond, , George W., 124, 131
J. Albert, 128
Hannaford
  Green, 63
  Mary Webb, 63
Hanson
  Benjamin, 188
  Cordelia, 185
  William, 185
Hanson shoe repair, 188

Harding
  Edward, 101
  Irene, 187
Hardy, Lewis, 135
Harmon
  Adalbert R., 166
  William Valentine, 166
Harpswell, 130
Harris
  Nathan, 135, 204
  Rebecca, 204, 205
Harrison, 197
Harrison, Maine, 84
Harrow House, 159
Harvard College, 67, 139
Haskell
  Abigail Libby, 25
  Alexander, 35
  Anna, 25, 102
  Barri, 25, 30, 31, 32
  Benjamin, 21, 22, 25, 30, 31, 33, 35, 36, 39, 84, 102, 110, 211
  Catherine, 25
  Catherine Jordan, 31
  Daniel, 102
  Deacon, 121
  Dexter, 90
  Edwin J., 35, 100, 120, 127, 169, 170
  Eugenia, 191
  Frank, 35, 167, 169, 170
  Grist Mill, 31, 32
  Hannah, 25, 31
  Hannah Freese, 34
  James, 35, 167, 169, 170
  John, 25, 39
  Lucy, 25
  Lydia, 22, 23, 30, 31, 33
  Mark, 25, 110, 134, 135
  Mary, 25, 33, 35, 39
  Mary Riggs, 21
  Mary Tybbott, 34
  Mary White, 25

Moses, 30
Nathaniel, 87, 124, 135
Parsons, 25, 31
Polly Partridge, 34
Rachel, 25
Reuben, 25
Roger, 21, 34
Sally Berry, 25
Sally March, 48
Sarah, 31
Sarah Brackett Fabyan, 84
Sarah Pike, 36
Solomon, 20, 22, 25, 34, 39, 56, 87, 110, 190, 211
Solomon, Jr., 25, 48, 84, 110
Thomas, 21, 22, 24, 25, 26, 27, 30, 31, 34, 39, 46, 52, 90, 102, 109, 110, 211
Walter F., 128, 148
William, 25, 30, 31, 34
Haskell Household, 184
Haskell Silk Mill, 35, 168, 169, 170,
Haskell Street, 90
Haskell, Deacon, 26
Hatch
   Capt., 112
   Hannah Johnson, 104, 105
   J. W., 114
   N., Capt., 105, 134
   Nathaniel, 111, 134, 136
   Sarah Newcomb, 136
   Sisters, 28
Hawkes
   Abner L., 84
   Ann, 204
   Betsey, 101
   E. Leory, 137, 187
   Ferdinand, 28
   Joshua Lowell, 201
   Louise, 204
   Wesley M., 188
Hawthorne, Nathaniel, 105

Hay, Harry F. G., 126, 128
Hayes
   David, 118, 120, 121, 123, 124
   David G., 30, 32
   George, 135
   Nancy, 117
Hazelton, Joseph H., 168
Healy, James A., Rev., 153
Henderson, John, 167
Henshaw, Mehitabel, 136
Hicks,
   Kerenhappuck, Widow, 83
   Samuel, 77
Hide, William, 88
Higgins, Enoch, Dea., 119
Highland House, 188
Highland Lake, 15, 162
Hills, Louis, Dr., 191
Hilton
   Margaret, 113
   Roger, 113, 114
Hinds, Walter, 158
Hodgkins
   Charles Edwin, 107
   Freeland D., 108
   George Freeland, 107
   John Webb, 107
   Leonard Franklin, 107
Hodgkins
   Deborah Crandell, 107
   Ebenezer, 107
   Mary Webb, 107
Hodsdon, Minnie, 208
Holbrook
   Bethiah, 106
   Persis, 106
   William, Capt., 106
Holden, Nathan, 120
Hollowell, Elizabeth, 208
Holston, William H., 59, 131
Holt, Hannah, 31
Honest Quaker, 198
Hopkinson, Stephen, 191

Horr
    Adeline Files, 99
    J. L., Dr., 99
Horse Beef, 159
Horsebeef Falls, 105
Hospital
    Thomas and Guy, 16
Howard, Judge, 85
Howe, Nathaniel, 195
Hudson, Dorr A., Rev., 128
Hughes, Clarence A., 190
Hunnewell
    Andrew, 62
    Dorothy Webb, 62
    Hannah, 34
    Zerubabel, Hannah, 24
Hunt
    Ichabod, 86, 88
    Mary Haskell, 33
    Nathan, 114
    Nathaniel, 33
Huston, Annie, 96

—I—

Ida May, 43
Ilsley
    Dr., 115
    George B., Dr., 114
    Isaac, 71
India Street, 89
Indian Wars, 83
Indians
    Abnakis, 3
    Abnekis, 5
    Aucociscos, 5
    First deed, 6
    Fishing, 11
    Language, 10
    Planting ground, 3, 8, 9, 11
    Polin, 5
    Sacarabeag, 3
    Sagamore, 3, 6, 10, 18
    Squitterrygusset, 4, 6, 18

Industry, 157, 159
Ingalls, E. C., Rev., 125
Ingersoll
    Benjamin, 13, 47
    Daniel, 28
    Deborah, 62
    Governor, 12
    John, 28, 62
    Nathaniel, 64
Iron industry, 42
Iron production, 41
Isaac, A. E., 114
Island of Saccarappa Falls, 178
Isleborough, 106

—J—

Jack, David, Rev., 151
Jack Downing, 198
Jackson
    Thomas, 54
Jameson
    Bethany Webb, 63
    Ruth Webb, 63
Japanned ware, 181
Jewett
    Hannah, 14
    Henry, 203
    Henry C., 109, 119
    Sarah, 14
    Thomas, 14
Hay, 189
Johnson
    Anna Quinby, 104, 105
    Benjamin, 104
    Charles, 104
    Elizabeth, 118
    Francis, 105
    Gardner, 104
    George, 28, 104, 105
    Hannah, 105, 117
    Hannah Hatch, 104
    James, 104, 211
    Jane, 83

Jeremiah, 104, 105
John, 104
Nancy, 105
Robert, 27, 104, 105
Rufus, 5, 104, 122, 135
Sam, Rev., 119
Jones
  Benjamin, Dr., 78
  Beverly, 78
  Eliza, 101
  Elizabeth, 14, 42, 54, 70
  Ephraim, 42
  Ezekial, 14
  Jane, 204
  John, Capt., 143
  Lydia, 78
  Mary Pearson, 70
Jordan
  Almira, 100
  Caroline, 205
  Dominicus, 119
  George A., 187
  Jonathan, 100
  Robert, 147
  Rufus K., 126, 205
  Samuel, 144
Jose, Nathaniel, 102
Judge of the court of Common Pleas, 70
June, Adrian T., Rev., 115

—K—

Kearney:, 151
Keddy, Edward E., 132
Kellogg, Elijah, 30, 130, 132
Kennebec Street, 117
Kennington, Thomas W., 151
Kent's Hill, 135
Kents Lock, 196
Kerr, William, 168
Kimball, John W., 167
King
  Caroline, 204
  Cyrus, 188
  Miss, 206
  Richard, 158
  Rufus, 188, 205
King Farm, 170
King George II of England, 157
King Street, 89
King's Mark, 160
King's Mast Agents, 9
Knife factory, 186
Knight
  Betsey March, 49
  George, 28
  Henry, 211
  John, 158
  Johnson, 49
  Leland W., 188
  Nathan, 158
  Nathaniel, 26, 105, 158, 211
  Sarah, 83
  Walter V., 168
Knight Brothers, 189
Knight Farm, 60
Knowlton, John J., 137
Knowlton Machine Company, 137
Knox
  General, 95
  Hannah Waldo, 94
  Henry, 94
Knox County, 94

—L—

LaFond Department Store, 194
LaFond Estate, 194
Lamb
  John, 65
  Marrett, 47, 88
  Mary Haskell, 25
  Samuel, 65, 135
  Sarah, 65

William M., 86
William W., 88
William, Jr., 87
William, Mary, 26
Lancaster
  Lydia Jones, 78
  Thonas, Parson, 78
Land
  Early claims, 18
  Early settlers, 21
  Largest purchase, 18
Landslides
  Boody slide, 2, 3
  Cumberland Mills, 2
  Old cellar field, 4, 26
  Prehistoric, 3
Lane
  Charles, 191
  Charles W., 166
  Lemuel, 166, 170
Larrabee
  Abigail, 65
  Alfred H., 97
  Amy Pride, 62, 68
  Benjamin, 15, 62, 64, 65, 68, 86, 87
  Benjamin, Jr., 13, 30
  Captain, 12
  Catherine, 64
  Deborah Ingersoll, 62
  Elizabeth, 62, 63, 65, 68
  John, 65, 87
  Lydia Bayley, 64
  Mark, 87
  Mary Quimby, 40
  Sarah Brackett, 65
Larrabee, John, 159
Larraby, Benjamin, Jr., 88
Lary
  Elizabeth, 136
  Joseph, 198
Lawrence
  Mary Munjoy, 8
  Robert, 6, 8, 9

Lawrence & Horne, 169
Lawyers, 38
Leavitt
  Asa P., 141
  Leonora, 140
LeBel, Ernest, 155
Lee, Jesse, Rev., 110, 134
Leighton
  Paul, 87
  Phebe, 87
  Sarah, 62
Letherbee, Mary, 65
Lewis
  Archelaus, 32, 38, 110, 162, 210
  Francis, 210
  James, Elder, 112, 134
  Squire, 210
  Temperance, 57
Lewiston Bleachery and Dye Work, 168
Lewiston Falls Academy, 177
Libby
  Alice B., 127
  Alonzo, 90, 191
  David B., 101
  Elliot, 198
  Joanna, 102
  Joseph, 124, 197
  Joseph P., Deacon, 40
  Julia, 132
  Julia E., 124
  Lothrop, 197
  Mary L. Babb, 101
  Melissa, 99
  Nathan, 101
  Peter, 40
  Phoebe, 63
  Roscoe F., 111
  Simeon, 63
  Tamsin Quimby, 40
Libby house, 191
Limington, 7, 31

Lincoln, Mary F., 113
Lindsay, John, 198
Linehan, Father, 153
Little Falls, 59, 105, 159, 197
Livermore, Maine, 41
Liverpool, Nova Scotia, 30, 34
Lombard, Solomon, 149
London, Charles, 185, 188
London blacksmith shop, 188
Long Level, 197
Longfellow, 185
  Henry Wadsworth, 41
  Stephen, 89, 107
Longfellow Street, 5, 40, 190
Lord
  Abigail Webb, 62
  Elbridge, 62
  James, 63
  John, 62
  Lucy Webb, 63
Lord, Haskell Neal, 189
Louisburg Expedition, 69, 70
Lowell, John R., 127
Lower Falls, 159
Lower Guard Lock, 197
Luce, Israel, Rev., 137, 191
Lumber yard, 192
Lumbering, 157
Lunt
  Benjamin, 82
  Charity, 44
  Daniel, 15, 73, 74, 77
  Eunice Conant, 75
  John, 74
  Mary Brackett, 82
  Samuel, 74
  William, 22, 24, 44, 73, 74, 77
  William's ledger, 73, 82
Lynn, Mass., 44

—M—

MacDonald, Roderick A., 132

Main Street, 26, 38, 84, 90, 118, 156, 172, 184, 193
Maine
  Denmark, 85
  Durham, 107
  Minot, 107
  Naples, 87
  Otisfield, 87
Maine Central, 190
Maine Historical, 148
Maine State Advent Christian Conference, 150
Mallison Falls, 28, 105
Manchester
  Isaiah, 132
  Margaret S., 132
  Stephen, 5, 105, 201
Mann
  W. G., Rev., 128
  William F., 132
Manufacturing Nails, 59
March
  Abigail, 40, 45, 49
  Betsey, 49
  Dorothy, 49
  Edmund, 30, 48
  Edwin J., Col., 49
  Jane, 49
  John, 49
  Joseph, 49
  Mary Brackett, 48
  Mary Weare, 48, 49
  Peletiah, 48, 49, 84
  Polly, 48
Mariner, George F., 125
Market Street, 44
Marr
  Brothers, 169
  Dennis, 41
Marrett, William, Dr., 123, 148
Marston, John, 67

Martha Washington
  Charitable Society of
  Saccarappa, 212
Martin
  David, 132
  Noah R., Dr., 113, 184, 189
Mason
  Herbert, 175
  John, Capt., 83
  Lizzie, 113
  M. B., 173
Massachusetts
  Amesbury, 48
  Barnstable, 57, 70
  Boston, 60
  Cape Cod, 34
  Charlement, 128
  Charlestown, 83, 169
  Danvers, 44
  Dighton, 91
  Highham, 106
  Hingham, 51
  Hopkinson, 59
  General Court of, 8, 12, 195
  Gloucester, 21
  Ipswich, 44
  Lowell, 150
  Lynn, 139
  Middleton, 53
  Newbury, 69
  North Adams, 207
  Northampton, 129
  Old Salem, 44
  Rockport, 167
  Roxbury, 114
  Salisbury, 39
  Sharon, 139
  Stoughton, 55
  Sturbridge, 15
  Taunton, 91
  Weymouth, 51
  Waltham, 33

Massachusetts Society (of the Cincinnati), 75
Mast industry, 160
Maxfield, William, 53
Maxwell,, Clements P., 19, 65
May, Elizabeth Wescott, 100
Mayberry
  George, 192
  Philene Babb, 102
  Sally Brackett, 84
  Simon H., 87
  Susanna Webb, 50
  Thomas, 50, 84, 106
  William, 102, 106, 107
Mayflower, 33
Mayhew
  Lillian, 208
  Hebron, 188
Mayo, Ebenezer, 64, 88
Mayor of Westbrook, 155
McCann
  Carrie, 118
  Frank H., 118, 191
McCausland, Samuel, 47
McEwen, Thomas, 178
McFarland
  Earl K., 137
  Jane, 124, 131
McIntire, Mary, 51
McKay
  Letitia, 113
  Maggie, 113
  Mary, 113
McLellan
  Arthur, 195
  Colonel, 58
  Henry, 186
  Hugh D., Hon., 57
  Samuel E., 186, 192
  William R., 186
Meade, H. B., Rev., 189
Mechanics Fair, 181
Memorial Day, 189
Memorial Library, 32, 123

Men's Furnishing Store, 188
Merrill
  Abigail Brackett, 82
  Elias, 32, 33
  Jacob, 77
  James, 66, 82
  Ruth, 118
Methodist Lane, 190
Michigan, Hillsdale, 49
Middle Street, 67
Middleton, Mass., 36
Mill Brook, 46, 68, 162
Mill Lane, 166
Miller, Dr., 191
Millions
  Ellen R., 124, 131
  George, 124, 131
Millions, George, 203
Mills, 157, 178
  Bates, 177
  Bayley's, 27, 56
  Carding and fuling, 163
  Continental, 177
  Dana Warp, 27, 116, 179
  Double saw mill, 105
  Duck and denim, 177
  Duck Mill, 186
  Gingham mill, 166-168, 178
  Godfrey, 27
  Grist Mill, 8, 37, 159, 163
  Haskell Silk Mill, 136
  Keeler and Bailey
    underwear mill, 188
  Lewiston, 177
  Lincoln Cotton Mill, 177
  Lumber, 47
  Proctor, 45
  Quimby, 38
  Quinby's saw mill, 136
  S. D. Warren Paper, 130
  Saccarappa, 54
  Saw mills, 8, 13, 37, 38, 54, 56, 159, 161, 163
  Scottish worker, 166
  Strikes, 174
  Titcomb Saw Mill, 71
  Union, 174
  W. K. Dana & Co., 71
  Water Power, 54, 62, 71
Mississippi, 176
Mitchell
  William H., 150
  Willis C., 190
Mitchell, Howard A., 152
Mitton
  Ann, 81
  Mary, 81, 83
  Michael, 81, 83
Moody
  Joshua, 65, 89
  Major, 62
Moore, Asabil, Rev., 135
Mordough
  J. H., Rev., 130
  John H., 122
Morrill
  James, 211
  Levi, Mrs., 41
Morrill's Corner, 41, 47, 144, 145
Morris, James W., 127
Morse
  Anthony, 211
  Jonathan, 81
  Sarah Brackett, 81
Moses, Frank, 190
Mosher
  Daniel, 58, 81
  James, 58
  Jane Brackett, 81
  Merrill W., 58
Mountfort, Edmund, 89
Mountjoy, John, 10
Mousam House, Kennebunk, 206
Mowatt, 42
Mower, F. O., 207

Munjoy
 Claim, 15
 George, 6-10, 18, 93
 John, 9
 Land, 210
 Mary, 7
Munjoy Hill, 7
Murch
 A. F., Dr., 190
 Eleanor, 207
 Fred, 190
 G. Fred, 166
 George, 166
 Harlan P., 124, 166, 188, 204
 Helen, 207
 Mary, 120
 Nancy, 118
 Nathaniel, 166
Murray, June, 113

—N—

Nahant, 5
Nail manufacturing, 184
Naples, 45
Nashua Division, 3
Nason's Corner, 143
Naumkeag, 14
Neale, Francis, 18
Neil, Nancy, 30
New England Family History, 34, 39
New Gloucester, 34
New Gloucestor Society of Shakers, 45
New Hampshire, 39, 157
 Dover, 7
 Exeter, 87
 Greenland, 83, 102
 Hampton, 82
 Keene, 135
 Lee, 84
 Londerry, 104
 Portsmouth, 98
 Somersworth, 105
New Jersey
 Closter, 128
 Hackensack, 79
 Newark, 114
New Marblehead, 5, 18, 20, 45, 50, 104, 106, 107
New Netherlands, 148
New York Tribune, 43
Newbury, 42
Newcomb
 Elisha, 124, 131
 Phoebe, 124, 131
Newton, Eleanor, 95
Nichols
 Ed., Rev., 63
 James Albert, 151
Normans of DeWellessley, 133
Norridgewock, 139
North Adams, 167
North and Pierce's Store, 121
North Berwick, 210
North Clemsford, 128
North School, 202, 205
North Yarmouth, 18, 30, 34, 62
Nova Scotia, 46
Noyes, Joseph, 36, 65, 89

—O—

O'Brien
 Sarah, 33
 Thomas, Colonel, 33
Oakdale, 12, 81
Ocean Street, 47, 167
Odd Fellows Block, 40, 190, 192
Odd Fellows Hall, 208
Ohio, Astabula, 129
Old Gorham Road, 83
Old Iron Works, 43, 112
Old Ironworks, 134

Osborne
    Elizabeth Shove, 91
    Paul, 91
Oxford County, 195
    Peru, 75

—P—

Padden, Mary, 60
Palmer
    John, 10
    Mary, 9
Park Hill, 118, 160, 200
Parker
    Alvin L., 191
    Lydia, 31
    Maurice, 185
Parkman
    Francis, Jr., 60
    George, Dr., 60
    Samuel, 60
Parkman, Maine, 60
Parris, Albion K., 195
Parsonfield, 83
Parsons
    Abigail, 24, 30
    Mary, 24, 34
Partridge
    Azuba, 40
    Benj., 135
    Capt., 77
    Jesse, 56
    Jotham, 110
    Nathan, 15
    Nathaniel, 55, 111
    Polly, 34
    Rosina, 40
Passadumkeag, 108
Patrick, Charles, 120
Patten
    Elizabeth, 113
    Robert, 113
Patterson, General, 73

Peabody
    Dorothy, 53, 54, 58
    Francis, 15, 36, 53, 54
    Joseph, 53
    Mary, 36, 37
Pearce, Robert, 13
Pearl Diver, 215
Pearson
    Anne, 70, 71
    Elizabeth, 70
    Eunice, 70
    Lois, 70
    Mary, 70
    Moses, 27, 28, 42, 56, 69, 71, 90, 210
    Sarah, 70, 71, 210
Pearsontown, 70
Pease, Lydia, 117
Penebscot County, 62
    Newfield, 107
Pennell
    Bertha, 209
    Clement, 211
    James, 191
    Jones, 186
Pepperell
    Andrew, 94
    Samuel, 94
Perley, Enoch, 195
Perry, John, 47
Pewter manufacturing, 181
Phaneug, Jeff, 185
Philadelphia Textile School, 179
Phillips
    John, 6, 9, 159
    Mary, 9
    Willia Andrews, 71
Phinney
    E. B., 125
    Edward, 191
    Fred, 192
    James, 192
    William, 5

Phippen
  Claim, 18
  David, 18
Pierce
  Daniel, 136
  Daniel T., 148, 162
  Josiah, 148
  Lewis Q., 141
Pierce Street, 87
Pike
  Charles, 135
  Elizabeth Jones, 42, 54, 70
  Frederick A., 43
  George, 135
  Hopey, 135
  James S., 43
  Mark, 135
  Mary Webb, 31, 42, 54
  Samuel, 31, 32, 33, 36
  Samuel Deane, 31, 42, 54
  Samuel G., 31, 43, 54
  Sarah Haskell, 31, 36
  Timothy, 41, 42, 43, 54, 135
Pine Tree State, 157
Piscataquis County, 61
Pleasant Street, 191
Plummer
  Anne, 39
  Henry B., 100
  Jane, 100
  Jesse, 198
  Josiah, 29
  Lucy Babb, 100
  Major, 100
  Maria, 137
  Mrs., 66
  Samuel, 100
Poland, 60
Polin, Chief, 200
Pomeroy, Thaddeus, 119
Poole, William W., 170
Poor, Enoch, Gen., 79
Pork Hill, 36, 118, 160, 200, 215

Porter
  A., 183
  Billy, Major, 78
  Freeman, 181, 183
  John, 106
  Joseph, 106
Porterfield, William, 104
Portland, 13
  Capisic, 65
  Center Street, 64
  City Farm, 87
  Congress Street, 65
  Deering district, 65
  First Parish, 109
  Harper's Hill, 65
  Love Lane, 64
  Middle Street, 64
  The Neck, 64
Portland, 139
Portland & Rochester Railroad, 165, 187, 192
Portland and Rochester Depot agent, 193
Portland City Home, 65
Portland Harbor, 165
Portland Neck, 8
Portland Public Library, 118, 215
Portland Transcript, 181
Post, E. H., 137
Post Office, 191
Pote, William, 18, 27
Potter, Dr., 10
Pottle, A. W., Rev., 136
Poughkeepsie, 181
Pownal, Gov., 92
Powsland, Richard, 28
Pratt
  Asa W., 104
  Cushing, 104
  Henry, 100
  John, 100
  Joseph P., 100

Preble
  Bridadier, 67
  Edward, 67
  Lucy, 67
Preble Street, 169
Press Herald, 179
Presumpscot House, 53, 56
  Presumpscot Town, River, Bridges, Ferries &/or Falls, 1-5, 8, 10, 12-15, 18, 19, 20, 26, 28, 36, 44, 45-47, 52, 54, 56, 62, 67, 68, 75, 77, 82, 86, 87, 89, 90, 93, 96, 101, 107, 119, 143, 159, 160-163, 167, 172, 175, 192, 195, 196, 200-202
Presumpscot Valley, 1
Pride
  Amy, 62, 68
  B. G., 190
  Harry L., 137
  Joseph, 46, 68
  Merritt, 190
  Sarah, 68
  William, 77
Pride's Bridge, 14, 36, 46, 47, 62, 63, 64, 82
Pride's Corner, 44, 74, 82, 85, 102
Proctor
  Anthony, 45
  Charity Lunt, 44
  Charles Henry, 45
  Elizabeth Quimby, 40, 49
  Ellen Babb, 99
  Frederick, 45, 49
  Harriet Quimby, 49
  James, 40, 45, 49
  John, 44, 45, 48, 77, 99
  John, Jr., 44, 45, 49
  Joshua, 99
  Mary, 40
  Mary Brackett, 44
  Mary W. Babb, 99
  Nathaniel, 45, 101
  Rebecca, 101, 136
  Richard, 45
  Sally, 48, 136
  Samuel, 44, 45, 47, 83, 86
  Sarah Brackett, 44, 46, 83
  William, 44, 45
Proctor Mill, 82
Proctor Stream, 48
Proctor's Bridge, 45
Proctor's Mill Stream, 46, 47, 68
Purington
  Francis, 204
Puritans, 83

—Q—

Quaker preacher, 205
Quakers, 96
Quimby
  Aaron, 45, 49
  Abigail March, 40, 45, 49
  Albion M., 40
  Anne, 71
  Benjamin, 34, 38, 39, 40, 49
  Betsey Walker, 40
  Daniel T., 40
  Edward F., Rev., 41
  Eleanor Starboard, 34
  Elizabeth, 40, 49
  Esther Cloudman, 40
  George, 40, 41
  Governor, 34
  Harriet, 49
  Henry Cole, 34
  Isaac F., Capt., 40, 72
  John, 56
  Joseph, 25, 39, 40
  Levi, 71
  Mary, 39, 71
  Mary Haskell, 25, 39
  Moses, 40, 45, 49, 71

Nancy, 40
Nathan, 40
Reliance Cloudman, 40
Robert, 39
Sally Brackett, 84
Sarah, 40, 41
Simeon, 40, 84
Tamsin, 40
Twins, 40
Quinby
  Aaron, 141
  Abel, 101
  Anna, 105
  Benjamin, 105
  Betsey, 204, 206
  Charlotte, 118
  Edward W., 140
  Eunice Akers, 101
  George, 204, 206
  George W., 140
  Ida Griggs, 204
  Isaac F., Capt., 193
  Johnson, 190
  Joseph, 88
  Rhoda, 101
  Sally, 118
  Sophronia, 204
Quinby
  Isaac F., 141
  Moses, 2nd, 135

—R—

Rand
  Dorothy Hamblen, 57
  N., 57
Randall
  Catherine, 62
  Elmer, 104
  John, Capt., 52
Ray
  Albus, Dr., 206
  Fabius M., 1, 204, 206

Raymond, 31, 45
  George E., 188
  George H., 127, 191
  Harlan M., 86
  Lucy Haskell, 35
Read, John, 47
Reed
  Joseph, 81
  Thomas B., 81, 84
Register of Deeds of
  Cumberland County, 32
Remnant Store, 153
Revere, Paul, 122
Revolutionary Army, 210
Revolutionary War, 68, 75
Rhea, Caleb, 197
Rhode Island
  Tiverton, 51, 53, 105, 106
Rich
  Hiram B., 126
  William A., 196
Richardson
  Freeman, 58
Richmond, 63
Richmonds' Island, 4, 5, 147
Ricker hous, 191
Ridlon's Hall, 153
Riggs
  Anne, 61
  Jeremiah, 21, 211
  Joseph, 211
  Josiah, 35
  Mary, 21
  Mary Collins, 35
  Mary Haskell, 35
  Thomas, 35
Ritchie, Charles, 191
River Road, 201
Robbins, Frederick E. C., 207
Roberts
  B. F., 40, 84, 190, 204
  Elizabeth Webb, 50
  James, 2
  Joanna, 99

Jonathan, 50
Joshua S., 101
Robie
   Frederick, Gov., 119
   Tappan, 119
Rockameecooks, 200
Rocky Hill, 205, 210
Rollins, Charles, 167
Ropes, George, 186
Ross
   Amy, 65
   David, 65
   Maurice, 175
Rowe, Irving, 190
Rowley, Mass., 39
Royal Navy of King George III, 160
Royallsborough, 29
Royalsborough, 14
Rumford, Count, 148

—S—

S. D. Warren Company, 43, 45, 172
Saccarappa, 1, 14, 26, 36, 38, 39, 41, 42, 43, 62
   First Permanent Settlement, 36
   First settler, 67
Saccarappa Bridge, 35
Saccarappa Falls, 15, 18, 19, 47, 178
Saccarappa Village, 66, 158
Saccarappy Road, 19
Saco, 181
Saco River, 200
Saco Street, 5, 43, 58, 72, 105, 110, 111, 134, 192
Salem, 14
Salem Village, 44
Salem Witchcraft, 44
Sands
   Henry, 189

Henry F., 99
   Maria Babb, 99
Sargent
   Thomas M., 27
   William M., 49
Saunders
   Capt., 92
   Harry W., 126
   John, 10
Savage, Isaac, 68
Sawyer
   Elizabeth Webb, 62
   Isaac, 46, 81
   Judith, 82
   Lauiston W., 189
   Myril, 204
   Sarah Brackett, 81
Scarborough, 40, 42, 59, 98, 157
Scates Block, 119, 192
Scates Building, 53, 54
Schools
   Bridge Street Grammar, 25, 30, 207, 209
   Divinity School, 151
   Duck Pond, 209
   Forest Street, 207
   High School, 207, 208
   Highland Lake, 209
   Main Street, 209
   Manual Training, 215
   Pride's Corner, 207, 209
   Rocky Hill, 209
   Saco Street, 209
   Spruce Swamp, 209
   Warren, 190
Schwartz
   Charles, 192
   John C., 191
Scotch Hill, 43, 166
Scotch-Irish, 104
Searle, Joseph, 118, 121
Seavey
   Eunice, 59

Milton, Dr., 206
Seavey Street, 206
Sebago, 198
Sebago Lake, 3, 56, 170, 195, 200
Sebego Pond, 18
Senate, Ann, 117
Settlements
 First permanent, 13
Shackford
 D. D., 99
 Hannah, 15
 Joanna Babb, 99
Shakers, 31, 45, 85
Shaw
 Daniel B., 19
 Deacon, 198
 Thomas, 105
Shinn, Q. H., 141
Shirley, Governor, 200
Shore
 Edward, 95
 James, 95
 Nathaniel, 95
Shove
 Edward, 90, 91
 Elizabeth, 91
 George, Rev., 91
 Nathaniel, 91
 Ruth, 91
 Theophilus, 91
Shrove, Edward, 88
Sibley, Stephen, 169
Silber Street, 44
Simonton, Dolly, 188
Simpson, James, 27
Sinnet
 Anne Johnson, 105
Skillings
 A. T., 192
 Rebecca, 102
 Timothy, 197
Slavery, anti, 43
Slaves, 193

Slocum, Joel B., 114
Small
 Ashely, 127
 Charles, 136
 David, 6, 19, 42, 55, 65, 87, 119
 Edward, 7
 Emily, 100
 Francis, 6, 8, 42, 46, 55, 65, 87, 119, 127
 George, 148
 Jermina Gilman, 87
 Sarah, 100
 Zachariah, 87, 204
Smith
 Charles Linn, 152
 F. O. J., 199
 Henry, 167
 Henry St. John, 167
 James, 84
 John, 91
 John, Capt., 55
 Jonathan, 144
 Mary Brackett, 84
 Mary Shove, 91
 Parson, 16, 67, 69
 Peter T., Rev., 109
 Rev. Thomas, 12
 Sarah, 22
 Susanna, 55
 Thomas, 15, 157
 Thomas Laurens, 105
 Thomas P., Dr., 191
 Thomas, Rev., 16, 63, 109
Smith, Parson, 162
Smith, Frank, Dr., 131
Snow
 John, 46, 47
 Mary, 82
 Temple H., 125, 128
Society of the Cincinnati, 75
Sokokis, 200
Somerworth, NH, 38, 40
South Hadley Falls, 168

South Portland, 4
South Windham, 105, 198
Southwick
　Paul, 91
　Ruth, 91
Sparrow, Lydia, 34
Spear
　Abigail, 50
　Bethiah, 50, 106
　Bethiah Farrar, 52
　Bethiah Holbrook, 106
　Charles, 137
　David, 50
　David, Capt., 50, 52, 106
　Eli, 50
　Elizabeth, 50
　Ezekial, 50
　James, 50
　John, 50
　Josiah, 50
　Seth, 50
　Susanna, 50
Speewell, 198
Speirs, Alexander, 167
Speirs Hall, 155
Spinning wheel, first, 140
Spring Street, 5, 37, 38, 45, 98, 102, 162, 166, 189, 191, 209
Springer
　George T., 189
　Joanna, 81
Springer Block, 184, 189
Sproul
　Hiram B., 168
　James, 168
Spurwink, 8, 147
Spurwink River, 4
St. Giles Cripple-gate, 98
Stackpole
　Alice, 85
　Lindette, 85
Standish, 70, 148
Stanley, Curtis L., 152

Star Theatre, 192
Starbird
　Capt., 77
　Thomas, 77
Starboard, Eleanor, 34, 40
State of Maine Edition, 179
Steamer Portland, 108
Steel, Eben, 182
Stephenson, Jesse, 69
Steven Plains, 181
Stevens
　Ansel, 190
　Betsey Webb, 60
　Henry, 66
　John, 150
　Mrs., 113
Stevens Plains, 82, 139, 182
Stiles
　Albion P., 168
　Fred W., Dr., 33
　Hannah, 33
　John, 33
　Merritt W., 33
Stimson, John, 188
Storor, Woodbury, 195
Stowe
　Calvin, 206
　Harriet Beecher, 206
Strawberry Bank, 98
Streeter, Russell, 139
Strong, Elnathan, Rev., 130
Stroudwater, 39, 59, 60, 70, 144, 158, 210
Stroudwater Falls, 38, 158, 162
Stroudwater River, 3, 161
Stroudwater Road, 40
Stroudwater Street, 90, 104, 116, 154, 191
Strout, S. F., Rev., 125
Sturgis
　Ebenezer G., 99
　Mary Ann Babb, 99
Sunday, Captain, 7

Sutermeister, Edwin, 99, 111, 134
Swedenborganism, 122
Sweetser
  Alfred F., 166
  Benjamin, 67
Swett
  Israel, 31
  Jane March, 49
  Nathaniel, 188
  Stephen, 49, 59
  Susanna, 59, 60, 62

—T—

Taylor
  John Webb, 46
  Jonas, 132
Tead, Edward S., 132
Teft, Warren N., 151
Ten Broeck, Petrus Stuyvesant, 148
Tenney, Thomas, 119
Thatcher
  Edward, 38
  Lydia, 38
  Peter, 38
  Ruth, 38
  Samuel, 38
The Neck, 64
The Waterwitch, 198
Thomas Pond, 195
Thomaston, Maine, 75, 94
Thompson
  Annie, 113
  Benjamin, 148
  David, 32
  Frederick, 140
  William, 113
  Zenas, 139
Thurlow, Hannah, 101
Thurrell, Family, 58
Tibbets, Robert P., 179, 188
Tibbetts, Catherine, 64

Tilton, Burton H., Rev., 116
Titcomb
  Anne Pearson, 70, 71
  Benjamin, 69, 70, 71
  Moses, Col., 70
  Sarah, 70, 71
  William, 70
Tobey
  Harriet L. Bunker, 107
  Tabitha Brackett, 82
  William H., 107
Tobin
  Eunice Webb, 63
  William, 63
Tolman
  James H., 114, 115
Topsham, 78
Torrey
  David, 96
  Dr., 135
Townsend
  D. Harry, 142
  Harry E., 142
Trafton, Mark, 135
Treadwell, C. A. C., 113
Treadwill
  Mary, 98
  Thomas, 98
Trelawney Plantation, 147
Trickey
  Edward, 104
  William, 189
Tuckfield, Mary, 65
Tupper, Col., 73
Turner, 140
Two Years Before the Mast, 162
Tybbott, Mary, 34
Tyng
  John, 22, 27, 90
  Sarah, 22
  William, Col., 70
Tyngsboro, 22

—U—

Underground Railroad, 193, 194
Union Army, 176, 177
Union Mutual, 101
United States Hotel, 181

—V—

Valentine
  Caroline, 60
  Leander, 60, 141, 184, 187, 203, 206
  Leonard, 192
  William, Major, 60
Valentine Street, 189, 207, 209
Valley Forge, 210
Varnum, Alice, 191

—W—

Wadsworth, Peleg, 41, 56
Wadsworth-Longfellow house, 42
Waite, John, Capt., 46
Wakeley, John, 18
Waldo
  Francis, 92
  General, 9, 104
  Hannah, 92, 94
  Jonathan, 92
  Lucy, 92, 95
  Samuel, 3, 8, 18, 22, 28, 90, 92, 93, 95, 98, 104, 157, 210
Wales, 39
Walker
  Ann Johnson, 104
  Betsey, 40
  Caroline Valentine, 60
  Hannah Webb, 59
  Helen Murch, 207
  Henry B., 22, 73
  Isaac Gibbs, 59, 60
  Isaac N., 60
  J. B., 120
  James, 118
  Joseph, 104, 162, 167, 189
  Lois Gibbs, 60
  Lowell N., 60
  Lucinda, 118
  Moses B., 60
  Timothy, 60
  William, 14, 46
Walker Memorial Library, 42, 104, 167, 191, 215
Walker Street, 154
Walker, Deacon, Mrs., 189
Walker, Joseph, 123
Walker-Brigham block, 153
Wallace
  John, 57
  Katy Hamblen, 57
  L., 57
  Orvin H., 150
  Sally Hamblen, 57
Walsh, A. A., Rev., 115
Warren, John W., 192
Warren
  Albert F., 29
  Charles, 179
  Cornelia, 175
  George, 4, 87, 162, 179, 191
  Jane Johnson, 83
  John, 83, 162
  John E., 22, 176
  John L., 176
  John W., 29, 188
  John, Capt., 87
  Joseph A., 110, 209, 210
  Lewis, 162
  Lewis P., 4, 87
  Nathaniel, 83, 162
  S. D.& Co., 22, 72, 130, 175
  Samuel Dennis, 130
  William, 179

Warren Aveune, 111
Warren Furniture Company,
   38, 119, 210, 148, 188
Warren Paper Mill, 175
Washington, George, 196
Water power, 54
Waterford, 195
Waterhouse
   Charles M., 128
   Gardner, 101
   Israel, Rev., 119
   Jane Babb, 101
   Leon E., 128
   Martha, 141
Waterman, John, 119
Waters
   Mary, 15
   Mrs., 41
Watson
   Bethiah Hamblen, 57
   Henry, 190
   John, 190
   Marcus, 208
   Nathaniel, 57
Watson House, 156
Weare
   Joseph, 48
   Mary, 48, 49
Webb
   Abbie, 204
   Abigail, 62, 63
   Anna, 63
   Anne Riggs, 61
   Benjamin, 63
   Bethany, 63
   Bethiah, 52, 54, 57, 62
   Betsey, 59, 60, 63
   Catherine Randall, 62
   David, 53, 54, 57, 58
   Dorothy, 62
   Dorothy Peabody, 53, 58
   Eli, 50, 62
   Elizabeth, 50, 54, 62, 100
   Elizabeth Larrabee, 62, 63,
      65, 68
   Eunice, 63
   Hannah, 59
   Hannahette, 60
   Henry, 60, 61
   Hezkiah, 50
   James, 60
   Jane Bailey, 54
   John, 14, 50, 59, 60, 62, 63,
      64, 68
   John, 3rd, 60
   John, Jr., 59, 60, 62, 63
   Jonathan, 25, 31, 32, 39,
      42, 53, 54, 56, 58, 66, 67,
      100, 119
   Joshua, 54, 56, 66, 100, 110
   Kiah, 58
   Lucy Preble, 67
   Lydia Bickford, 59
   Mahlon H., 19, 60
   Margaret, 50
   Mary, 31, 42, 54, 63, 107
   Mary Connely, 100
   Mary Coverly, 54, 55
   Mary Padden, 60
   Phoebe, 63
   Polly, 59
   Ruth, 63
   Samuel, 50, 51, 52, 58, 62,
      106
   Sarah, 107
   Sarah Leighton, 62
   Seth, 51, 52, 62
   Stephen, 60
   Susan, 63
   Susanna, 50, 52
   Susanna Smith, 55
   Susanna Swett, 59-62
   Thomas, 51, 59, 63
   William, 58, 60, 63
Webb, 67
Webster, Eugene, Rev., 127

Wescott
  Elizabeth Babb, 99
  Esther, 99
  Levi, 99
  Post, 100
Wesley, Samuel, 133
Wesley
  Arthur, 133
  John, 133
Wesley Chapel, 111
West Bridge Street, 68
Westbrook, 1, 14, 19
  Thomas, Col., 9, 18, 83, 157, 159, 160, 200
Westbrook Chronicle, 208
Westbrook Hardware Company, 141
Westbrook Hospital, 190
Westbrook Inn, 65
Westbrook Junior College, 139
Westbrook Manufacturing Company, 28, 31, 32, 35, 54, 114, 148, 165, 167, 177
Westbrook Manufacturing District Nursing Association, 33
Westbrook Seminary, 139, 142
Westcott, Mrs., 191
Weston, James P., 142
Weymouth, Mabel, 100
Wheeler
  Henry, 89
  John, 124, 132
  John W., 190
  Mary East, 89
  Sarah, 89
  Susan R., 124, 132
Wheet, Dr., 167
Whitcher, H., Rev., 125
White, Mary, 25
White Hills, 144
White House, 87, 135
White's Bridge, 201

Whitman
  Charles, 195
  Josiah, 195
Whitney
  Asa P., 191
  W. B., 114
Whittier, Joseph, 101
Wight
  Donald, 114
  John, Rev., 26, 109
  Rev. Mr., 58
Williams, Jenkin, 18
Willis, William, 5, 39, 67, 68, 81, 147
Wilson
  George S., 115
  John, 86, 88
Wilton, Maine, 58
Windham, 18, 19, 42, 44, 45, 102, 105, 107, 201
  First burials, 106
  Proprietors, 26
Windham Hill, 104
Windham Road, 87
Windham Society, 109
Winslow
  Annie Huston, 96
  Benjamin, 89, 96
  Charity Hall, 96
  Edward, 95
  Eleanor Newton Adams, 95
  Elizabeth, 96
  George H., 168
  Governor, 95
  Hope Cobb, 96
  Horatio Gates, 100
  Isaac, 92, 95
  Jacob S., 167
  James, 90, 96, 97
  Job, 95
  Joseph, 44
  Kenelm, 95
  Lucy Waldo, 92
  Margaret Barbour, 96

Mary Babb, 100
Nathan, 13, 86, 96, 198
Nathaniel, 90
Sarah B., 206
Sarah W., 204
Stephen, 204
Winslow Street, 100
Winter
  John, 147
  Sarah, 147
Wisconsin, Wanwatosa, 176
Wise
  Ann V., 118
  Elizabeth, 56
  Elizabeth Pearson Birney, 70
  Joseph, 70
Wood, William R., 167
Woodard, E. P., 151
Woodbury
  Edmund, 185, 189
  Edmund M., 100
  Elizabeth, 100
  Hugh, 100
  Lowell H., 201
Woodfords, 145
Woodfords Society, 145

Woodman
  B. J., 203
  Benjamin J., 101
  Charles B., 101, 125, 191
  Charlotte, 207
  Charlotte Babb, 101
  George M., 191
  George M., Dr., 125, 203
  Ruel W., 189
Worcester
  Hannah, 36, 107
  Timothy, 36, 46, 107
Wright
  Colley, 19
  Inkhorn, 19
Wuhu, China, 152
Wyer
  Joe, 48
  Otis, 191

—Y—

Y.M.C.A., 175
York County, 185
York County Registry of Deeds, 27

www.ingramcontent.com/pod-product-compliance
Lightning Source LLC
Chambersburg PA
CBHW050346230426
43663CB00010B/2004